ACTION GU

ACTION GUIDE
EUROPE

Steve Watkins and Paul Grogan

QUEENSGATE PUBLICATIONS

First published in 2000 by Queensgate Publications,
Cookham, Berkshire

ISBN 1-902655-06-0

A catalogue record of this book is available
from the British Library.

Cover design by Charlie Webster
Book design by Production Line, Minster Lovell, Oxford
Production by Landmark Consultants, Princes Risborough,
Buckinghamshire
Printed by Cox & Wyman Ltd, Reading, Berkshire

CONTENTS

INTRODUCTION

As you have got this far in reading this book it means that we have at least one thing in common: a desire to inject a sense of adventure into our lives. We may lead completely different lives and harbour completely different adventure aspirations, yet the feeling that we want to prevent life simply passing us by without at least once pushing our physical and mental barriers is shared. If you have already found the elixir that adventure sports provide, then we hope we can tempt you with a few new ideas for trying something different. If this is your first foray into the adventure world, then how lucky you are to have arrived at the threshold during such an exciting phase of adventure sport development. Thrill seekers have never had it so good. The last decade has seen an explosion of operators offering more exciting, well-organised and better-supervised sports, and the emergence at the commercial level of a significant number of completely new adventures, such as canyoning. Seriously, if you cannot find a sport to thrill you these days then you must already be in the grave.

The book is laid out in alphabetical order by sport, with indices at the back of the operators and the activities by country. The sports themselves were chosen on a basis of exposure to the elements: so, for example, microlighting made it in but gliding did not. We also tried to avoid including noisy machine-based sports: so, no quad bikes, car rallying or jet skis. Again, microlighting was accepted due to the ethereal nature of flying out in the open and heli-skiing just made it because the chopper is only a means of getting to the start of the adventure. The operators all have bases in the country where they operate the sport, so there are no middlemen to take more of your money and you know that you are supporting local business. I'm sure there will be many willing to argue with the logic of our selection; if you want to cry foul, or if you want to buy us a beer for our choices, then please feel free to get in touch. And don't be afraid to point out mistakes or suggest additions for the next edition.

Though we do not have first-hand experience of every centre in these pages, the credentials of all are sound. Every centre in the guide uses fully qualified or very experienced instructors and all have been operating for sufficient years (some from the outset of the sport they offer) to suggest that they are here to stay. With communication becoming ever easier via Internet technology, we have ensured that every centre has either an email address or a website, and the vast majority have both. If you have access to the Internet then we recommend looking up the websites to gain more insight into companies you are interested in and what they offer. Requesting information and making bookings are so much easier and cheaper by email. We declined to include information about buying your own gear. Basically, if you are already involved in the sport then you will have a good idea about the equipment available, and if you just want to taste a sport then you aren't going to spend a stack of cash on kitting yourself out. If you want to find out about the necessary kit for going it alone, then talk to the centre you're planning to visit or check out the specialist magazines that have sprung up around most of the sports. They will have up-to-date information on current market trends and prices and can advise on buying second-hand gear where appropriate.

If this book helps you get just one day of excitement that you otherwise would have missed out on, then the long nights at the keyboard and the way we made our friends and families suffer our writers' moods will all seem worthwhile – though the friends and families may disagree!

Get out there and have a blast!

Steve and Paul
e-mail: *actioneurope@aol.com*

A NOTE OF CAUTION

Adventure sports inherently involve more risk than some other sports. Personal risk of injury or even death can be quite substantial; and there is risk of damaging other people's property. Readers of this guide are strongly advised to take out relevant insurance policies to cover themselves in the event of such occurrences. The readers are solely responsible for choosing to undertake any activity included in this guide and assume responsibility for any or all of the risks involved. Readers should make all the necessary enquiries to the chosen centres to ascertain the operators' capabilities and standards. The publishers, authors and all parties and their agents associated with the production of this guide do not make any warranties as to the competence and safety of the tour operators included herein. All of the entries are provided free of charge to the operators, so there is no bias resulting from financial interest. The entries have been compiled from information request forms submitted by the operators between May and September 1999. The entry details have been checked, but the publishers, authors and all parties and their agents associated with the production of this guide cannot guarantee the accuracy of the information. Prices are an obvious area where change is likely. Nor can they accept responsibility for any error or misrepresentation, or be liable for any loss suffered as a result of anybody using the information in this guide.

ACKNOWLEDGEMENTS

Steve and Paul would like to say a big thank you to all the operators who took the time to get in touch and whose best wishes always boosted our determination to finish the book. They would also like to thank Steve's dad, Don, for his unpaid but highly professional help with the editing process when they could no longer bear to read it again! Also a big thanks to Steve's mum, Dilys, for keeping the coffee supplies going during the Big Weekend, and to Rich, Jonesy and Brewster for making them see sense when that same sunny weekend almost passed without any climbing. Ta mucho to Dom and Kev for their ideas on the cover. And now, ladies and gentleman, it is time to be free!

Help us keep this guide as up-to-date as possible, by sending all your comments, corrections and additions to:

actionguide@queensgategroup.co.uk

ABBREVIATIONS

AALA	UK Adventure Activities Licensing Authority
ABRS	Association of British Riding Schools
AEGM	Asociacion Espagnola de Guias de Montaña
AFF	Accelerated Free Fall
AIRaf	Associazione Italiana Rafting
ANTE	National Association of Equestrian Tourism
ATE	Accompagnateurs de Tourisme Equestre
BCU	British Canoe Union
BFSLYC	British Federation of Sand and Land Yachting Clubs
BHPA	British Hang Gliding and Paragliding Association
BMAA	British Microlighting Aircraft Association
BMC	British Mountaineering Council
BPA	British Parachute Association
BSA	British Surfing Association
BSAC	British Sub Aqua Club
CAA	Civil Aviation Authority
CACL	Accelerated Free Fall Course (Spain)
CMAS	Confederation Mondiale des Activites Subaquatiques
CPCL	Progressive Free Fall Course (Spain)
DGAC	French civil aviation authority
FFVL	French Federation of Free Flight
FICK	Federazione Italiana Canoa Kayak
MIA	Mountaineering Instructors Award
MIC	Mountain Instructor Certificate
MLTB	Mountain Leader Training Board
NCA	National Caving Association
PADI	Professional Association of Diving Instructors
RYA	Royal Yachting Association

SAF	Icelandic Travel Industry Association
SPSA	Single Pitch Supervisors Award
UIAGM-IVM	Mountain Guide
WCA	Welsh Canoeing Association

ACTION GUIDE EUROPE

ABSEILING

Although more commonly associated with climbing, abseiling has none the less assumed its own place in the annals of adventure sports. Also known as rapelling, abseiling involves descending a rope using a device cunningly referred to as a descender, which allows participants to control their rate of descent. The potential for places to abseil from is limited only by the need to anchor the rope to something solid at the top.

More often than not abseiling is included in climbing courses, but for those who would rather not have to climb to the top before coming back down, there are a number of companies in Europe offering abseiling as an activity in its own right. After being given a briefing on the basic principles, you'll be provided with a helmet, a sit harness and a descender (which is attached to the sit harness using a karabiner). Once you're attached to the rope via your descender, you'll be ready to lower yourself over the edge. After that, it's downhill all the way. The good news is that because the descender controls the rate of descent, you can go as fast or as slow as you want, and there'll always be someone on hand to talk you through every step.

The most recent incarnation of abseiling is known as rap-jumping. Instead of sliding upright down the rope, participants actually descend face first. It's probably not considered good practice among the climbing fraternity, but who's to say it's not fun?

Feeling ropey – a cautionary tale
Andy lowered himself carefully over the edge of the aqueduct, head first and facing outwards, with his back to the pillar. Carefully aligning his feet above his head, he let go of the rope, spread his

arms wide and dropped like a stone. Abseiling down the rope, he fell the 120 feet in a little over 6 seconds. Just yards from the bottom, he tugged hard on the rope and locked it off. But he didn't stop there. Instead of coming to a halt just feet from the ground, he kept on going, his helmet bouncing off the concrete at the base of the pillar. For days he couldn't remember who he was or what had happened. Only when his memory returned did he realise why he hadn't stopped in time.

The rope he was using was designed for climbing and not abseiling. To avoid shock on climbers and their gear, climbing ropes are designed to stretch up to 10%; abseiling ropes, which are not expected to take any sort of fall, are designed with very little stretch. It doesn't take a mathematician to figure out that the stretch in 120 feet of climbing rope is going to be more than a couple of feet. And so Andy's rope didn't stop him where he expected it to. He was an experienced climber who made a simple mistake.

All accredited abseiling and climbing centres will take care that you use the proper ropes for the job, but if you're ever abseiling – or climbing – with someone else's rope, make sure you look before you leap.

IRELAND

CELTIC ADVENTURES
Caherdaniel, Co. Kerry
Phone: +353 (0)66 9475 277
Fax: +353 (0)66 9475 277
Email: info@activity-ireland.com
Website: www.activity-ireland.com

Back down the Irish cliffs
South-west Ireland is one of the most unspoilt parts of Europe and Celtic Adventures is based in the heart of some of the best outdoor activity locations there. You can get a taste of abseiling on the sea cliffs or in the mountains, both of which offer spectacular scenery and

drops to suit all levels of ability. The professional guides ensure that your safety is paramount and courses can be tailor-made to suit your requirements. At the end of the day, you can share daring tales with your fellow abseilers while listening to Irish music and supping a pint of Guinness or Murphys in one of the cosy local pubs.

Activity prices: Trips are tailor-made to suit the clients' needs. Prices are based around I£20 per person per day from June to mid-August, I£18 otherwise. Discounts are available for students and school/scouting groups.

Accommodation: Hostel accommodation at I£8 or B&B at I£20, both per person/sharing basis. Holiday cottages and four-star campsite also available.

Food: Available at centre for approximately I£14 per day for all meals.

Equipment supplied: All specialist equipment provided.

What to take: Personal clothing and footwear.

When to go: Year round except December and January, depending on weather.

Established: 1988

Safety: All guides are fully qualified in their fields. Celtic Adventures is a member of the Irish Association of Adventure Sports and is promoted by the Irish Tourist Board, Bord Failte.

Insurance: Centre has insurance but it is recommended that clients arrange their own.

Methods of payment: VISA or personal cheque.

Booking information: Advance booking is recommended with payment requested at least 42 days in advance.

Nearest airport: Cork (2.5 hours) or Kerry (1.5 hours). Groups of clients travelling together can be collected from the airport.

Nearest rail station: Killarney (80 mins). Groups of clients travelling together can be collected from the station.

UNITED KINGDOM

ADVENTURE SPORTS
Carnkie Farmhouse, Carnkie, Redruth, Cornwall TR16 6RZ
Phone: +44 (0)1209 218 962

Fax: +44 (0)1209 314 118
Email: holidays@adventure-sports.co.uk
Website: www.adventure-sports.co.uk

Abseil down Cornish sea cliffs
Cornwall is blessed with some of the UK's most stunning coastal scenery and the sea cliffs make for a great place to take your first walk backwards off a cliff edge. Your well-qualified instructor will take you through the rope techniques and safety measures needed to make your descent a real thrill. Adventure Sports change the abseiling location to suit the prevailing weather conditions so you are always getting the best option. The centre offers a range of sports so you can mix climbing with other adventures during your stay.

Activity prices: A three-day camping stay with two days of activities costs from £76 (low season) to £100 (high season) and prices go up to £329 for a seven night/seven activity days course.

Accommodation: Included in price. You have a choice of camping, self-catering chalets or a converted self-catering farmhouse. There are many social options nearby or on the site.

Food: Not included.

Equipment supplied: All specialised equipment is provided.

What to take: Personal clothing and suitable footwear.

When to go: Summer months only.

Established: 1982

Safety: All the centre's abseiling instructors hold nationally recognised qualifications and are very experienced. The centre is a member of the West Country Tourist Board.

Insurance: Insurance is required. The centre offers policies.

Methods of payment: VISA, cheque and cash.

Booking information: Advance booking is required. A £50 deposit is payable.

Nearest airport: Newquay.

Nearest rail station: Redruth. Transfers can be arranged.

AVALON ADVENTURE

The Mill House, Dulford, Cullompton, Devon EX15 2ED
Phone: +44 (0)1884 266 646
Fax: +44 (0)1884 266 646
Email: avalon-adventure@dial.pipex.com
Website: http://dialspace.dial.pipex.com/avalon.adventure/

A down sort of day

Avalon Adventure is based in Devon, but they offer abseiling days throughout the UK. The courses are run by qualified instructors and are often on cliffs or off disused bridges. You learn to set up your own abseils using safe equipment and ropework techniques, and the experience is bound to get you enthused about other adventure sports such as climbing. The centre can organise charity abseiling events.

Activity prices: Course prices vary, so contact centre for details.

Accommodation: Not included. The centre can help you arrange a place to stay.

Food: Not included.

Equipment supplied: All specialist equipment is supplied.

What to take: Personal clothing, suitable footwear.

When to go: April to November.

Established: 1992

Safety: All the instructors are fully qualified and hold first aid qualifications.
The centre is licensed by the AALA.

Insurance: The centre is insured though clients may wish to take out separate insurance too.

Methods of payment: VISA, Mastercard, cheques and cash.

Booking information: Advance booking is essential.

Nearest airport: Exeter. Transfers can be arranged.

Nearest rail station: Exeter. Transfers can be arranged.

BLACK MOUNTAIN ACTIVITIES

PO Box 5, Hay on Wye, Hereford HR3 5YB
Phone: +44 (0)1497 847 897
Fax: +44 (0)1497 847 897
Email: enquiries@blackmountain.co.uk
Website: www.blackmountain.co.uk

Backward down 50 metre high Welsh cliffs

Abseiling is one of the most accessible but also one of the most thrilling sports for complete beginners. Black Mountain Activities offer abseiling as part of their rock climbing taster days, where you get the chance to build up your skills to the point where you can tackle a 50 metre high cliff. No matter how brave you are, there is always a tense moment as you edge backwards over the edge.

Activity prices: £30 per day, including rock climbing.

Accommodation: Not included in the price. There is a range of accommodation available locally and the centre will advise you.

Food: Not included in price. Packed lunches can be arranged at extra cost.

Equipment supplied: All specialist equipment is supplied.

What to take: Personal clothing, swimsuit and suitable footwear.

When to go: Year round.

Established: 1992

Safety: All the centre's staff are fully qualified in their respective sports, hold first aid qualifications and are highly professional. All equipment used meets national safety standards. The centre is licensed by the AALA and the Welsh Tourist Board.

Insurance: The centre is insured though clients may wish to take out separate insurance too.

Methods of payment: Personal cheque and cash.

Booking information: Advance booking is recommended though late bookings may be possible.

Nearest airport: Depends on tour. Cardiff and Bristol are nearest to the centre.

Nearest rail station: Depends on the itinerary. Hereford and Abergavenny are nearest to the centre.

HIGH TREK SNOWDONIA

Tal y Waen, Deiniolen, Caernarfon, Gwynedd LL55 3NA
Phone: +44 (0)1286 871 232
Fax: +44 (0)1286 870 576
Email: high.trek@virgin.net
Website: www.hightrek.co.uk

A personal descent in Wales

Abseiling is often a popular way for people to get their first taste of mountain sports, and High Trek Snowdonia specialise in making that experience as personal as possible. On their Mountain Adventure course, which includes abseiling, there are just four clients to every instructor, ensuring that you get every opportunity to be in action and learning new skills for the maximum amount of time. The abseiling takes place in Snowdonia's spectacular deep gorges, which have descents to suit all levels of ability. No previous ropework experience is necessary, but you need to be fit with a good head for heights or a willingness to conquer your fear!

Activity prices: Abseiling forms part of the three-day Mountain Adventure course that costs £235 fully inclusive. The other adventures on offer include scrambling, gorge walking, night hikes and bivouacs.

Accommodation: Included in the price. You stay at the homely Tal y Waen farmhouse in bunk-bed accommodation.

Food: Included in price. You get full board including wine with dinner and a packed lunch.

Equipment supplied: All specialist equipment is supplied.

What to take: Personal clothing, suitable footwear.

When to go: April to August.

Established: 1985

Safety: All the centre's abseiling instructors hold the Mountain Instructor Award and a first aid qualification. The centre is approved by the Association of Mountaineering Instructors and the Wales Tourist Board.

Methods of payment: VISA, Mastercard, Switch, cheques, cash.

Booking information: Advance booking is recommended though late bookings may be possible. A £75 deposit is payable and full payment is due four weeks in advance. Sliding scale for cancellation depends on time of cancellation.

Nearest airport: Manchester.

Nearest rail station: Bangor.

PEAK ACTIVITIES
Rock Lea Activity Training Centre, Station Road, Hathersage,
Hope Valley, Derbyshire S32 1DD
Phone: +44 (0)1433 650 345
Fax: +44 (0)1433 650 342
Email: admin@iain.co.uk
Website: www.iain.co.uk

Over the Peak edge
Abseiling is one of Peak Activities' most popular courses. Whether
you are just a beginner or very experienced, the guides know places to
match your ability. For novices, a thorough lesson in the correct rope
and movement techniques instils confidence but cannot stop the
pounding heart as you walk backwards over the edge of a cliff. In that
moment, the lovely scenery of the Derbyshire Peak District will be lost
on you. For braver clients, a nearby disused railway viaduct provides a
sterner test of courage as you can dangle in mid-air, 100 feet above a
fast-flowing river. The instructors are all nationally qualified, so your
safety will not be compromised no matter how extreme the experience feels to you. In a half-day or full-day session you can have as
many goes as you want.

Activity prices: Abseiling is usually included as part of a multi-activity
weekend. It costs around £149 per person. Personal one-to-one tuition can
also be arranged.
Accommodation: Not included in the tour price. There is a large range of
options within easy reach of the centre, ranging from hostels and B&B to
farmhouses and hotels.
Food: Not included in tour price but there are plenty of local eateries to suit all
budgets.
Equipment supplied: All specialist equipment and bad weather gear if
necessary.
What to take: Personal clothing and suitable footwear. Full list supplied on
booking.
When to go: Year round.
Established: 1979

Safety: All the guides and instructors used by Peak Activities are qualified in their relevant fields and have first aid qualifications too. Staff carry radios and first aid kits. The company is licensed by the AALA and is a member of the Heart of England Tourist Board. Supplied specialist equipment is of a high standard and regularly maintained and replaced.

Insurance: All Peak Activity tours are fully insured for public and third party liability. Optional additional insurance can be taken out to guard against cancellation, illness, loss of property etc.

Methods of payment: VISA, Mastercard, Eurocard, personal cheque.

Booking information: A 50% deposit is requested with all bookings.

Nearest airport: Leeds (45 mins), Manchester (45 mins), Birmingham (90 mins) or Sheffield (12 mins). Transfers can be arranged.

Nearest rail station: Hathersage. Transfers can be arranged.

ROCK AND ICE

Birch Tree House, Shirley, nr. Ashbourne, Derbyshire DE6 3AS
Phone: +44 (0)1335 360 490
Fax: N/A
Email: rock.ice@bigfoot.com
Website: www.rockandice.demon.co.uk

Just down in the Dales

Rock and Ice are based in the stunning Peak District National Park, home to some of the most famous crags in the country. Their abseiling courses are offered both there and throughout the rest of the UK. Although it is possible just to book an abseiling course, the activity is often included as part of a multi-sports break or as part of a beginners' rock climbing course, so don't limit yourself to just one thrill. The centre uses a quick-release backup system for all their abseil courses to ensure complete safety.

Activity prices: Prices are based around £80–100 per day for one to one tuition and £50 per person on a one instructor to two clients basis. Contact the centre for other activities that can be included.

Accommodation: Not included in the tour price. The centre will help you to arrange accommodation in the local area.

Food: Not included in price but there are local places to suit all budgets.

Equipment supplied: All specialist equipment.

What to take: Personal clothing and suitable footwear. Suggested list supplied on booking.

When to go: Year round, depending on weather.

Established: 1987

Safety: The instructors employed by Rock and Ice are all qualified by the national governing bodies.

Insurance: The centre recommends outdoor pursuits travel insurance that starts at £12.50 for up to four days.

Methods of payment: personal cheque and cash.

Booking information: A 50% deposit is requested with all bookings. Balance is due 28 days before course. Cancellation penalties are applied.

Nearest airport: Manchester.

Nearest rail station: Derby. Transfers can be arranged.

THE ROCK CENTRE

Chudleigh, Devon TQ13 OEE
Phone: +44 (0)1626 852717
Fax: +44 (0)1626 852717
Email: trc@globalnet.co.uk
Website: www.rockcentre.co.uk

Abseiling in Devon

When it comes to cliffs and crags, The Rock Centre is spoilt for choice. Ideally situated in the heart of Devon, it's within easy reach of the infamous tors of Dartmoor and the spectacular sea cliffs of the south coast. The centre even has its own cliff onsite, making it the perfect place for beginners to learn beyond the prying eyes of more practised posers. From gentle introductory slopes to the towering vertical walls of Chudleigh Rock, abseiling can be arranged on a half-daily or daily basis. Further afield, cliffs, bridges, buildings and viaducts abound – if there's somewhere safe to set up an anchor, the chances are you can abseil down it.

Activity prices: £10 per half-day, £20 per full day for groups of four or more. For individuals or groups smaller than four, an instructor costs £40 per half-day and £80 per full day.

Accommodation: Not included in the price, although a good range of accommodation is available locally. Camping at the Rock Centre costs £1 per person, bunkhouse accommodation £2 per person. B&B accommodation can be arranged at a price to suit.

Food: Clients to arrange their own.

Equipment supplied: All specialist equipment is provided.

What to take: Personal clothing and footwear suitable for the prevailing conditions; if in doubt, call ahead for advice.

When to go: Year round.

Established: 1978

Safety: All staff hold national governing body qualifications and the centre is licensed by the AALA.

Insurance: The centre carries indemnity insurance for all activities and can advise on personal accident insurance if required.

Methods of payment: Cash or cheque.

Booking information: Reservations must be made in advance. A deposit is not normally required.

Nearest airport: Exeter or Plymouth.

Nearest rail station: Exeter or Newton Abbot. Clients can be picked up by prior arrangement.

BALLOONING

Over two centuries ago, hot air ballooning became the first way humans ever flew and the thrill those brave pilots must have felt is something that can easily be relived today, with substantially less risk! In fact, it is one of the safest sports around, but certainly not one of the cheapest to commit yourself to. However, the serenely thrilling experience is unique and taster flights are within the means of most, so you should justify spending the money at the very least once in a lifetime. The roar of the burner, the adventure of having just a wicker basket stopping you from tumbling to earth and the short-lived drama of landing mix seamlessly with the peace and quiet of drifting wherever the wind feels like taking you. The pilot reads subtle changes in the wind conditions and steers by controlling the altitude of the balloon to take advantage of varying wind speeds and directions at various levels. Despite their expertise, even the pilots don't know where or when the balloon is likely to land, and so radio contact is kept with support crews on the ground who drive to the eventual landing spot to retrieve you. If you want to become a qualified pilot and fly regularly, then get out your chequebook. Balloons are not cheap and so airtime costs on a par with learning to fly an aircraft. However, if you want a way to snap out of your daily rut without exerting yourself, then ballooning is the ideal choice. It is a remarkable and memorable way to fly.

Around the world in twenty days

Over the last few years of the 1990s there was a rash of efforts by teams in heavily sponsored and highly technical balloons to become the first people to balloon non-stop around the world. There were some dramatic and heroic failures, most notably Steve Fossett's 1998 attempt that ended in flames in the Coral Sea after travelling 14,236 miles. When Breitling Orbiter 3 took off from Switzerland on 1 March 1999, the succession of previous failures had started to cast doubts on whether this was one record too far for current balloon technology. Twenty days later, the Breitling pilots, Bertrand Piccard and Brian Jones, stepped triumphantly out into the Egyptian desert as the first people to fly non-stop round the world.

FRANCE

FRANCE MONTGOLFIERES BALLOON COMPANY
16 passage de la Main d'Or, 75011 Paris
Phone: +33 1 47 00 66 44
Fax: +33 1 47 00 66 55
Email: dlabeaume@teaser.fr
Website: www.franceballoons.com

A French hot air treat
Imagine floating over the châteaux of the magnificent Loire Valley or the beautiful valleys and hills of the famous Beaujolais region. France Montgolfières offer all this and more with their range of balloon flights. It was the Montgolfières brothers who constructed the first hot air balloon in 1783. The programmes are suitable for individuals or groups, and the flights can take place in the early morning or in the hours leading up to sunset. The experienced and qualified pilots all speak French and English and they will ensure you are informed of exactly what you are flying over. As well as the Loire Valley and Beaujolais flights, the company also has flights around Paris, in the Château D'Oex area of Switzerland and over the wondrous fairy chimney landscapes of Cappadocia in Turkey.

Activity prices: The Loire flight costs US$250 for a one hour flight. The Beaujolais flight costs US$250 for a one hour fifteen minute flight. The Paris flight costs US$295 including hotel transfer. The Swiss trip costs US$235 and the Turkish trip US$220. All prices per person.

Accommodation: Not included in the price, but can be arranged. Packages in the Loire include the flight and one night at a hotel or château and dinner. Prices from US$320.

Food: Not included, except the Loire packages as stated above.

Equipment supplied: No specialist equipment is required.

What to take: Warm wind-proof clothes, depending on the conditions.

When to go: Year round, weather permitting.

Established: 1984

Safety: All pilots are CAA qualified and the company is certified by the French civil aviation authority.

Insurance: Insurance is advised. Clients to arrange own policy.

Methods of payment: VISA, Mastercard, travellers' cheques and cash.

Booking information: Advance booking is essential. If a flight is cancelled due to weather conditions a full refund or rearrangement of the flight is offered, depending on type of ticket purchased.

Nearest airport: Depends on flight location.

Nearest rail station: Depends on flight location.

SPAIN

FLYING CIRCUS
Miguel Moya 6-28004, Madrid
Phone: +34 91 531 94 96
Fax: +34 91 531 40 80
Email: reservas@flyingcircus.es
Website: www.flyingcircus.es

Fly high in Spanish skies
Flying Circus is an established ballooning company that offers flights from prestigious launch sites, including ones near Madrid, Aranjuez and Segovia. Each flight lasts between one and two hours – they usually fly first thing in the morning and at weekends – and they reach a height of between 500 and 1,500 feet. Flight vouchers are available if you wish to give the flight as a gift.

Activity prices: Flights cost Pta20,000 per person.

Accommodation: Not included in the price, but can be arranged locally.

Food: Not included.

Equipment supplied: No specialist equipment is required.

What to take: Warm wind-proof clothes, depending on the conditions.

When to go: Year round, weather permitting. If flights are cancelled due to weather then the flight can be rearranged for later.

Established: 1989

Safety: All the Flying Circus pilots are CAA qualified. The balloons are all maintained to CAA standards and they fly only in light winds.

Insurance: Insurance should be arranged by client.

Methods of payment: VISA, Mastercard, travellers' cheques and cash.

Booking information: Advance booking is essential.

Nearest airport: Madrid.

Nearest rail station: Madrid.

UNITED KINGDOM

ACORN ACTIVITIES

PO Box 120, Hereford HR4 8YB
Phone: +44 (0)1432 830083
Fax: +44 (0)1432 830110
Email: sales@acornactivities.co.uk
Website: www.acornactivities.co.uk

Ballooning over the Herefordshire countryside

It's clear and still, early morning perhaps, or at dusk when the wind has dropped to a whisper. The world glides by as you float above the treetops. The only sound is the occasional roar of the burner boosting the balloon. All around lies the spectacular Herefordshire countryside. Acorn Activities is ideally situated for this unique experience which provides a full hour of airtime. An additional one or two hours are required as you take part in a safety briefing and help to set up the balloon for your flight. While you are flown by a qualified commercial pilot, a retrieval vehicle follows the balloon as far as its touchdown before transporting you back to the launch site. If weather prevents ballooning, you have the option of substituting your balloon flight for a 20 minute spin in a Robinson R-22 helicopter. Children must be at least 12 years old and all participants should be agile enough to climb in and out of the basket!

Activity prices: £145 per person for a one-hour flight, plus one to two hours' safety briefing and setting up.

Accommodation: Not included in the price, but can be arranged locally.

Transport to the airfield can be arranged at a small extra cost.

Food: Not included.

Equipment supplied: No specialist equipment is required.

What to take: Warm wind-proof clothes, depending on the conditions.

When to go: Year round, weather permitting.

Established: 1990

Safety: All pilots are CAA qualified.

Insurance: Insurance is required, although this can be arranged through Acorn Activities.

Methods of payment: VISA, Mastercard, cheque and cash.

Booking information: Late bookings are welcomed. A non-refundable deposit of £10 per day is required. Cancellation charges apply on a sliding scale from 80% for over 43 days before departure to 100% for up to 14 days.

Nearest airport: Cardiff or Birmingham International.

Nearest rail station: Depends on the itinerary.

A big balloon party

Every two years, Lorraine in Switzerland hosts the second biggest balloon get-together in the world. Over 1,000 hot air balloon teams from over 55 countries bring an amazing collection of weird and wonderful balloons to the Alps in a colourful spectacle to rival any other festival. First held in 1989 to commemorate the bicentennial of the French Revolution, the party has gained in recognition and now lasts for almost two weeks. Every day there is a mass take-off at dawn and dusk which is ideal for photography.

BUNGEE JUMPING

Of all the adventure activities mentioned in this book, few capture the imagination as much as bungee jumping. Fleeting, intense and vaguely hedonistic, there's something distinctly unnerving about stepping out into space with nothing but a bunch of elastic between you and a hard place.

SCAD-fad

Pioneered in Hamburg, the latest craze to have people leaping headlong into space is SCAD-jumping, or Suspended Catch Air Device. While this sounds more like a police breathalyser than a breath of fresh air, it may yet prove to be as popular as its big-bungee brother. A SCAD is actually an enormous square net with tubular inflatable sides, suspended 150 feet or more beneath a tower. Instead of being attached to a bungee cord, you are secured in a harness with a solid back brace, neck brace and helmet. You're then directed to sit in an ominous-looking pair of bomb-bay doors at the top of the tower. On the count of three the doors swing open and you drop like a 200-pounder onto the SCAD net below.

While this might sound like the perfect way to break a bone, the SCAD net gives as much as 30 feet, and slows you down so gently you won't even notice it happening. In the unlikely event that you decide to give yourself to a lifetime of leaping, you might like to try it out of a helicopter 250 feet above the net. Or you might not.

Bungee jumping was pioneered in New Zealand, but actually originated and continues today as a rite of passage in the Vanuatu Islands of the South Pacific, where instead of industrial-strength elastic, teenage boys tie vine ropes around their ankles and leap off wooden towers.

Whether you're jumping from a tower, a bridge or a cable car, you'll be asked to remove any loose objects from your person, strapped into the ankle harness and then pitched into space on the count of one. There really isn't much more to it than that, apart from to mention that the rebound is almost as exciting as the downward journey.

Recent alternatives to the original adrenaline rush include reverse or 'catapult' bungee: participants are harnessed at the waist to the length of elastic and are then clipped to a bolt behind them with a quick-release attachment. The bungee rope is then stretched by a crane (or something similar) until it is tighter than an e-string. Those accelerating from 0 to 60 mph in 0 seconds for the first time have been known to start running through the air on the way back down!

AUSTRIA

HIGH 5
Bahnhof 248, 6951 Lingenau
Phone: +43 5513 4140
Fax: +43 5513 4150
Email: office@outdoor.at
Website: www.outdoor.at

Dive off Austria's Highest bungee bridge
High 5 is one of the leading outdoor centres in the country and their bungee jumping course is the highest bridge jump in the country at a whopping 106 metres high. The bridge is at Lingenau near the beautiful Lake Constance and you will be given full instructions by nationally qualified bungee jump masters on how to go about leaping off. After all the excitement you even get the option of spending the night sleeping in a teepee.

Activity prices: Bungee jumps cost 80 euros.

Accommodation: Available at centre, including teepees for exotic nights under canvas.

Food: Available at centre.

Equipment supplied: All specialist equipment is supplied.

What to take: Nothing special.

When to go: 1 May to 31 October.

Established: 1989

Safety: All the instructors at High 5 are nationally qualified. The centre is a member of the Austrian Outdoor Association.

Insurance: Full liability insurance cover is included in the price of the jump.

Methods of payment: Bank draft and cash.

Booking information: Advance booking is recommended.

Nearest airport: Zurich (1 hour).

Nearest rail station: Bregenz. Transfers can be arranged.

ITALY

NO LIMITS BUNGEE CENTRE – TRIORA

Exploring Bungee Srl, 44 via Tadino, 20124 Milan
Phone: +39 (0)2 2940 3136
Fax: +39 (0)2 2940 6787
Email: info@bungee.it
Website: www.bungee.it

Don't dive for me Argentina

The Triora No Limits Bungee Centre is located in an ancient medieval village. The jump site is at the 119 metre high Loreto Bridge which crosses a deep gorge cut by the fast-flowing River Argentina. Once you are all strapped into the harness and have got over your wobbly legs, you plunge 30 metres in free fall, experiencing forces of 1.65G and speeds of up to 87 kph, before the rope takes effect to slow you over the next 74 metres. Say hello to the nearby water before you rebound back up to start falling again. No doubt you will soon be queuing again for another go. It only takes a few hours, so you will have plenty of time to explore the many other adventure sport opportunities in the area.

Activity prices: First jump L120,000, second jump L100,000 or a tandem jump for L200,000. Special night jumps (10 p.m.–1 a.m.) cost L150,000 and an 18 minute video costs L20,000. Group discounts available.

Accommodation: Not included. B&B accommodation is available locally.

Food: Not included. Available locally.

Equipment supplied: Full body harness and ankle harness – all you need.

What to take: A good dose of courage.

When to go: Year round except December and January.

Established: 1994

Safety: All bungee equipment is subject to rigorous independent testing and regular checking. The elastic ropes are replaced after only 10% (every 300 jumps) of their expected lives and the rope sustains a maximum of only 18% of its maximum load capability during each jump. All other equipment is changed every two years. Each jump has a Jump Master who has passed a technical exam and has over 5 years of experience.

Insurance: Full liability insurance cover is included in the price of the jump.

Methods of payment: VISA, travellers' cheques, and local or foreign currency.

Booking information: Advance booking is recommended but not essential.

Nearest airport: Torino or Nice.

Nearest rail station: Sanremo.

NO LIMITS BUNGEE CENTRE – VEGLIO-PISTOLESA (BIELLA)

Exploring Bungee Srl, 44 via Tadino, 20124 Milan
Phone: +39 (0)2 2940 3136
Fax: +39 (0)2 2940 6787
Email: info@bungee.it
Website: www.bungee.it

A colossal leap

Operated by the same company as the Triora Bungee Centre, this No Limits Centre offers an even higher jump from the daunting and impressive eight-tier, 152 metre high bridge called Colossus. It is located just 40 km off the A4 Milan to Torino motorway. On this jump, you get to experience 43 metres of breathtaking free fall before the bungee cord kicks in and the full jump is a spine-tingling 140 metres long. Your body will experience around 1.7G of acceleration force, so don't go after breakfast!

Activity prices: First jump L150,000, second jump L130,000 or a tandem jump for L260,000. Special night jumps (10 p.m.–1 a.m.) cost L180,000 and an 18 minute video of your jump costs L20,000. Group discounts available.

Accommodation: Not included. B&B accommodation is available locally.

Food: Not included. Available locally.

Equipment supplied: Full body harness and ankle harness – all you need.

What to take: A good dose of courage.

When to go: Year round except December and January.

Established: 1994

Safety: All bungee equipment is subject to rigorous independent testing and regular checking. The elastic ropes are replaced after only 10% (every 200 jumps) of their expected lives, and the rope sustains a maximum of only 18% of its maximum load capability during each jump. All other equipment is changed every two years. Each jump has a Jump Master who has passed a technical exam and has over 5 years of experience.

Insurance: Full liability insurance cover is included in the price of the jump.

Methods of payment: VISA, travellers' cheques, and local or foreign currency.

Booking information: Advance booking is recommended but not essential.

Nearest airport: Torino or Nice.

Nearest rail station: Cossato.

SLOVENIA

TOP EXTREME
TOP d.o.o., Vojkova 9, 5000 Nova Gorica
Phone: +38 (0)66 522 006
Fax: +38 (0)66 522 006
Email: info@top.si
Website: www.top.si

A Unique Slovenian flying experience
Top Extreme is the only bungee jumping centre in Slovenia and their principal jump site is the 55 metre high Solkan bridge near Nova

Gorica. You can take the leap alone and stay dry, get dunked into the River Soča or team up with a friend for a tandem jump. Whichever method you choose, the results are the same . . . sheer terror followed by an overwhelming overdose of adrenaline, always accompanied by enormous grins and shrieks. The centre also has a mobile bungee crane that travels around the country, so enquire as to its whereabouts if you fancy seeing a bit more of the country while plummeting upside down.

Activity prices: Jumps cost DM70 per person. Group and student discounts available.
Accommodation: Not included. Available locally.
Food: Not included. Available locally.
Equipment supplied: Full bungee harness.
What to take: Personal clothing.
When to go: April to October.
Established: 1993
Safety: The centre's bungee staff are all qualified instructors.
Insurance: Full liability insurance cover is included in the price of the jump.
Personal accident insurance is advised.
Methods of payment: Cash only.
Booking information: Advance booking is essential.
Nearest airport: Trieste (30 km).
Nearest rail station: Nova Gorica (2 km). Transfers can be arranged.

SWITZERLAND

ALPIN RAFT
Postfach 78, 3800 Matten
Phone: +41 33 823 4100
Fax: +41 33 823 4101
Email: mail@alpinraft.ch
Website: www.alpinraft.ch

Bungee jump from a gondola in the Swiss Alps
Situated in the heart of the Swiss Alps in the shadow of the Eiger's spectacular and foreboding North Face, Interlaken is ideally situated for every adrenaline activity you could care to mention, and bungee jumping is no exception. Instead of a crane or a bridge, jumpers are cast out into space from a gondola over a mountain lake. Open every evening from May to October, the bungee jump is best experienced at sunset, when the entire scene is bathed in the warmth of alpenglow. If you only ever bungee jump once in your lifetime, strap into your harness here – it may well be the most scenic bungee jump in Europe.

Activity prices: Bungee jumps cost SFr120.
Accommodation: Backpacker accommodation available at the centre.
Food: None provided.
Equipment supplied: Harness.
What to take: No special equipment required.
When to go: May to October.
Established: 1988
Safety: Instructors receive full bungee jump training and are qualified first aiders.
Insurance: Clients must arrange their own insurance.
Methods of payment: All common Methods of payment accepted.
Booking information: Book by phone or email. Full payment is charged for cancellation on the day of trip.
Nearest airport: Bern.
Nearest rail station: Interlaken.

WALLIS-PUR ADVENTURE PARK – EUROBUNGY
Rue de la Place 24, CH 3965 Chippis
Phone: +41 79 447 2800
Fax: +41 274 56 18 00
Email: swiss@eurobungy.ch
Website: www.eurobungy.ch

Leap off Europe's highest bungee sites

The Wallis-Pur Sports and Adventure Park is home to EuroBungy. They have some amazing jump sites both in and outside of the park, ranging from a 190 metre high leap in the park to a whopping heart stopper from 300 metres at the Gemmibahn bridge in Leukerbad, the highest bungee jump in Europe. That should blow away the cobwebs! All you have to do is turn up with enough bottle to jump. Just in case you are really crazy and the bungee jumps get a bit monotonous, they also have the world's largest giant swing, 150 metre high bridge swing where you reach 200 kph. Hold on to your hat!

Activity prices: Bungee jumps cost SFr120 for a 100 metre jump, SFr190 for the 190 metre jump and SFr320 for the big one. The giant swing costs SFr135.

Accommodation: Not included in the price. Hotel accommodation is available in the valley, or you can sleep in an Indian teepee just 15 minutes from the park.

Food: None provided.

Equipment supplied: All specialist equipment.

What to take: No special equipment required.

When to go: April to November.

Established: 1996

Safety: Instructors receive full bungee jump training from the centre and hold national qualifications. The centre is a member of the IAAPA.{?}

Insurance: The centre has full insurance for its activities. Clients should arrange their own travel policy.

Methods of payment: All major credit cards and cash.

Booking information: Advance booking is recommended but you can just turn up on the day too.

Nearest airport: Geneva, Milan or Zurich.

Nearest rail station: Sierre. Transfers are not available. A bus runs from the station to Val d'Annviers and the centre is just after the village of Niouc.

UNITED KINGDOM

ACORN ACTIVITIES
PO Box 120, Hereford, HR4 8YB
Phone: +44 (0)1432 830083
Fax: +44 (0)1432 830110
Email: sales@acornactivities.co.uk
Website: www.acornactivities.co.uk

Bungee jumping throughout the UK
Acorn Activities use a number of bungee towers in England, Scotland and Wales from April to October. Three mobile cranes tour the UK, meaning there's more than likely to be a bungee opportunity within easy driving distance. Gift vouchers are available, which can then be redeemed at a date and location to suit you. Participants must weight at least 6.5 stone and less than 30 stone, and must be at least 14 years of age. Those aged 17 or under must have a parent or guardian present, or have written permission.

Activity prices: £50 per person.
Accommodation: Not included in the price.
Food: Not included.
Equipment supplied: Harness provided.
What to take: No special clothing required.
When to go: Year round.
Established: 1990
Safety: All instructors are highly experienced.
Insurance: Insurance is required, although this can be arranged through Acorn Activities.
Methods of payment: VISA, Mastercard, cheque and cash.
Booking information: Late bookings are welcomed. A non-refundable deposit of £10 per day is required. Cancellation charges apply on a sliding scale from 80% for over 43 days before departure to 100% for up to 14 days.
Nearest airport: Cardiff or Birmingham International.
Nearest rail station: Depends on the itinerary.

CANYONING

Pioneered in the Alps in the early 1990s and fast gaining popularity all over Europe, canyoning is the latest adventure activity to make the most of the mountains. Clad in wetsuits, helmets and buoyancy aids, participants navigate steep, narrow waterways by swimming, sliding and abseiling their way downstream, scrambling around boulders and leaping into deep plunge-pools.

Also known as gorge walking, canyoning is actually nothing new, particularly in America where outdoor adventurers have been exploring the backwaters of National Parks and wilderness areas for decades. Combining the skills of climbing, caving and white water navigation, canyoning opens up previously inaccessible areas of the landscape to exploration and enjoyment.

There are now dozens of companies all over Europe offering introductory taster sessions and a few which organise longer, multi-day trips. If you'd like to do more of the sliding and less of the leaping, trips can usually be tailor-made to suit individual or group requirements. No previous experience is required, although participants are usually expected to be able to swim. As you jump, splash and scramble your way downstream, what started as a tentative tip-toe into the unknown might soon become the outdoor experience of a lifetime.

AUSTRIA

ALPIN CLUB GESÄUSE – CANYONING ADVENTURE TEAM
Hall 10, A-8911, Admont, STMK
Phone: +43 3613 4269
Fax: +43 3613 4269
Email: acg-cat@canyoning.at
Website: www.canyoning.at

The hills are alive with canyoners

Being based in the middle of the eastern Alps allows ACG-CAT access to some of the country's best gorges and canyons. Their tours range from one to six days in length and cover three distinct levels of ability. Blue runs last for approximately three hours and are ideally suited to beginners. You master swimming through natural pools and traversing fallen trees. Red courses last from four to six hours, during which you learn about roping techniques and then abseil down cliffs and waterfalls up to about 25 metres in height. The ultimate black courses last from six to eight hours and you must have completed a red run beforehand.

Activity prices: Blue tours cost Sch690, Red tours Sch890 and the ultimate black trip costs Sch990. A canyoning weekend costs from Sch2,290.

Accommodation: For multiple day courses the price includes one grill dinner, hotel accommodation and breakfast.

Food: Some food is included in the multiple day courses.

Equipment supplied: All specialist equipment is supplied, including canyoning harness, helmet, wetsuit and jacket.

What to take: Swimsuit and suitable footwear.

When to go: May to October.

Established: 1993

Safety: All guides are UIAGM-IVM and Guide de Montagne qualified.

Insurance: Clients are covered by centre's insurance.

Methods of payment: Bank transfer.

Booking information: Advance booking is recommended.

Nearest airport: Graz-Salzburg.

Nearest rail station: Liezen-Austria.

HIGH 5

Bahnhof 248, 6951 Lingenau
Phone: +43 5513 4140
Fax: +43 5513 4150
Email: office@outdoor.at
Website: www.outdoor.at

Explore the canyons of Constance

High 5 is at the forefront of organised adventure sports in Austria and offer a range of canyoning trips to suit all levels of ability. All the trips take place near Lingenau on the shores of the spectacularly beautiful Lake Constance, near the border with Switzerland and Germany. The canyons all have alluring names, such as Merlin's World, Jungle's End and Angel Falls, and you can link several of them together over a longer stay if you really want to test your endurance. Whichever you choose, you are going to get seriously wet and seriously excited, so be prepared.

Activity prices: The canyoning trips cost from Sch80 per day. There are also three-day options.

Accommodation: Available at centre, including teepees for exotic nights under canvas.

Food: Available at centre.

Equipment supplied: All specialist equipment is supplied.

What to take: Swimsuit and towel.

When to go: 1 May to 31 October.

Established: 1989

Safety: All the canyoning instructors at High 5 are nationally qualified.

The centre is a member of the Austrian Outdoor Association.

Insurance: Full liability insurance cover is included in the price.

Methods of payment: Bank draft and cash.

Booking information: Advance booking is recommended.

Nearest airport: Zurich (1 hour).

Nearest rail station: Bregenz. Transfers can be arranged.

SPORTSCHULE FANKHAUSER – TIROL RAFTING

Dorfstrasse 17, A-6382 Kirchdorf, Tirol
Phone: +43 5352 62233
Fax: +43 5352 62587
Email: fanky@netwing.at
Website: www.tirolrafting.com

Deep into a canyon maze

Sportschule Fankhauser is based in the dramatic and beautiful Tirol region of Austria and has access to an incredible network of canyons in the Haiming area. Within a 10 sq km section of mountains there are no fewer than seven canyons for you to explore, with technical challenges to suit every level of ability. The well-qualified and experienced guides will take you through the basic techniques needed for abseiling, scrambling and leaping into pools from the cliffs. If you have the bottle and the experience, then there are canyons here to test the best.

Activity prices: The canyoning trips start from Sch490 per person.

Accommodation: Available at centre, either camping or in a bunkhouse.

Food: Breakfast and half board packages are available at the centre.

Equipment supplied: All specialist equipment – wetsuits, neoprene shoes, helmets, lifejackets, harnesses and climbing gear – is supplied.

What to take: Swimsuit.

When to go: Year round, daily.

Established: 1985

Safety: All the canyoning guides hold national qualifications. The centre is approved by the Austrian Tourist Office and the Austrian Canyoning Association.

Insurance: The centre has liability insurance but clients should arrange their own accident policy.

Methods of payment: VISA, Mastercard, Eurocard, travellers' cheques and cash.

Booking information: Advance booking is essential at least one day ahead. No deposit is required and there are no cancellation penalties.

Nearest airport: Innsbruck. Transfers can be arranged.

Nearest rail station: Ütztal-Bahnhof. Transfers can be arranged.

BULGARIA

BULGARIAN MOUNTAINS ADVENTURE

Kancho Shipkov, Kv. Dianabad bl 18 vh.A, 1172 Sofia

Phone: +359 2 620 688

Fax: N/A

Email: kancho@bglink.net

Website: http://pss.bglink.net/mysite/explorebg.html

A personal taste of Bulgarian adventure
Bulgaria is one of the least explored adventure destinations in Europe, yet it has some outstanding locations. Bulgarian Mountains Adventure is a company based around members of the national mountain rescue service. They offer personal and tailor-made guiding services. It would be hard to find somebody better qualified to take you on great adventures there. The beautiful Bulgarian mountain ranges are dissected by numerous canyons that are suitable for canyoning. You get the chance to abseil through waterfalls, scramble up gullies, slide down river chutes and leap into pools. At night, if you wish, you can camp out around a campfire.

Activity prices: The trips are all tailor-made to suit your requirements and cost around US$50 per day, or less, depending on what you do and where you go. The centre will advise you on the possibilities. The price also includes local transportation.

Accommodation: Food and lodging during the activity are included in the price and organised by the centre. Hotels and meals at the start and end of your trip are not included but the centre can help you arrange these.

Food: Food is included during the activity, but not at the start and end of your trip.

Equipment supplied: All specialist equipment is supplied.

What to take: Personal clothing, suitable footwear, swimsuit and towel.

When to go: Year round, though winter is only for the crazy!

Established: 1997

Safety: At least one of the guides in every group is a qualified rescuer from the Bulgarian Mountain Rescue Service. They have plentiful experience and excellent local knowledge.

Insurance: Clients should arrange their own policy; or the centre can arrange it on the spot.

Methods of payment: Bank transfer and cash.

Booking information: Advance booking is essential and a 30% deposit is payable. Cancellation penalties may apply.

Nearest airport: Sofia. Transfers can be arranged.

Nearest rail station: Sofia Central. Transfers can be arranged.

FRANCE

SNOW SAFARI LIMITED
Chalet Savoy, 1351 route des Chavants, 74310 Les Houches
Phone: +33 (0)4 50 54 56 63;
UK bookings & information +44 (0)1279 600 885
Fax: +33 (0)4 50 54 57 19
Email: Chalsavoy@aol.com
Website: www.chaletsavoy.com

Canyoning the rivers of the Mont Blanc Massif
This relatively new adventure sport has become one of the most popular mountain activities in the French Alps, and involves abseiling down waterfalls, leaping into plunge pools and sliding down chutes of fast-moving water. The Chalet Savoy offers a half-day introductory course that includes basic instruction on an indoor climbing wall followed by a spectacular descent of the Balme Canyon. For the more experienced or more adventurous, a full-day trip takes in some of the most dramatic canyons in the Mont Blanc region.

Activity prices: FFr350 per half-day, FFr630 per full day, including a video of the whole adventure.
Accommodation: Available at the Chalet. Summer prices start from FFr140 per person for B&B, or FFr2050 per person for seven days and seven nights.
Food: Half-board included in the accommodation price.
Equipment supplied: All equipment supplied.
What to take: Swimsuit and towel.
When to go: May to September.
Established: 1987
Safety: All guides and leaders are fully qualified for the relevant activity.
Insurance: Clients must arrange their own insurance.
Methods of payment: VISA, Mastercard.
Booking information: Contact Snow Safari for booking form and full terms and conditions.
Nearest airport: Geneva.
Nearest rail station: Les Houches.

ITALY

CANYON ADVENTURES
Via Mateotti 57/b, 38069 Torbole sul Garda (TN)
Phone: +39 (0)464 505 072
Fax: +39 (0)464 505 647
Email: flipper@anthesi.com
Website: www.garda.com/flipper

Explore secluded Garda canyons
Lake Garda is one of the most beautiful parts of Italy and there are over 20 different canyons to which Canyon Adventures offer trips, including some in other parts of northern Italy. You get to swim through rivers, slide and abseil down waterfalls and leap from rocks into crystal clear pools. There are courses to suit every level of ability, so even if you have never done anything like it before you can have a go (providing you can swim, of course!). The guides are all experienced and qualified and many speak other languages including English, German and French. There can be no better way of getting close to nature and in summer the climate is wonderful too.

Activity prices: Half-day canyoning trips costs from L70,000 to L100,000 while full-day trips cost from L120,000 to L200,000. Longer trips are possible.
Accommodation: Not included in course price. Clients normally arrange their own but the centre can help.
Food: Full-day tours include lunch, otherwise clients arrange their own. There are many options in the Garda area.
Equipment supplied: All specialist equipment is provided.
What to take: Sports shoes or walking boots, a towel, t-shirt and dry clothes for changing into afterwards.
When to go: Daily from April to end of October.
Established: 1992
Safety: All canyoning guides are nationally qualified. The centre is also a member of Associazione Italiana Canyoning and the Commission Européenne de Canyon.

Insurance: The centre has full liability insurance. Clients are advised to take out their own accident insurance.

Methods of payment: Travellers' cheques and cash.

Booking information: Advance booking is essential. Full payment is due at time of booking. Cancellations must be notified in writing at least one week before activity date.

Nearest airport: Verona.

Nearest rail station: Rovereto.

SLOVENIA

TOP EXTREME

TOP d.o.o., Vojkova 9, 5000 Nova Gorica
Phone: +38 (0)66 522 006
Fax: +38 (0)66 522 006
Email: info@top.si
Website: www.top.si

Up a Slovenian canyon without a paddle

Slovenia is one of the least explored parts of Europe yet it has some stunning scenery. Top extreme's half-day canyoning trips take you into the country's upper Posoèje region where there are several fascinating canyons. The easier course on offer lasts for around three hours and involves swimming through pure pools, sliding down rock chutes and scaling waterfalls. A more challenging course lasts for around five hours and gives you the chance to test your skills and endurance further. June to September are the best months for tackling the canyons.

Activity prices: The half-day courses cost DM75 per person. Group and student discounts are available.

Accommodation: Not included. Available locally.

Food: Not included. Available locally.

Equipment supplied: Wetsuits, shoes, helmet, lifejacket and waterproof jacket are supplied.

What to take: Shorts, t-shirt and towel.

When to go: April to November (it gets rather cold during the winter months).

Established: 1993

Safety: The centre's canyoning staff are all qualified instructors.

Insurance: Accident insurance is included in the price. The company also has liability insurance.

Methods of payment: Eurocard, Mastercard and cash.

Booking information: Advance booking is essential.

Nearest airport: Ljubljana (100 km).

Nearest rail station: Most na Soci (30 km).

SPAIN

EXPEDICIONES SC

Las Almunias de Rodellar, E-22144 Huesca
Phone: +34 974 34 30 08
Fax: +34 974 34 30 08
Email: expediciones@mad.servicom.es
Website: www.expediciones-sc.es

Canyoning in the Pyrenees

Reputed to be the birthplace of canyoning, Spain's Sierra de Guara features more than 70 canyons in an area of barely 20 sq km. Based in Huesca, about 80 km south of the Pyrenees, Expediciones has been running canyoning trips in the region for more than 20 years. Trips vary from one or two days to week-long expeditions, but all include a healthy helping of vertiginous canyon walls, enormous waterfalls and idyllic plunge pools. Wild and inaccessible, the canyons are a world apart from the surrounding mountains and longer trips involve carrying all equipment and supplies and camping out overnight in bivouacs. Beginners are especially welcome, but some of the canyons require abseiling experience.

Activity prices: From Pta5,500 for one day, Pta22,000 for two days and Pta79,000 for one week.

Accommodation: Two-day and one-week trips include accommodation in four-person, igloo-type tents. The campsite features hot showers, bar, restaurant and a climbing wall.

Food: Two-day and one-week trips include all food. Other requirements by arrangement.

Equipment supplied: All specialist equipment provided.

What to take: Old trekking shoes, day sack, swimsuit, shorts and t-shirt, lightweight waterproof, water bottle, cap, sun glasses, sun cream, etc.

When to go: June to September.

Established: 1978

Safety: All guides are nationally certified as canyoning or climbing guides and are multi-lingual.

Insurance: Obligatory activity-specific insurance is included in the price.

Methods of payment: Spanish or French currency, travellers' cheques, Eurocheques.

Booking information: Contact directly by phone, fax or email to make a booking. A 10% deposit is usually required.

Nearest airport: Huesca.

Nearest rail station: Huesca.

EXPEDICIONES SC

Las Almunias de Rodellar, E-22144 Huesca
Phone: +34 974 34 30 08
Fax: +34 974 34 30 08
Email: expediciones@mad.servicom.es
Website: www.expediciones-sc.es

Canyoning in Majorca

Mallorca is renowned for its deep gorges and precipitous canyons, and nowhere more so than the Sierra de Tramuntana, a mountain range that dominates the north coast of the island. The wild, rugged coastline guards a treasure-trove of emerald-green pools and untouched ravines, many of which can only be reached from the canyons above. The landscape is characterised by 200 metre walls, 150 metre tunnels and canyons so deep that they rarely see direct sunlight. Black vultures are common in many of the canyons, and ancient terraces provide evidence of human habitation. Expediciones offers week-long expeditions that include all food, equipment, and accommodation. First-timers are welcome but participants must be able to swim 100 metres.

Activity prices: From Pta79,000 for one week.

Accommodation: Two-day and one-week trips include accommodation in four-person, igloo-type tents. The campsite features hot showers, bar, restaurant and a climbing wall.

Food: Two-day and one-week trips include all food. Other requirements by arrangement.

Equipment supplied: All specialist equipment provided.

What to take: Old trekking shoes, day sack, swimsuit, shorts and t-shirt, lightweight waterproof, water bottle, cap, sun glasses, sun cream, etc.

When to go: June to September.

Established: 1978

Safety: All guides are nationally certified as canyoning or climbing guides and are multi-lingual.

Insurance: Obligatory activity-specific insurance is included in the price.

Methods of payment: Spanish and French currenty, travellers' cheques, Eurocheques.

Booking information: Contact directly by phone, fax or email to make a booking. A 10% deposit is usually required.

Nearest airport: Palma de Majorca Airport. Clients can be picked up at the airport by arrangement.

Nearest rail station: N/A.

SWITZERLAND

ADVENTURE'S BEST
PO Box 9, Via Basilea 28, CH-6903 Lugano
Phone: +41 91 966 11 14
Fax: +41 91 966 12 13
Email: info@asbest.ch
Website: www.asbest.ch

Canyoning in southern Switzerland
A relatively young company, Adventure's Best has been organising outdoor activities in Ticino for the last five years. The most southern state (canton) in Switzerland, Ticino is a region 90 km by 40 km characterised by lakes, rivers and an extensive mountain range rising

as high as 3,400 metres. Available only from May to October, canyoning is one of the best ways to explore the hanging valleys and remote gorges of the region, and Adventure's Best offers a choice of over 20 different itineraries. All canyoning trips are led by a nationally certified Alpine Guide. Activities are available on a daily basis, and a variety of accommodation options are available at the centre (see below).

Activity prices: There are numerous trips on offer. Contact the centre for a full price list.

Accommodation: Not included in the price, but is available at the centre. Shared dormitoriess cost SFr20 per person, a double room SFr40 per person, a double room with en suite bath/shower SFr50 per person and a single room with en suite bath/shower SFr60 per person.

Food: Not included in the price, but is available at the centre. Buffet breakfast costs SFr15 per person.

Equipment supplied: All specialist equipment is provided.

What to take: Personal clothing.

When to go: May to October.

Established: 1994

Safety: All instructors hold recognised qualifications from the relevant national or international governing body.

Insurance: Clients are responsible for arranging their own insurance.

Methods of payment: VISA, Mastercard, Amex, travellers' cheques and cash.

Booking information: No deposit required.

Nearest airport: Lugano-Agno (5 km).

Nearest rail station: Lugano (200 metres).

ALPIN CENTER ZERMATT

Mountain Guides' Association, 3920 Zermatt
Phone: +41 (0)27 966 2460
Fax: +41 (0)27 966 2469
Email: alpincenter@zermatt.ch
Website: www.zermatt.ch/alpincenter

Canyoning for water lovers and haters

Deep among the high mountains surrounding Zermatt are deep, feature-filled canyons that make great adventure playgrounds. If you like the idea of canyoning but hate the idea of getting soaked, try the Alpin Center's tour up the Gorner Gorge. You can scramble up rocks alongside thundering waterfalls and feel the force of the water without taking the plunge! For water babies, the full-day trip up the Massa Gorge is more suitable. With thick wetsuits to protect against the cold river, you hike, glide, jump and swim your way past impressive rock formations up the valley. For real adventure junkies, the Zwischbergen Gorge adds a few bigger challenges.

Activity prices: The Gorner Gorge trip costs SFr95; the Massa Gorge SFr150; the Zwischbergen Gorge SFr235. Group size varies from three to six depending on tour.

Accommodation: A wide range of accommodation is available in the Zermatt area. The centre can assist with arranging it.

Food: Not included. There are plenty of eating options in Zermatt.

Equipment supplied: Specialist equipment is provided.

What to take: Personal clothing and suitable footwear.

When to go: Generally June to October.

Established: 1982

Safety: All the Alpin Center guides are fully licensed, qualified and highly experienced. You are in very safe hands.

Insurance: Clients must arrange their own personal accident insurance and it is recommended that you also take out Rescue Insurance with Air Zermatt for SFr20 per week or SFr30 per year. Forms are available from the Alpin Center.

Methods of payment: VISA, cash or bank transfer.

Booking information: Advance booking is essential.

Nearest airport: Zurich.

Nearest rail station: Zermatt.

ALPIN RAFT

Postfach 78, 3800 Matten
Phone: +41 33 823 4100

Fax: +41 33 823 4101
Email: mail@alpinraft.ch
Website: www.alpinraft.ch

Swiss canyoning
Situated in the heart of the Alps, Interlaken is arguably the centre of adventure activity in Switzerland, offering snow-capped summits, foaming rivers and year-round opportunity. Canyoning involves natural waterslides, abseiling down waterfalls and leaping into bottomless plunge pools. Alpin Raft offer several different canyoning experiences all within half an hour's drive of Interlaken. Canyons range in difficulty from easy to extreme, the latter boasting big slides and even bigger jumps. Half-day and full-day options are offered and all equipment is provided – all you need is a swimsuit, a towel and a thirst for white water!

Activity prices: From SFr88 for a half-day to SFr140 for a full day.
Accommodation: Backpacker accommodation available at the centre.
Food: Lunch included.
Equipment supplied: Wetsuit, harness, booties, helmet and buoyancy aid.
What to take: Swimsuit and towel.
When to go: May to October.
Established: 1988
Safety: Instructors are fully trained in canyoning and are qualified first aiders.
Insurance: Clients must arrange their own insurance.
Methods of payment: All common Methods of payment accepted.
Booking information: Book by phone or email. Full payment is charged for cancellation on the day of trip.
Nearest airport: Bern.
Nearest rail station: Interlaken.

UNITED KINGDOM

ACORN ACTIVITIES
PO Box 120, Hereford HR4 8YB
Phone: +44 (0)1432 830083

Fax: +44 (0)1432 830110
Email: sales@acornactivities.co.uk
Website: www.acornactivities.co.uk

Canyoning in south Wales
Hills and fast-flowing streams provide breathtaking locations for this wet and wild day out, but be warned – you will get wet! The day's adventure involves walking behind waterfalls, traversing rock walls, scrambling over rocks and even crossing rivers on a Tyrolean zip wire – if you don't know what one is, can you afford not to find out for yourself? None of the individual components is obligatory, and for those on family holidays less demanding locations are used. Wetsuits, helmets and buoyancy aids are all provided as a matter of course.

Activity prices: £40 per day (minimum booking six people, although individuals may join groups).

Accommodation: Not included in the price.

Food: Not included.

Equipment supplied: All specialist equipment is supplied.

What to take: Swimsuit, suitable footwear and a towel.

When to go: Year round.

Established: 1990

Safety: All instructors are highly experienced in ropework and river rescue techniques.

Insurance: Insurance is required, although this can be arranged through Acorn Activities.

Methods of payment: VISA, Mastercard, cheques and cash.

Booking information: Late bookings are welcomed. A non-refundable deposit of £10 per day is required. Cancellation charges apply on a sliding scale from 80% for over 43 days before departure to 100% for up to 14 days.

Nearest airport: Cardiff or Birmingham International.

Nearest rail station: Depends on the itinerary.

BLACK MOUNTAIN ACTIVITIES

PO Box 5, Hay on Wye, Hereford HR3 5YB
Phone: +44 (0)1497 847 897
Fax: +44 (0)1497 847 897
Email: enquiries@blackmountain.co.uk
Website: www.blackmountain.co.uk

Gorge walking in the Black Mountains
The UK's version of canyoning may at first glance not seem as exciting as the bigger canyon trips in the rest of Europe but the UK tour is capable of giving an adrenaline boost to the toughest adventure junkies. In the Black Mountains and the Brecon Beacons you traverse rock walls, jump boulders, climb waterfalls and squeeze through small rock holes as well as the more traditional abseiling into sinkholes! To top it all off, you get the chance to zip on a rope over a raging river. Bored? You won't be.

Activity prices: £30 per day or £20 for a half-day trip.
Accommodation: Not included in the price. There is a range of accommodation available locally and the centre will advise you.
Food: Not included. Packed lunches can be arranged at extra cost.
Equipment supplied: All specialist equipment is supplied.
What to take: Personal clothing, swimsuit, suitable footwear.
When to go: Year round.
Established: 1992
Safety: All the centre's staff are fully qualified in their respective sports, hold first aid qualifications and are highly professional. All equipment used meets national safety standards. The centre is licensed by the AALA and the Welsh Tourist Board.
Insurance: The centre is insured though clients may wish to take out separate insurance too.
Methods of payment: Personal cheques and cash.
Booking information: Advance booking is recommended though late bookings may be possible.
Nearest airport: Depends on tour. Cardiff and Bristol are nearest to the centre.

Nearest rail station: Depends on the itinerary. Hereford and Abergavenny are nearest to the centre.

CROFT-NA-CABER
Kenmore, Loch Tay, Perthshire
Phone: +44 (0)1887 830 236
Fax: +44 (0)1887 830 649
Email: info@croftnacaber.co.uk
Website: www.croftnacaber.co.uk

Threading through Perthshire gorges
Croft-na-Caber is based near to Loch Tay and there are a number of forest-clad gorges in the area that are great fun to explore. The centre's guides will take you through the basic skills needed for abseiling down the waterfalls and then you can combine this with plunging into pools, climbing up rocks and sliding down water chutes. The centre offers half- and full-day trips to suit a variety of abilities.

Activity prices: Gorge walking trips start from around £30 per person.
Accommodation: Self-catering log cabins or hotel accommodation at centre.
Food: Hotel restaurant and bar at centre.
Equipment supplied: All specialist equipment is supplied.
What to take: Personal clothing, swimsuit, suitable footwear.
When to go: Year round.
Established: 1974
Safety: All the centre's staff are fully qualified in their respective sports, hold first aid qualifications and are highly professional. All equipment used meets national safety standards. The centre is licensed by the AALA.
Insurance: The centre is insured up to £6 million for liability but clients may wish to take out separate insurance for accidents/cancellation too.
Methods of payment: VISA, Mastercard, cheques and cash.
Booking information: Advance booking is essential. Payment of 20% deposit is required. Tour must be confirmed or cancelled at least seven days in advance.
Nearest airport: Edinburgh. Transfers can be arranged.
Nearest rail station: Perth, Pitlochry. Transfers can be arranged.

PEAK ACTIVITIES

Rock Lea Activity Training Centre, Station Road, Hathersage,
Hope Valley, Derbyshire S32 1DD
Phone: +44 (0)1433 650 345
Fax: +44 (0)1433 650 342
Email: admin@iain.co.uk
Website: www.iain.co.uk

Gorge yourself in the Derbyshire Peaks

The Peak District National Park is one of the most beautiful locations in the country and brims with adventure opportunities. A great way to explore places that few people ever get to is to take off on a gorge-walking trip. Peak Activities run several courses that take you through some spectacular local gorges, swimming through rivers, scrambling up rocks and jumping into pools – generally, getting wet and soggy! You will soon understand why this is one of fastest-growing sports in Europe.

Activity prices: Prices vary depending on group size and length of course. They start from £20 per person for a two-hour session.

Accommodation: Not included in the course price. There is a large range of options within easy reach of the centre, ranging from hostels and B&B to farmhouses and hotels.

Food: Not included in course price but there are plenty of local eateries to suit all budgets.

Equipment supplied: All specialist equipment, including wetsuits.

What to take: Swimsuit and suitable footwear. Full list supplied on booking.

When to go: Year round, though winter windsurfing is only for the hardy.

Established: 1979

Safety: All the windsurfing instructors used by Peak Activities are RYA qualified. Boardsailing Instructors and have first aid qualifications. Staff carry radios and first aid kits. The company is licensed by the AALA and is a member of the Heart of England Tourist Board. Supplied specialist equipment is of a high standard and regularly maintained and replaced.

Insurance: All Peak Activity tours are fully insured for public and third party liability. Optional additional insurance can be taken out to guard against cancellation, illness, loss of property, etc.

Methods of payment: VISA, Mastercard, Eurocard, personal cheques.

Booking information: A 50% deposit is requested with all bookings.

Nearest airport: Leeds (45 mins), Manchester (45 mins), Birmingham (90 mins), Sheffield (12 mins). Transfers can be arranged.

Nearest rail station: Hathersage. Transfers can be arranged.

CAVING

You would be hard pushed to gather enough people to make up a soccer team from people who are indifferent to caving and pot-holing. It is a sport that seems to engender either love or hate, with few people sitting in between. If you want to be like an explorer of old, discovering new places, seeing things that no one has seen before, then you are already out of luck on the earth's surface. However, underground there are still plenty of cave systems all over the world that are yet to be fully explored. There are relatively few companies offering caving as a commercial activity, not because it lacks excitement or challenge but more likely because it is hard to put a glossy cover on tight dark tunnels full of water and sliding around on muddy slopes. However, everyone should consider trying caving, because it gives you a completely different perspective on our planet and how it is formed. And it is not all muck and no glamour. There are massive, theatre-like chambers in the cave systems where weird, marvellous shapes are sculpted by the drip of limestone-heavy water from the ceiling. Some chambers are so impressive that if they were on the surface, they would be national treasures. For beginners, there are simple cave systems where you can stand up most of the time; and there are dry systems too if you want to avoid getting soaked. For more experienced cavers, there are endless places to challenge your skills and technical expertise with rewards to match your effort.

Actually, the lack of commercial caving companies may well be due to the sport being so damned good that established cavers want to keep their wonder world for themselves. I'd go and check it out soon if I were you, though you may have to do it via a club.

Europe's top ten deepest caves

1   Lamprechtsofen-Vogelschacht, Salzburg, Austria, –1,632
       metres (the world's deepest, too)
2   Gouffre Mirolda/Loucien Bouclier, Haute-Savoie, France, –
       1,610 metres
3   Reseau Jean Bernard, Haute-Savoie, France, –1,602 metres
4   Torca del Cerro, Asturias, Spain, –1,589 metres
5   Sistema del Trave (La Laureola), Asturias, Spain, –1,441 metres
6   Il Laminako Aterneko Leizea, Nararra, Spain, –1,408 metres
7   Sustav Lukina jama, Trojama, Velebit, Croatia, 1,393 metres
8   Evren Gunay sinkhole, Cukurpinar, Turkey, –1,377 metres
9   Ceki II, Rombonski Podi, Slovenia, –1,370 metres
10 Reseau de la Pierre Saint Martin, Pyrenées-Atlantigues,
       France/Spain, 1,342 metres

Europe's top ten longest caves

1   Holloch, Schwyz, Switzerland, 175,150 metres
2   Siebenhengste-hohgant Hohlensystem, Switzerland, 140,000
       metres
3   Systeme de Ojo Guarena, Burgos, Spain, 100,000 metres
4   Reseau de la Coumo d'Hyouernedo, Haute-Garonne, France,
       94,843 metres
5   Hirlatzhöhle, Oberösterreich, Austria, 90,200 metres
6   Easegill System, Yorkshire Dales, United Kingdom,
       70,500 metres
7   Raucherkarhöhle, Oberösterreich, Austria, 65,000 metres
8   Ogof Draenen, Wales, United Kingdom, 62,000 metres
9   Reseau de Lalpe, Isère/Savoie, France, 60,247 metres
10 Red Del Rio Silencio, Cantabria, Spain, 60,000 metres

UNITED KINGDOM

ACORN ACTIVITIES
PO Box 120, Hereford HR4 8YB
Phone: +44 (0)1432 830083
Fax: +44 (0)1432 830110
Email: sales@acornactivities.co.uk
Website: www.acornactivities.co.uk

Caving in the largest underground complex in Europe
Exploring the depths of the countryside with experienced cave leaders, this unique experience is an opportunity not to be missed. Helmet and headlamp are both provided – all you need is some old clothes and overalls. The longer the session, the deeper you will venture into the cave system.

Activity prices: £25 for a half-day, £40 for a full day (minimum booking four people, although individuals may join groups).
Accommodation: Not included in the price.
Food: Not included.
Equipment supplied: Helmet and headlamp are provided.
What to take: Old clothes, overalls and shoes that can get wet.
When to go: Year round, weather permitting.
Established: 1990
Safety: All instructors are experienced cave leaders.
Insurance: Insurance is required and this can be arranged through Acorn Activities.
Methods of payment: VISA, Mastercard, cheques and cash.
Booking information: Late bookings are welcomed. A non-refundable deposit of £10 per day is required. Cancellation charges apply on a sliding scale from 80% for over 43 days before departure to 100% for up to 14 days.
Nearest airport: Cardiff or Birmingham International.
Nearest rail station: Depends on the itinerary.

AVALON ADVENTURE

The Mill House, Dulford, Cullompton, Devon EX15 2ED
Phone: +44 (0)1884 266 646
Fax: N/A
Email: avalon-adventure@dial.pipex.com
Website: http://dialspace.dial.pipex.com/avalon.adventure/

Explore Britain's best caves

Although Avalon Adventure is based in Devon, they operate trips to all the major caving areas of the United Kingdom, including south Wales and the Mendips. Whether you wish to try a course where you squeeze through a series of tight tunnels or a walk through some enormous caverns, the centre can arrange it. They can offer tailor-made trips too. Their 'Try Caving' days are for those looking for a taste of the underground world using simple cave systems where the challenge can be changed en route to reflect how you are feeling about the experience.

Activity prices: The principal caving trips last five days and cost around £155. The 'Try Caving' day costs just £30.

Accommodation: Not included. The centre can help you arrange a place to stay.

Food: Not included.

Equipment supplied: All specialist equipment is supplied.

What to take: Personal clothing, suitable footwear.

When to go: April to November.

Established: 1992

Safety: All the instructors are fully qualified and hold first aid qualifications. The centre is licensed by the AALA.

Insurance: The centre is insured though clients may wish to take out separate insurance too.

Methods of payment: VISA, Mastercard, cheques and cash.

Booking information: Advance booking is essential.

Nearest airport: Exeter. Transfers can be arranged.

Nearest rail station: Exeter. Transfers can be arranged.

BLACK MOUNTAIN ACTIVITIES

PO Box 5, Hay on Wye, Hereford HR3 5YB
Phone: +44 (0)1497 847 897
Fax: +44 (0)1497 847 897
Email: enquiries@blackmountain.co.uk
Website: www.blackmountain.co.uk

Exploring the caves of the Brecon Beacons
The southern part of the Brecon Beacons is riddled with caves, caverns and passages. There are over 300 caves in the National Park with challenges to suit every level of ability from beginners to the most experienced cavers. With a headlamp on your helmet and wearing a protective suit, you will scramble and squeeze your way through enchanting caverns full of weird formations. If you fancy something a little more challenging then try a pot-holing course where you take on vertical cave systems using abseiling techniques and caving ladders. Some previous caving experience is preferable for this activity.

Activity prices: £30 per day or £20 for a half-day trip. Pot-holing costs £35 for a full day.

Accommodation: Not included in the price. There is a range of accommodation available locally and the centre will advise you.

Food: Not included. Packed lunches can be arranged.

Equipment supplied: All specialist equipment is supplied.

What to take: Personal clothing, swimsuit, suitable footwear.

When to go: Year round.

Established: 1992

Safety: All the centre's staff are fully qualified in their respective sports, hold first aid qualifications and are highly professional. All equipment used meets national safety standards. The centre is licensed by the AALA and the Welsh Tourist Board.

Insurance: The centre is insured though clients may wish to take out separate insurance too.

Methods of payment: Personal cheque and cash.

Booking information: Advance booking is recommended though late bookings may be possible.

Nearest airport: Depends on tour. Cardiff and Bristol are nearest to the centre.

Nearest rail station: Depends on the itinerary. Hereford and Abergavenny are nearest to the centre.

PEAK ACTIVITIES

Rock Lea Activity Training Centre, Station Road, Hathersage, Hope Valley, Derbyshire S32 1DD
Phone: +44 (0)1433 650 345
Fax: +44 (0)1433 650 342
Email: admin@iain.co.uk
Website: www.iain.co.uk

Deep, deep down in Derbyshire

If you are looking for a deep and possibly spiritual experience then join one of Peak Activities' caving for beginners courses and you could find yourself exploring the aptly named Giant Hole, England's deepest cave system. With safety helmet on and your lamp lit, you can see the wondrous and sometimes grotesque limestone formations that riddle the region's hills. Your nationally qualified instructors will show you some of the techniques needed for the final abseil into a pot-hole. The beginners' courses are largely weather independent as they only access higher levels that are not so suscep-tible to water level changes. Once you have completed that course, you can move on to the more advanced pot-holing courses where you abseil, descend caving ladders and squeeze your way into deeper, more technical sections.

Activity prices: Novices' 'Introduction to Caving' weekend courses cost £129 per person, while a pot-holing extreme weekend costs £180. Caving is also included on the multi-activity weekend at £149 per person. Personal one-to-one tuition can also be arranged.

Accommodation: Not included in the tour price. There is a large range of options within easy reach of the centre, ranging from hostels and B&B to farmhouses and hotels.

Food: Not included in tour price but there are plenty of local eateries to suit all budgets.

Equipment supplied: All specialist equipment and bad weather gear if necessary.

What to take: Personal clothing and suitable footwear. Full list supplied on booking.

When to go: Year round, depending on weather.

Established: 1979

Safety: All the caving instructors used by Peak Activities are nationally qualified and have first aid qualifications. Staff carry radios and first aid kits. The company is licensed by the AALA and is a member of the Heart of England Tourist Board. Supplied specialist equipment is of a high standard and regularly maintained and replaced.

Insurance: All Peak Activity tours are fully insured for public and third party liability. Optional additional insurance can be taken out to guard against cancellation, illness, loss of property, etc.

Methods of payment: VISA, Mastercard, Eurocard, personal cheques.

Booking information: A 50% deposit is requested with all bookings.

Nearest airport: Leeds (45 mins), Manchester (45 mins), Birmingham (90 mins) or Sheffield (12 mins). Transfers can be arranged.

Nearest rail station: Hathersage. Transfers can be arranged.

ROCK AND ICE

Birch Tree House, Shirley, nr. Ashbourne, Derbyshire DE6 3AS
Phone: +44 (0)1335 360 490
Fax: N/A
Email: rock.ice@bigfoot.com
Website: www.rockandice.demon.co.uk

Under the skin of the Derbyshire Dales

The Peak District National Park and the limestone areas of Derbyshire are riddled with caves and old mines suitable for exploring. Rock and Ice's highly experienced and well-qualified instructors ensure that your journey to the centre of the earth is both safe and exhilarating. Their courses cater for beginners or advanced cavers and they provide all the specialist rigging needed for getting into the cave systems. Not all the caves are restricted in space so there is always something suitable for most people. You get to see underground caverns and strange rock formations, and in one cave there is the biggest fossilized oyster bed in Europe.

Activity prices: Prices are based around £100 per day for one to one tuition and £50 per person on a one instructor to two clients basis. Call the centre with your requirements to get an exact price.

Accommodation: Not included in the tour price. The centre will help you to arrange accommodation in the local area.

Food: Not included in price but there are local places to suit all budgets.

Equipment supplied: All specialist equipment.

What to take: Personal clothing and suitable footwear. Suggested list supplied on booking.

When to go: Year round; entry to some caves depends on rainfall conditions. Established: 1987

Safety: The instructors employed by Rock and Ice are all qualified by the national governing bodies.

Insurance: The centre recommends outdoor pursuits travel insurance that starts at £12.50 for up to four days.

Methods of payment: Personal cheques and cash.

Booking information: A 50% deposit is requested with all bookings. Balance is due 28 days before course. Cancellation penalties are applied.

Nearest airport: Manchester.

Nearest rail station: Derby. Transfers can be arranged.

THE ROCK CENTRE
Chudleigh
Devon
TQ13 OEE
United Kingdom
Phone: +44 (0)1626 852717
Fax: +44 (0)1626 852717
Email: trc@globalnet.co.uk
Website: www.rockcentre.co.uk

Caving in Devon

Set in 10 acres of outstanding natural scenery, The Rock Centre could hardly be better placed for caving. There are a number of caves on site, which are suitable for a basic introduction to the underground world. For the more adventurous, off-site options abound. Often intricate and complex, Devon's caves provide the perfect environment for introductory trips, as well as challenging routes for the more experienced. In addition to booking on a daily basis, more committed cavers can opt for a nationally recognised caving qualification. Offered under the auspices of the National Caving Association (NCA), the Local Cave Leadership Award (LCLA) Level 1 qualifies the candidate to lead others in non-vertical cave systems. The course covers personal skills, equipment, access, hazards, weather, flooding, emergencies and first aid, as well as leadership and group management. Level 1 training courses last for two days and assessment courses a further two days.

Activity prices: £10 per half-day, £20 per full day for groups of four or more. For individuals or groups smaller than four, an instructor costs £40 per half-day and £80 per full day. LCLA Level 1 course training course costs £50 per head, the Assessment course £60 per head.

Accommodation: Not included in the price, although a good range of accommodation is available locally. Camping at the Rock Centre costs £1 per person, bunkhouse accommodation £2 per person. B&B accommodation can be arranged at a price to suit.

Food: Clients to arrange their own.

Equipment supplied: All specialist equipment is provided.

What to take: Personal clothing and footwear suitable for the prevailing conditions; if in doubt, call ahead for advice.

When to go: Year round.

Established: 1978

Safety: All staff hold national governing body qualifications and the centre is licensed by the AALA.

Insurance: The centre carries indemnity insurance for all activities and can advise on personal accident insurance if required.

Methods of payment: Cash or cheque.

Booking information: Reservations must be made in advance, although a deposit is not normally required.

Nearest airport: Exeter or Plymouth.

Nearest rail station: Exeter or Newton Abbot. Clients can be picked up by prior arrangement.

COASTEERING

This is the newest adventure craze to hit the commercial market and it is easy to see why it has caught on. Coasteering involves scrambling, swimming and leaping along dramatic cliff-lined coasts, taking you to places previously thought to be inaccessible. The sport was born in Pembrokeshire in West Wales in the late 1980s and it has recently seen a boom in popularity. Dressed up in special reinforced wetsuits, buoyancy jackets and helmets, participants face the challenge of traversing the coastline, scrambling up cliffs to get around obstacles, swimming through crashing waves at the mouths of inlets and crevices and occasionally (and usually optionally!) leaping from the rocks into the sea below. Oh yes, it certainly is exciting. And it is open to virtually anyone, as you do not need any specific technical training or experience, though you should be able to swim well. When you add in the stunning coastal scenery, you can see that while coasteering may be the new kid on the block, it is certainly around to stay and will thrive.

UNITED KINGDOM

ACORN ACTIVITIES
PO Box 120, Hereford, HR4 8YB
Phone: +44 (0)1432 830083
Fax: +44 (0)1432 830110
Email: sales@acornactivities.co.uk
Website: www.acornactivities.co.uk

Coasteering the spectacular Welsh coast

Pembrokeshire is the birthplace of coasteering, and remains an unspoilt and spectacular location for a lot of leaping, scrambling and climbing. Much of the activity takes place at sea level, scrabbling to keep your feet out of the water while exploring the caves, crannies and hidden coves of this isolated coastline. Occasionally, however, the route heads up and over the headland, providing an ideal vantage point for a few piked belly-flops. All the guides are of course extremely experienced and know where the water is deep enough to jump. Wetsuits and helmets also provide much-needed protection against the abrasive rocks.

Activity prices: £25 for a half-day, £40 for a full day.

Accommodation: Not included in the price.

Food: Not included.

Equipment supplied: Wetsuits and helmets are provided.

What to take: A warm change of clothes and shoes to get wet.

When to go: Year round.

Established: 1990

Safety: All leaders are highly experienced.

Insurance: Insurance is required, although this can be arranged through Acorn Activities.

Methods of payment: VISA, Mastercard, cheque and cash.

Booking information: Late bookings are welcomed. A non-refundable deposit of £10 per day is required. Cancellation charges apply on a sliding scale from 80% for over 43 days before departure to 100% for up to 14 days.

Nearest airport: Cardiff or Birmingham International.

Nearest rail station: Depends on the itinerary.

ADVENTURE SPORTS

Carnkie Farmhouse, Carnkie, Redruth, Cornwall TR16 6RZ
Phone: +44 (0)1209 218 962
Fax: +44 (0)1209 314 118
Email: holidays@adventure-sports.co.uk
Website: www.adventure-sports.co.uk

Clamber along Cornish cliffs

Cornwall's rugged coastline is one of the most spectacular in the UK and the best way of all to get to see every nook and cranny is to go coasteering. You can scramble along checking out the coves and caves under the guidance of an experienced instructor. No previous experience is necessary as all the training you need is given beforehand. The centre also offers other sports, so you can combine coasteering with other adventures during your stay.

Activity prices: A three-day camping stay with two days of activities costs from £76 (low season) to £100 (high season); prices go up to £329 for a seven night/seven activity days course.

Accommodation: Included in price. You have a choice of camping, self-catering chalets or a converted self-catering farmhouse. There are many social options nearby or on the site.

Food: Not included.

Equipment supplied: All specialist equipment is provided.

What to take: Swimsuit and suitable footwear.

When to go: Summer months only.

Established: 1982

Safety: All of the centre's coasteering guides hold nationally recognised qualifications and are very experienced. The centre is a member of the West Country Tourist Board.

Insurance: Insurance is required. Policies are offered by the centre.

Methods of payment: VISA, cheque and cash.

Booking information: Advance booking is required. A £50 deposit is payable.

Nearest airport: Newquay.

Nearest rail station: Redruth. Transfers can be arranged.

PRESELI VENTURE

Parcynole Fach, Mathry, Haverfordwest, Pembrokeshire SA62 5HN
Phone: +44 (0)1348 837 709
Fax: +44 (0)1348 837 656
Email: sophie@preseliventure.com
Website: www.preseliventure.com

Scramble, scale and leap from Welsh cliffs

Coasteering is a relatively new adventure sport and Preseli Venture has been offering it pretty much from its inception. Ideally located near to the dramatic Pembrokeshire coastline, the centre offers daily half-day trips that can also be combined with sea kayaking and mountain biking for a longer break. Scrambling along the base of the cliffs, swimming across narrow inlets as the waves crash around you and leaping from as high a cliff as you dare make for completely addictive entertainment. The instructors are all qualified and ensure that your safety is paramount. To round off your adventure, you get the chance to leap into a turquoise-coloured, crystal clear quarry pool from a multi-level, ruined building. Simply exhilarating.

Activity prices: £30 for a half-day, £159 for an inclusive weekend course. You can also combine coasteering with mountain biking and/or sea kayaking.

Accommodation: Included in the weekend course price. The Preseli Venture Lodge sleeps up to 30 people.

Food: Great home-cooked food is available at the centre and is included in the weekend course price.

Equipment supplied: Full wetsuit, buoyancy jacket, helmet and windproof jacket (winter months only).

What to take: Swimsuit, training shoes, towel.

When to go: Year round, daily.

Established: 1987

Safety: All the guides have relevant national qualifications, specific on-site training, and life saving and first aid qualifications. Preseli Venture is a member of the BCU and the WCA {?} and is part of the Welsh Tourist Board Accreditation Scheme.

Insurance: Clients should arrange their own insurance; it is available via Preseli Venture.

Methods of payment: VISA, Mastercard, Amex, travellers' cheques and cash.

Booking information: Advance booking is recommended. A non-refundable 50% deposit is required with booking.

Nearest airport: Cardiff.

Nearest rail station: Haverfordwest. Transfer from this station, or from Fishguard ferry port or Fishguard station, can be arranged.

TWR-Y-FELIN NO LIMITS

The TYF Group, 1 High Street, St Davids, Pembrokeshire SA62 6QS
Phone: +44 (0)1437 721 611
Fax: +44 (0)1437 721 692
Email: info@tyf.com
Website: www.tyf.com

Scramble along Pembrokeshire's dramatic coastline
Based in Britain's smallest city, the TYF No Limits centre has access
to some of the UK's most dramatic coastline. In 1986, TYF was the
first centre in the world (probably!) to introduce coasteering as an
organised tour, and they have been at the forefront of developing the
sport into what it is today. You get to taste the unique mixture of
climbing, scrambling, swimming and cliff jumping as you make your
way along the coast. Courses are chosen to suit the group's ability
and it is not essential to be a strong swimmer as the buoyancy jacket
means you never sink. The instructors are all trained in life saving and
first aid so you are in safe hands.

Activity prices: Coasteering is normally combined with other sports in a two-
day stay. Prices range from £89 for camping to £160 for full board.
Accommodation: Included in price. You can either camp or have B&B, half
board or full board accommodation in the Twr-y-Felin Hotel, a beautiful
converted 18th-century windmill.
Food: Included in hotel-based course prices (see above).
Equipment supplied: All specialist equipment and clothing is provided.
What to take: Personal clothing.
When to go: April to October.
Established: 1986
Safety: All instructors hold first aid and life saving qualifications and are
trained in-house for coasteering. The centre is approved by the AALA and is a
member of the Welsh Tourist Board.
Insurance: The centre has liability insurance but recommends that clients take
out independent insurance against curtailment and cancellation of their
course (available from the centre) and a personal accident policy.
Methods of payment: VISA, Mastercard, Switch, cheque and cash.

Booking information: Advance booking is required.

Nearest airport: Cardiff.

Nearest rail station: Haverfordwest. Transfers may be arranged.

CYCLING

Whether it's a day-trip with a bum-bag or a tour around the world, travelling by bike is limited only by your imagination. Touring by car has its advantages, but only from the saddle of a bike does the world roll by slowly enough to take it all in.

On an end to end tour

Europe is blessed with an abundance of classic cycle routes on its quiet, country roads, ranging from a week's racing to a month's ambling. In the UK, the most famous tour traces a nearly straight-line route from Land's End at England's most southerly point to John O'Groats on Scotland's northernmost tip. The distance covered is approximately 880 miles, which has been ridden (non-stop) in less than two days, but usually takes between one and two weeks.

In mainland Europe, the Tour de France is undoubtedly the best-known cycling race in the world. While few have the time, ability or inclination to cycle 3,000 miles in 21 days over some of the highest mountain passes in the world, anyone can follow the route before or after the race at their own pace. You can take in the infamous Col du Tormalet or the awe-inspiring Alpe d'Huez. For the fanatically fit, it's even possible to ride the route on the same day as the riders. The roads are usually closed a few hours before the start – if you're prepared to get up early and ride like a demon, you might just reach the finish before the riders. But of course, you don't have to get up and do it all over again the next morning.

Cycle touring is as old as cycling itself, and today it's not uncommon for hardy veterans to cycle across entire continents in search of adventure. Most, however, are quite content with a few days or weeks exploring places closer to home, from the quiet country roads of South Wales to the high mountain passes of the Alps. No specialist skills or training are required, and because you can go as fast or as slow as you like, fitness is barely a consideration. All you need is a start point, a destination and a little determination to make it all happen.

For anything longer than a couple of days, most people will pack panniers on the front or back of their bike. As any touring cyclist will tell you, these bags soon become a home from home, and can carry more than enough equipment to keep you on the road for months at a time. If that sounds too much like hard work, there are a number of companies across Europe offering organised tours. All equipment is provided, the most scenic and suitable routes are planned in advance, and a support vehicle carries all your bags and equipment to your destination at the end of each day. It doesn't offer quite the same flexibility or freedom as going it alone, but if you don't want to ride with your home on your bike, why not ride your bike to your home?

CYPRUS

CYPRUS BIKE TRAVEL
Machis Kritis , 118GR 74100 Rethymnon, Crete, Greece
Phone: +30 831 53 328
Fax: +30 831 52 691
Email: info@hellasbike.com
Website: www.hellasbike.com

A Cypriot cycle week
Cyprus Bike Travel is linked to Hellas Bike Travel which operates in Greece; they provide similar packages and all booking is done through the Crete office. The Level 1 Cyprus rides aim to show you

the best of the country's quieter regions without excessive effort. The routes are on paved back roads and have slight ascents but plenty of downhill parts to compensate. They are suitable for beginners or casual cyclists. The bicycles supplied are all high quality Scott bikes. Tours last from six to eight hours with breaks.

Activity prices: A one-week Level 1 course, including five guided tours, costs US$290 and includes the Scott hire bike, a permanent support vehicle, transfers to and from your hotel, guiding and third party insurance. You also get a free t-shirt and water bottle to keep. Cycle hire is available separately too.
Accommodation: Not included in price. The centre can help you arrange accommodation to suit your budget.
Food: Not included in price. The tours pass by typical Cypriot taverns where home-cooked foods may be sampled.
Equipment supplied: Scott mountain bike and helmet.
What to take: Personal cycling clothing and footwear.
When to go: Mid-March to mid-November.
Established: 1988
Safety: All the guides have bike mechanic training or substantial experience in the field. They have first aid qualifications and speak German and English well. All guides are skilled at dealing with clients of all abilities and have good local knowledge.
Insurance: Third party insurance and accident insurance is included. Clients should arrange their own travel policy.
Methods of payment: Bank transfer prior to arrival only.
Booking information: Bank transfer should be credited to Cyprus Bike Travel at least 14 days before arrival. Cancellation penalties apply on a sliding scale.
Nearest airport: Paphos.
Nearest rail station: N/A.

GREECE

HELLAS BIKE TRAVEL
Machis Kritis , 118GR 74100 Rethymnon, Crete, Greece
Phone: +30 831 53 328
Fax: +30 831 52 691

Email: info@hellasbike.com
Website: www.hellasbike.com

A multiple Greek experience
Hellas Bike Travel has the enviable job of providing cycling tours on
no fewer than five of the most spectacular Greek islands. They have
bike centres on Corfu, claimed as 'my island of magic' by Empress
Sissi in Homer's Odyssey, and Halkidiki, with its wide beaches and
secluded bays surrounded by pine forests and gentle hills. Or you can
go to Rhodes, the sunniest island in Greece, with its old Byzantine
ruins; Paros, the 'princess of the Cyclades'; or Crete. With its unique
character, mountains and wonderful beaches, Crete has it all for
cyclists looking for a break away. The company's Level 1 tours are on
asphalt roads with slight ascents and lots of downhill and are suitable
for beginners, families and children. The bicycles are all high quality
Scott bikes and they have racing bikes too. Tours last from six to eight
hours with breaks.

Activity prices: A one-week Level 1 course, including five guided tours, costs
US$300 and includes the Scott hire bike, a permanent support vehicle,
transfers to and from your hotel, guiding and third party insurance. You also
get a free t-shirt and water bottle to keep. Cycle hire is available separately
too.
Accommodation: Not included in price. The centre can help you arrange
accommodation to suit your budget.
Food: Not included in price.
Equipment supplied: Scott mountain bike and helmet.
What to take: Personal cycling clothing and footwear.
When to go: Mid-March to mid-November.
Established: 1988
Safety: All the guides have bike mechanic training or substantial experience in
the field. They have first aid qualifications and speak German and English
well. All guides are skilled at dealing with clients of all abilities and have good
local knowledge. The tours are mainly conducted in German and English. The
Crete centre runs English tours only, or French on request.

Insurance: Third party insurance and accident insurance is included. Clients should arrange their own travel policy.

Methods of payment: Bank transfer prior to arrival only.

Booking information: Bank transfer should be credited to Hellas Bike Travel at least 14 days before arrival. Cancellation penalties apply on a sliding scale.

Nearest airport: Depends on the island chosen.

Nearest rail station: Depends on the island chosen.

IRELAND

IRISH CYCLING SAFARIS
Belfield House, University College Dublin, Dublin 4
Phone: +353 1 260 0749
Fax: +353 1 706 1168
Email: ics@kerna.ie
Website: www.kerna.ie/ics/

Cycling tours in Ireland and Europe
Irish Cycling Safaris offers week-long cycling tours throughout Ireland, Scotland, France, Italy and Spain. Each tour involves a group of 15–20 people, together with a guide and a luggage van, exploring some of the hidden country roads and cycling some of the most scenic parts of each country. Each day includes 30–35 miles of cycling, although there are longer options for those who want to stretch their legs. A mixture of B&B and hotel accommodation is included in the price, as is breakfast. Lunches and evening meals are organised by the guide and must be paid for locally. Hybrid touring bikes and all other equipment are provided. No previous experience is required, but clients must arrange third party insurance.

Activity prices: Week-long tours in Ireland from £350, France from £470, Spain from £440 and Italy from £400.

Accommodation: B&B accommodation and small, family-run hotels are included in the price.

Food: Breakfast is included in the price and the guide organises lunch and dinner.

Equipment supplied: All specialist cycling equipment, including 21-speed Trek hybrid bikes and helmets, is provided.

What to take: Personal cycling clothing.

When to go: May to September inclusive.

Established: 1988

Safety: All guides are over 25 years old, hold a full driving licence and have excellent local knowledge.

Insurance: Insurance is mandatory and can be arranged if required.

Methods of payment: VISA, Mastercard and travellers' cheques all accepted.

Booking information: A non-refundable £60 deposit is required to secure a booking, with the balance to be paid two weeks prior to departure.

Nearest airport: Depends on the tour.

Nearest rail station: Depends on the tour.

SPAIN

ESPANA BIKE TRAVEL

Avenida de Tirajana 25, Lokal 8, 35100 Playa del Ingles, Gran Canaria

Phone: +34 609 549 324

Fax: +34 928 773 317

Email: jose@sas-sports.de or sasmax@arrakis.es

Website: www.espanabike.com

Riding the Canaries

España BikeTravel are based on the gorgeous island of Gran Canaria in the Canary Islands. They are linked to the company that owns Hellas Bike Travel in Greece and offer a similar high level of service in their packages. Gran Canaria has some superb cycling routes on quiet back roads and this operator uses these for their Level 1 tours. Designed for beginners and casual cyclists, the routes are all on surfaced roads and have only slight ascents but plenty of downhills. The centre supplies good quality Scott mountain bikes for the tours. The rides last from about six to eight hours per day, including breaks for lunch and drinks.

Activity prices: A one-week Level 1 course, including five guided tours, costs US$300 and includes the Scott hire bike, a permanent support vehicle, transfers to and from your hotel, guiding and third party insurance. You also get a free t-shirt and water bottle to keep. Cycle hire is available separately too, as are shorter biking packages.

Accommodation: Not included in price. The centre can help you arrange accommodation to suit your budget.

Food: Not included in price, except a picnic on the tours.

Equipment supplied: Scott mountain bike and helmet.

What to take: Personal cycling clothing and footwear.

When to go: Year round.

Established: 1996

Safety: All the guides have experience in the field and first aid qualifications.

Insurance: Third party insurance and accident insurance is included. Clients should arrange their own travel policy.

Methods of payment: VISA or bank transfer.

Booking information: Bank transfer should be credited to España Bike Travel at least 14 days before arrival. Cancellation penalties apply on a sliding scale.

Nearest airport: Las Palmas (32 km).

Nearest rail station: N/A.

UNITED KINGDOM

ACORN ACTIVITIES
PO Box 120, Hereford HR4 8YB
Phone: +44 (0)1432 830 083
Fax: +44 (0)1432 830 110
Email: sales@acornactivities.co.uk
Website: www.acornactivities.co.uk

Cycling in Wales, Herefordshire and Shropshire
Acorn Activities are one of the largest adventure sport providers in the United Kingdom. They offer a range of two- to seven-day self-guided cycling tours through the beautiful rolling hills and villages around Wales and the English Borders. Detailed route plans are

provided and they are designed to include the best scenery without too much hill climbing within two to four hours of riding per day. Your luggage is transported to the overnight stops, so you only have to carry a picnic. There are both group and individual trips available and some of the rides follow a theme, for example taking in castles or real ale pubs. Tandem bikes and trailers for children are also offered.

Activity prices: Range from £120 for a two-night trip to £595 for a one-week trip based in hotels. Includes accommodation, at least on B&B basis, luggage transport, bikes, maps and route guides.

Accommodation: Included in the price. Ranges from pubs and B&B to farmhouses and hotels.

Food: Depends on tour; minimum included is bed and breakfast.

Equipment supplied: Bikes, helmets, panniers, maps, puncture kits, cycle clips.

What to take: Lightweight waterproof jacket, cycling gloves and shoes (latter both optional).

When to go: Year round.

Established: 1990

Safety: All routes are selected to minimise travel on high traffic volume roads.

Insurance: Clients to arrange own; available via Acorn Activities.

Methods of payment: VISA, Mastercard, cheque and cash.

Booking information: Late bookings are welcomed. Deposit (non-refundable) of £10 per day. Cancellation charges apply on sliding scale from 80% for over 43 days before departure to 100% for up to 14 days.

Nearest airport: Cardiff or Birmingham International.

Nearest rail station: Depends on tour; contact Acorn Activities for details of how to get to the centre.

BICYCLE BEANO CYCLE TOURS
Erwood, Builth Wells, Powys LD2 3PQ
Phone: +44 (0)1982 560471
Fax: n/a
Email: bicycle@beano.kc3.co.uk
Website: www.kc3.co.uk/beano/

Cycle touring in the Welsh Borders

With traffic-free country lanes and long downhill descents, the stunning landscape of Wales and the Welsh Borders is a cyclist's paradise. Bicycle Beano's routes range from two to seven days and are designed to make the most of the mountains, taking in lush green valleys, dramatic seascapes, medieval castles and picturesque villages. A typical day's ride is a moderately paced 35-mile circular route, but there are plenty of short cuts and longer detours en route for those who want to cycle more or less. Cycling alone or with a group, everyone meets up for lunch and afternoon tea, to explore an ancient castle, or to go for a dip in a natural jacuzzi. Each group is accompanied by a guide and a helper, and accommodation varies from friendly guest houses to three-star hotels. Itinerary highlights include cycling Gospel Pass in the Black Mountains, riding the turf tracks over the Radnor Hills of mid-Wales and free-wheeling in the valleys around Snowdon.

Activity prices: From £120 for a two-day weekend, £210 for a three-day weekend and £390 for a seven-day tour.

Accommodation: A variety of three-star hotels, guest houses, bunkhouses and camping accommodation is included in the price, depending on the itinerary.

Food: Delicious, home-cooked vegetarian breakfasts, post-ride tea and cakes and evening meals are included in the price. Lunches, normally taken at quiet country pubs, are not included.

Equipment supplied: Bike rental is available, but most people bring their own.

What to take: Personal cycling clothing.

When to go: May to September.

Established: 1981

Safety: All participants are given a full safety briefing on safe cycling. Children are welcome, but must be accompanied by a responsible adult. All guides are highly experienced and qualified in first aid.

Insurance: At least third party insurance is recommended; an information leaflet is available.

Methods of payment: Cheques in sterling or foreign currency and Eurocheques are all acceptable.

Booking information: Advance booking required with £40 deposit.
Nearest airport: Birmingham or Manchester, depending on the itinerary.
Nearest rail station: Hereford, Ledbury, Bangor, Builth Road, Haverfordwest or Fishguard, depending on the itinerary.

BIKE RIDES

Bremhill, Calne, Wiltshire SN11 9LA
Phone: +44 (0)7000 560 749
Fax: +44 (0)7000 560 749
Email: tours@bike-rides.co.uk
Website: www.bike-rides.co.uk

Pedalling the UK's prime spots
Bike Rides offer a whole range of road tours in the UK and mainland Europe to suit every level of ability from beginners to very experienced. The popular UK weekend rides run alongside the mountain bike tours and include some of the country's best scenic spots. The North Downs, the Yorkshire Dales, Wiltshire and the Welsh Borders are all on offer, but the real challenge is the Sustrans Coast to Coast route from Whitehaven to Sunderland. It's not all about riding, though, and the tours have a good reputation for their social side too. Mainland Europe tours include the Loire Valley in France, the Algarve in Portugal and Spain's Picos de Europa. Riding distance is normally 15–60 miles a day with a back-up support vehicle for those wanting to rest. Accommodation is chosen for its location and charm so you can really relax after the day's ride and enjoy the wine and food.

Activity prices: The weekend trips cost between £85 and £95, including accommodation and food. The four-day Coast to Coast tour costs £195. Overseas tours cost around £395 per week.
Accommodation: Included in the price. Ranges from hotels and B&B to farmstays and camping.
Food: Some tours are full board and others are half board. Wine is included on some tours.
Equipment supplied: Bikes and helmets are available for hire; route plans are provided and guides carry repair kits.

What to take: Your own bike and helmet if you have one, personal cycling clothing, cycling gloves and shoes.

When to go: Selected departure dates all year round.

Established: 1992

Safety: Experienced guides are used on all tours.

Insurance: For overseas tours, clients can take out the Bike Rides insurance policy or arrange their own. Clients need to arrange their own insurance for UK trips.

Methods of payment: VISA, Mastercard, Delta, Switch, personal cheque, cash.

Booking information: Advance booking is advised. Payment is due eight weeks prior to departure. A deposit of £35 per person is required for UK rides and £75 for overseas. Cancellation charges apply.

Nearest airport: Depends on tour.

Nearest rail station: Depends on tour.

COMPASS HOLIDAYS

48 Shurdington Road, Cheltenham, Gloucestershire GL53 0JE
Phone: +44 (0)1242 250 642
Fax: +44 (0)1242 529 730
Email: compass.holidays@bigfoot.com
Website: http://dialspace.dial.pipex.com/town/road/xdt51/index.htm

Pedal away in the Heart of England
Cycling through the quiet lanes and back roads of the Cotswolds, Britain's largest Area of Outstanding Natural Beauty, and Wiltshire gives riders the chance to experience at first hand some of the loveliest countryside in the United Kingdom. The areas are easily accessible from the M4 and M5 motorways, making them ideal places for a short cycling break. Compass Holidays can put together a whole range of tour options, from one day to one week, to suit all ability levels. The majority of the rides are self-guided, using the maps and route directions supplied, so you can set your own pace and rest on a whim. At the end of it all, you can relax in your hotel, eat good food and recharge the batteries for the next day's ride.

Activity prices: There are a huge number of tours available at varying prices, starting from £66 per person for a one day/two night break in B&B accommodation.

Accommodation: Included in the price. Ranges from pubs and B&B to farmhouses and luxury hotels.

Food: Breakfast is included, all other meals are optional.

Equipment supplied: Bikes, helmets, locks, water bottles, maps, route directions.

What to take: Personal clothing, cycling gloves and shoes. You can take your own bike and equipment if you wish.

When to go: Year round.

Established: 1990

Safety: Qualified guides lead guided tours. Compass Holidays is a member of the Heart of England Tourist Board and the West Country Tourist Board.

Insurance: Clients need to arrange their own insurance. The bikes are insured by Compass.

Methods of payment: VISA, Mastercard, personal cheque, cash.

Booking information: Advance booking is advised. Payment is due eight weeks prior to departure. A deposit of £50 per person is required with booking.

Cancellation charges apply on a scale from 75% with 27 days' or more notice to 100% for less than 27 days.

Nearest airport: Depends on tour.

Nearest rail station: Depends on tour.

CYCLING ADVENTURE TOURS LTD

Flat 4, 74 Lexham Gardens, Kensington, London W8 5JB
Phone: +44 (0)207 835 0288
Fax: +44 (0) 207 835 0288
Email: cycling@venturetours.co.uk
Website: www.venturetours.co.uk

Touring on and off-road throughout the UK

With its extensive network of minor country roads and a temperate climate, the UK is ideally suited to biking year-round. Cycling Adventure Tours offers a range of cycling tours from relatively easy weekend trips to demanding, two-week off-road journeys across the country. Highlights include Sea to Sea rides, the Scottish Highlands and the Lake District. Services include arranging accommodation, providing a guide (self-led itineraries are available on request) and luggage transfer. Tranfers to and from the nearest rail station can also be arranged in advance. A number of trips – such as Cornwall and the Lake District – also include some hiking as part of the plan, for those wary of multi-day saddle sores. If you can't find a trip to match your needs, itineraries can be customised to order. Free Sunday rides in south-east England provide an ideal taster. Bikes are not provided but can be hired on request.

Activity prices: Guided weekend trips start from £58 with an early booking discount of £20. A two-week trip costs around £770, with an early booking discount of £30. Self-led trips start at £58 for a weekend and £530 for a two-week trip.

Accommodation: B&B accommodation is included in the price on all trips.

Food: Breakfast and packed lunches are included in the price and evening meals are usually taken in pubs near to the accommodation.

Equipment supplied: None provided, but bike hire can be arranged on request.

What to take: A bike. A rack and panniers are also recommended to carry luggage.

When to go: Year round.

Established: 1998

Safety: No formal qualifications, just four years' experience.

Insurance: Travel insurance is recommended but is not provided.

Methods of payment: Cash, cheques, travellers' cheques, electronic transfer, Transcash and Eurogiro. Foreign currency transactions may attract additional charges.

Booking information: A 5% deposit is required to secure a booking.

Nearest airport: Depends on the itinerary.

Nearest rail station: Depends on the itinerary. Travel can be arranged from any UK train station to the start point of a trip.

PEAK ACTIVITIES

Rock Lea Activity Training Centre, Station Road, Hathersage, Hope Valley, Derbyshire S32 1DD
Phone: +44 (0)1433 650 345
Fax: +44 (0)1433 650 342
Email: admin@iain.co.uk
Website: www.iain.co.uk

A Peak cycle

The Peak District is a beautiful place for cycling and Peak Activities run trips on some the nicest back roads through the National Park. Their qualified guides will take the route-finding load off your shoulders so that you can relax and enjoy the stunning scenery. Stops will be made en route at local cafés or pubs to savour some local cooking. Meanwhile, if you fancy a break, then the support vehicle is always there as a refuge from the hill climbs.

Activity prices: Cycling weekends cost from £129.

Accommodation: Not included in the tour price. There is a large range of options within easy reach of the centre, ranging from hostels and B&B to farmhouses and hotels.

Food: Not included in tour price but there are plenty of local eateries to suit all budgets.

Equipment supplied: Bikes and helmets and bad weather gear if necessary.

What to take: Personal cycling clothing and suitable footwear. Full list supplied on booking.

When to go: Year round.

Established: 1979

Safety: All the guides and instructors used by Peak Activities are qualified in their relevant fields and have first aid qualifications too. Staff carry radios and first aid kits. The company is licensed by the AALA and is a member of the Heart of England Tourist Board. Supplied specialist equipment is of a high standard and regularly maintained and replaced.

Insurance: All Peak Activity tours are fully insured for public and third party liability. Optional additional insurance can be taken out to guard against cancellation, illness, loss of property etc.

Methods of payment: VISA, Mastercard, Eurocard, personal cheques.

Booking information: A 50% deposit is requested with all bookings.

Nearest airport: Leeds (45 mins), Manchester (45 mins), Birmingham (90 mins) or Sheffield (12 mins). Transfers can be arranged.

Nearest rail station: Hathersage. Transfers can be arranged.

DOG SLEDDING

Few things are more gruelling, or more punishing, than the 1,500-mile Iditarod dog sled race across Alaska, but for most people that's not what running dogs is all about.

Alaskan Odyssey

In 1925, in the middle of winter, a small town in the far north-west of Alaska discovered an outbreak of diphtheria. Taken by surprise, the people of Nome were inadequately supplied with serum and, in an effort to stave off an epidemic, dog sled teams set off across Alaska's unforgiving interior from Anchorage to reach the stricken population. Every year since 1973, the Iditarod Trail Race has forged the same route across Alaska in memory of the first life-saving dog teams. Arguably the most dangerous and difficult race in the world, it definitely isn't for the faint-hearted, and has claimed a number of lives in its history. Many teams fail even to reach the finish. As for the winners, the very best can expect to cover the 1,151 miles in an astonishing ten days, as if their life depended on it. And it probably does.

Dog sledding originated in the wilds of northern Canada and Alaska, where the native Inuit population was dependent on dogs for hunting, transport and survival. Dog sled teams made their mark in the world of exploration when Amundsen used them to make his epic journey to the South Pole, and in a sense they've never looked back.

Dogs are attached to a sled by means of a padded harness and a rope, and a team can number as many as a dozen or more. They can either be raced, which is common in northern Canada and Alaska, or used for touring, as is popular in Finland and Norway. Unlike racing, touring with a dog sled is less about speed and more about exploration. There are a number of companies in Scandinavia that offer trips from a few hours to a few days. If you really want to get to know your team and the country you're travelling through, there's no better way than travelling for a week or more, staying in wilderness huts along the route.

Because the dogs are doing most of the work, there's no need to be especially fit, although standing on a moving sled and looking after your team all day can be tiring. No experience is needed either, as the dogs are usually well-trained and used to working for complete strangers. In fact, all you really need is a willingness to trust the dogs and let them take you where they will!

FINLAND

JIM'S WILDERNESS ADVENTURES LIMITED
Wolfbay Lodge, Rajaniementie 39, 93999 Kuusamo
Phone: +358 400 258 669
Fax: +358 8 856 101
Email: jwa.ltd@koillismaa.fi
Website: www.koillismaa.fi/wolfbay

Dog sledding in Finland
If you don't mind the cold, why not try a week of Arctic travelling on wilderness trails of old? Wolfbay Lodge offers adventurers the chance to explore Finland's magnificent Taiga and to experience the traditional means of winter travel on a week-long expedition along the Finno-Russian border, one of the last true wilderness areas left in Europe. After familiarisation with dogs and equipment, the first leg of the journey travels east through snow-clad forests and across frozen lakes as far as the Russian border. From here the route continues either north towards Oulanka National Park or south towards the

protected forests around Hossa. Accommodation is in basic winter shelters and clients drive their own dog team throughout.

Activity prices: FM7,500 for a week-long expedition, or personalised tours from FM1,250 per day.

Accommodation: Private cabins with sauna at Wolfbay Lodge and more basic cabins on the expedition.

Food: All meals included.

Equipment supplied: All specialist equipment provided.

What to take: Cold-weather clothing and footwear, including winter boots, thermals, hats, gloves, etc.

When to go: December to early April.

Established: 1995

Safety: Proprietor James Osch personally guides all expeditions and has seven years' experience driving sled dogs.

Insurance: Relevant insurance is provided.

Methods of payment: VISA, Mastercard and SWIFT bank transfers.

Booking information: No deposit required, but payment must be made at least one month before arrival. Cancellation within the final month will forfeit 50% of the full activity prices.

Nearest airport: Kuusamo.

Nearest rail station: N/A.

SAFARIS UNLIMITED
PO Box 80, FIN-94101 Kemi
Phone: +358 16 253405
Fax: +358 16 253406
Email: martti.niskanen@safarisunlimited.fi
Website: www.safarisunlimited.fi

Get mushing with huskies or reindeer
Safaris Unlimited specialise in running snowmobile trips, but they also offer the chance to get hooked up to a team of six or eight Siberian huskies for an exciting run across the Finnish wilderness. You will practise the basic commands to get the eager dogs off and running

and learn how to stop them too! Families with children can be accommodated with bigger sleighs. This trip is combined with snowmobiling. On the Adventure Safari trip in southern Lapland, there is a rare opportunity to drive a reindeer sledge at a reindeer farm. So get out your red outfit and white beard and start practising your Ho! Ho! Ho!

Activity prices: The snowmobile and husky safari costs FM825 per person for a four-hour trip. The reindeer sledging is part of the full-day Adventure Safari tour and costs FM1,500, including lunch and hot berry juice.

Accommodation: Not included in the price but the centre will organise it for you. Food: Not included, except as stated above, but again it can be organised for you.

Equipment supplied: All specialist equipment and clothing, jackets, boots, balaclava, mittens etc., is provided.

What to take: Personal clothing.

When to go: 10 December to 22 April.

Established: 1992

Safety: All the guides are trained by the company in relevant areas, including wilderness skills, safety measures, first aid etc. The centre is a member of the Association of Finnish Travel Agents and the Incentives Association Finland.

Insurance: Clients are protected by Finnish Traffic Insurance Act for personal injury while snowmobiling. Personal travel insurance is recommended. Client is responsible for vehicle damage (up to FM3,000 per vehicle).

Methods of payment: VISA, Mastercard, cash.

Booking information: Advance booking is advised. Payment is due 30 days in advance and cancellation more than 30 days before the trip is not penalised.

Nearest airport: Kemi. Transfers arranged at nominal charge.

Nearest rail station: Kemi. Transfers arranged at nominal charge.

HANG GLIDING

Perhaps it is the delta-shaped wing or the prone flying position, but there is something about hang gliding that makes it appear to be the closest humans can get to flying like a bird. Although the technology you see in modern hang gliders points to it being a relatively new sport, the basic principles of this type of human flight were some of the first to be tried over 100 years ago. Since then things have thankfully moved on from wooden frames coated in bird feathers, and today's hang gliders used at the schools are very stable, very strong and much easier to handle. It still requires skill and knowledge to get off the ground, but the training environments provided by the following centres are ideally suited to beginners. You don't have to commit to full-blown pilot training from the outset as all the centres offer a variety of taster courses which will see you flying but tethered to the ground by a rope to stop you going too high or too far. If the flying bug bites you then you can train to become an Elementary Pilot, and that course then counts towards becoming a Club Pilot, at which point you may fly solo. It is not cheap to become fully qualified but the cost can be reduced if you invest in or buy shares in a second-hand hang glider to train on. When you are soaring high above the Chamonix Valley soaking up the wonderful aerial views of Mont Blanc, the price will seem small indeed.

FRANCE

ALPINE FLYING CENTRE
The Flyer's Lodge, 216 rue de Bellevue, Les Houches, 74310
Phone: +33 (0)4 50 54 59 63

Fax: +33 (0)4 50 54 48 52
Email: flyerlodge@aol.com
Website: www.flyers-lodge.com

Fly high over the Chamonix Valley
Chamonix is right at the heart of one of the most beautifully dramatic mountain regions in the world and the flying conditions are second to none. The seasonal changes make it an ideal place to learn to cope with varying thermal and weather systems. For newly qualified pilots, this is as good a place as you will find for developing your hang gliding skills. The extensive cable car system and road access to launch sites means there is no carrying your gear back up hills. The centre does not cater for complete beginners. There are two five-day courses that help teach you how to get more from your flying. The Air Experience course is ideal for less-experienced pilots to learn about efficient flying techniques and accurate use of a variometer. The Mountain Thermal course covers these points but also looks more closely at weather conditions and mountain and valley conditions, so is more suited to pilots with a little experience. Other more advanced courses are also available.

Activity prices: The Air Experience and Mountain Thermal courses both cost FFr2,000. Daily fly guiding service costs FFr160 per day.
Accommodation: The centre is based at the lovely Flyer's Lodge. B&B accommodation costs FFr195 and half board FFr310.
Food: Included in accommodation costs (see above). Excellent three-course evening meals are cooked every night except one.
Equipment supplied: None.
What to take: You need to take all your own flying equipment and personal flying clothing. Check with centre for full list.
When to go: Year round.
Established: 1994
Safety: All instructors hold BHPA or FFVL {?} flying qualifications and are highly experienced.
Insurance: Clients must arrange their own medical, travel/cancellation and flying insurance.
Methods of payment: VISA, Mastercard, travellers' cheques, cash.

Booking information: Advance booking is essential. A deposit of FFr500 per person is required and full payment for accommodation is due six weeks prior to arrival. Less than 30 days' notice of cancellation means you still pay the full holiday cost. Course and guiding payments are made at the end of your stay.

Nearest airport: Geneva.

Nearest rail station: Les Houches.

SWITZERLAND

ALPIN RAFT

Postfach 78, 3800 Matten
Phone: +41 33 823 4100
Fax: +41 33 823 4101
Email: mail@alpinraft.ch
Website: www.alpinraft.ch

Hang gliding over the Swiss Alps

Interlaken is one of the very few places in the world where you can tandem hang-glide over mountain lakes and majestic Alpine scenery. Without the noise of an engine, hang gliding is as pure as it is peaceful, offering an unrivalled view of Europe's greatest mountain range. No experience is required as full training will be given, and all instructors are fully qualified passenger pilots.

Activity prices: From SFr155.

Accommodation: Backpacker accommodation available at the centre.

Food: None provided.

Equipment supplied: All specialised equipment is provided.

What to take: Normal hiking clothes.

When to go: April to October.

Established: 1988

Safety: All instructors are fully qualified passenger pilots.

Insurance: Clients must arrange their own insurance.

Methods of payment: All common Methods of payment accepted.

Booking information: Book by phone or email. Full payment is charged for cancellation on the day of trip.

Nearest airport: Bern.
Nearest rail station: Interlaken.

UNITED KINGDOM

ACORN ACTIVITIES
PO Box 120, Hereford HR4 8YB
Phone: +44 (0)1432 830083
Fax: +44 (0)1432 830110
Email: sales@acornactivities.co.uk
Website: www.acornactivities.co.uk

Hang gliding throughout the UK
Acorn Activities offers hang gliding courses for two, four or six days, depending on your time and commitment. Initially, three tether lines ensure stable flights, but as your confidence grows, the lines are gradually slackened until, weather permitting, you take your first solo flight. The six-day course leads to your Elementary Pilot's Certificate, enabling you to fly long distances solo. Weather is of course a crucial consideration when it comes to flying without a engine. With this in mind, accommodation can be booked through Acorn on the understanding that the dates might have to be rearranged, although this is at the discretion of the accommodation supplier. Acorn Activities will accept no responsibility for cancelled accommodation costs should they arise.

Activity prices: £140 for a two-day course, £280 for a four-day course and £420 for a six-day course.
Accommodation: Not included in the price, although accommodation can be arranged at a budget to suit.
Food: Not included.
Equipment supplied: All specialised equipment is provided.
What to take: Warm, wind-proof clothes and sturdy shoes or boots.
When to go: Year round, weather permitting.
Established: 1990
Safety: All instructors are BHPA qualified.

Insurance: Insurance is required, although this can be arranged through Acorn Activities.

Methods of payment: VISA, Mastercard, cheque and cash.

Booking information: Late bookings are welcomed. A non-refundable deposit of £10 per day is required. Cancellation charges apply on a sliding scale from 80% for over 43 days before departure to 100% for up to 14 days.

Nearest airport: Cardiff or Birmingham International.

Nearest rail station: Depends on the itinerary.

CAIRNWELL MOUNTAIN SPORTS

Gulabin Lodge, Spital of Glenshee, Blairgowrie PH10 7QE
Phone: +44 (0)1250 885 255
Fax: +44 (0)1250 885 256
Email: cairnwell@virgin.net
Website: http://members.tripod.co.uk/cairnwell

A Highland Fling off a hill

Austrian Gustav Fischnaller started his hang gliding school in Scotland in 1974 and has excellent experience at flying from some of the most dramatic locations. They have a range of course options including taster days for complete novices, all the way up to the BHPA Club Pilot certificate. The beginners' training hill is about 8 miles away from the centre and dual gliders are used to give flying exposure from the start. It takes about 12 days to get the Club Pilot certificate.

Activity prices: Taster days cost £65 including BHPA membership. The two-day basic introductory course costs £120, a four-day course £215 and a ten-day course £420.

Accommodation: The centre's own Gulabin Lodge provides accommodation for up to 30 people at £10 per night for self-catering, £13 for B&B.

Food: Not included. Meals can be provided if booked in advance.

Equipment supplied: All flying equipment is provided.

What to take: Personal clothing and sturdy footwear.

When to go: End of May to end of September.

Established: 1974

Safety: All instructors are BHPA qualified and the centre is licensed by the AALA.

Insurance: BHPA membership includes third party insurance. Personal insurance is up to the client. Policies are available from the centre.

Methods of payment: VISA, Mastercard, cheque and cash. Fee charged on credit card bookings.

Booking information: A non-refundable 50% deposit is required on booking.

Nearest airport: Edinburgh (70 miles). Transfers can be arranged.

Nearest rail station: Pitlochry (22 miles). Transfers can be arranged.

DERBYSHIRE FLYING CENTRE

Cliffside, Church Street, Tideswell, Derbyshire SK17 8PE
Phone: +44 (0)1298 872 313
Fax: +44 (0)1298 872 313
Email: hg-pg@d-f-c.freeserve.co.uk
Website: www.d-f-c.freeserve.co.uk

Peak time flying

There can be few more scenically attractive places to learn to fly in the UK than the Peak District National Park. The Derbyshire Flying Centre has negotiated access to over 20 training hills that allow flying in all wind directions and for all ability levels, including beginners. They offer a two-day Taster Introduction Course that gives you ample time to become acquainted with the basic principles of flying and how to control the hang glider. You experience the thrill of free flight, under the guidance of an expert instructor, from day one. If you wish to qualify for an Elementary Pilot Certificate then the five-day course should see you succeed. You can then spend a further five days going through the practical and written tests necessary to become a Club Pilot. Whatever you choose, you will have an exhilarating time.

Activity prices: The Taster course costs £85 with two -day BHPA membership costing a further £10. The Elementary Pilot Course costs £195 if booked in one block with BHPA membership for three months costing £35. The Club Pilot course also costs £195 with an upgrade to full BHPA membership costing £44.

Accommodation: Not included in the price, but the centre can help to organise it if necessary.

Food: Not included. Lunch is normally taken at local pub (alcohol not permitted) or café.

Equipment supplied: All flying equipment is provided.

What to take: Sensible, suitable clothing (warm layers is best) and strong, comfortable, supportive footwear.

When to go: Year round subject to weather.

Established: 1989

Safety: All instructors are BHPA qualified and the centre is a member of the same organisation.

Insurance: BHPA membership (compulsory) includes third party insurance. Personal insurance is up to the client. Policies are offered at the centre.

Methods of payment: Cheque and cash.

Booking information: Two weeks' advance booking is preferred. Courses or days that are cancelled due to weather are credited to the client.

Nearest airport: Manchester.

Nearest rail station: Hope. Transfers can be arranged.

HIGH ADVENTURE

Sandpipers, Coastguard Lane, Freshwater Bay, Isle of Wight PO40 9QX
Phone: +44 (0)1983 752 322
Fax: +44 (0)1983 755 063
Email: phil@high-adventure.demon.co.uk
Website: www.high-adventure.co.uk

A static Wight flight

High Adventure was the first operator in the UK to introduce static tow hang gliding and have an outstanding success record in training pilots. They now have a dedicated team of eight instructors who teach to all levels. The centre also has a weather advantage in that many of the low-pressure systems that can stop flying miss the Isle of Wight so they get more flying days per year. There are over a dozen sites to launch from, so wind direction is never an issue either. The courses available start with a one-day taster where you are introduced to the basic construction of a hang glider and then experience flying with an instructor. If you enjoy that then you can take on a two-day introductory course which counts towards your first licence should you wish to progress. Other courses qualify you as a student pilot and a club pilot.

Activity prices: A one-day taster course during the week costs £55 including BHPA membership. At weekends, the taster day costs £69. A two-day introductory course costs £100 weekday or £130 weekend, both plus £10 for BHPA membership. The three to four day Student Pilot course costs £225 (plus £35 BHPA fee); the four to five day Club Pilot course costs £295 (plus £35 BHPA fee).

Accommodation: Not included in the price. Choice of hotels nearby.

Food: Not included. Available on site.

Equipment supplied: All flying equipment is provided.

What to take: Sensible, suitable clothing (warm layers is best) and strong, comfortable, supportive footwear.

When to go: March to October.

Established: 1981

Safety: All the centre's instructors are qualified with the BHPA. The centre is a member of the Isle of Wight Tourist Board and the BHPA.

Insurance: Third party insurance, via BHPA, is included in the price. Personal insurance should be arranged by client.

Methods of payment: VISA, Mastercard, cheque and cash.

Booking information: Advance booking is necessary and a deposit is required. The deposit is non-refundable if cancellation is not for good reason.

Nearest airport: Southampton.

Nearest rail station: Lymington. Daily transfers from 10.15 a.m. ferry from Lymington.

LEJAIR

1 Manor Drift, Wendling, Dereham, Norfolk NR19 2NB
Phone: +44 (0)1362 687 000
Fax: +44 (0)1362 687 000
Email: rona@lejair.co.uk
Website: www.lejair.co.uk

A unique way to fly

In 1984 Lejair introduced safe tow launch hang glider training to the UK and it has been remarkably successful in taking students to pilot status, making it possibly the most experienced centre of its kind in Europe. The unique training method involves being towed behind a microlight up to a height of 2,000 feet. There are no long walks up hills (the centre is based on a flat airfield) so you get more flying time per day and the system functions whatever the wind direction. The longer flight times possible also means that you have more time to get used to the controls. Progression is very quick and most students by the fourth or fifth day are up to 400–500 feet, landing back at take-off. On introduction courses, clients are normally flying on their own by the fourth flight. If you want to become a pilot then this is the quickest way to do it.

Activity prices: A one-day introduction course costs £95. Five-day courses cost £500 and eight-day courses cost £750. Dual flights cost £75.

Accommodation: Not included in the price, but camping and caravan are available on-site.

Food: Not included. Client to arrange own.

Equipment supplied: All flying equipment is provided.

What to take: Sensible, suitable clothing (warm layers is best) and strong, comfortable, supportive footwear.

When to go: March to November from Wednesday to Sunday only.

Established: 1984

Safety: All instructors are BHPA qualified.

Insurance: Third party insurance is included in the price. Personal insurance needs to be arranged by client. Policies are offered at centre.

Methods of payment: VISA and cheque.

Booking information: Advance booking is essential and payment is due with booking.

Nearest airport: Norwich.

Nearest rail station: Norwich.

SUSSEX HANG GLIDING AND PARAGLIDING

Dairy Farm House, Wick Street, Firle, East Sussex BN8 6NB
Phone: +44 (0)1273 858 170
Fax: +44 (0)1273 858 177
Email: sussexhgpg@mistral.co.uk
Website: www.airbase.co.uk/sussexhgpg/

Soar over the South Downs
The South Downs offer some of the best flying conditions in England
and the Sussex school has launch sites that face every possible wind
direction. The centre operates several courses to take you from
novice to Club Pilot level. The weekend introductory courses take
place all year round and the aim is to get you flying your first top to
bottoms and usually much more. The five-day Elementary Pilot
Certificate course takes you from tethered flights to free flights where
you use radio helmets to stay in touch with the instructors. If you need
more than five days to reach the required level, they are provided free.
You can then take the Club Pilot course. So get soaring!

Activity prices: A one-day introductory course costs £75, a two-day weekend
introductory course £120. The Elementary Pilot Certificate and Club Pilot
courses cost £325 each.
Accommodation: Not included in course price. The centre can help you
organise accommodation in Brighton.
Food: Not included. Take some snacks and sandwiches with you.
Equipment supplied: All specialist flying equipment is provided.
What to take: Warm, windproof clothing with separate waterproof and strong
supportive boots.
When to go: Year round subject to weather.
Established: 1995
Safety: All the instructors used are BHPA qualified and the centre is a member
of the same organisation.
Insurance: BHPA membership (compulsory) includes third party insurance.
You will need to join on arrival. Other insurance is client's responsibility.
Methods of payment: Cheque and cash.

Booking information: Advance booking is advised.

Nearest airport: London Gatwick

Nearest rail station: Preston Park or Brighton.

WILTSHIRE HANG GLIDING AND PARAGLIDING CENTRE

Old Yatesbury Airfield, Yatesbury, Calne, Wiltshire SN11 8FA

Phone: +44 (0)1672 861 555

Fax: +44 (0)1672 861 555

Email: hamish.a@virgin.net

Website: http://business.virgin.net/hamish.a

Flying high over the Wiltshire Downs

Based near Avebury, this centre has access to some excellent launch sites on hills on the edge of the picturesque Vale of Pewsey and the Marlborough Downs. They have courses to suit all abilities including beginners. The one-day taster course uses tether ropes attached to the hang glider to get you flying as quickly as possible. The instructors pass more control to you as you progress, and you will get around 12 flights during the day. The two-day introduction is designed to give you enough flying time to get rid of the tether ropes for you to fly your first solos. You can then work towards your Elementary Pilot's licence where you move to unassisted take-offs, gentle turns and stand-up landings.

Activity prices: The one-day taster course costs from £59, the two-day course from £107; the Elementary Pilot Certificate course lasts four days and costs from £199.

Accommodation: Not included in course price. The centre can help you organise accommodation in the local area.

Food: Not included.

Equipment supplied: All specialist flying equipment is provided.

What to take: Warm clothing with separate windproof and waterproof top and supportive footwear.

When to go: Year round subject to weather.

Established: 1980

Safety: All the instructors used are BHPA qualified and the centre is a member of the same organisation and the Association of Free Flight Professionals.

Insurance: BHPA membership (compulsory) includes third party insurance. You will need to join on arrival. Other insurance is client's responsibility.

Methods of payment: Cheque and cash.

Booking information: Advance booking is advised.

Nearest airport: Bristol.

Nearest rail station: Chippenham

HIKING

Of all the adventure activities listed in this book, none is as simple or as accessible as hiking. Whether your goal is a stroll in the park or a coast to coast extravaganza, few things are more memorable than the first time you stand on a hill-top under cloudless skies and gaze out to the horizon in every direction.

Via la Vida Loca

'Via Ferrata' comes from the Italian phrase vie ferrate, *literally translated as 'steel roads'. In hiking terms, a Via Ferrata is an outdoor hike across steep ground, from rocky outcrops to vertical cliffs of 100 metres (300 feet) or more, using metal stairs, ladders, pitons and handrails as security. They were first built in the Dolomites by the Italian military at the turn of the century to make strategic mountain-tops more accessible. Today they are dotted throughout the French and Italian Alps and are becoming increasingly popular with hikers who want to go that little bit higher and that little bit steeper. Climbs vary in difficulty and demands on fitness, but are open to adventurers of every age, from 7 to 77. You don't have to be a rock climber or an alpinist to appreciate these aerial walks, but a head for heights definitely helps. On steeper sections you can actually clip your harness onto the wire for safety – going with a guide is highly recommended, at least for your first trip. Once you're familiar with the principles, the advantage over rock climbing is that no specific skills are required and you can climb safely on your own.*

Walking really is what you want to make it, come rain or shine, winter or summer. For most just getting outdoors is enough, but for many reaching the summit, and often as many summits as possible, is all part of the challenge. Some will be happy with a day-pack and a picnic, while others aren't satisfied unless they have a 50lb pack and an itinerary that would make a mountain goat think twice. Beyond that, there are hill walkers who want to put the hill back into walking, searching out the steepest routes to the summit. Where this requires hands as well as feet, walking becomes 'scrambling', often involving much steeper terrain and exposed rock ridges. In the extreme it may even require individuals to be roped to each other for safety, but at this end of the scrambling spectrum, the boundaries between walking and climbing become blurred.

In fact, many of the skills associated with climbing and mountaineering are fundamental to hiking in the hills. If you're just getting started, there are numerous companies offering hiking holidays and hill-walking courses that cover all the basics of route planning, navigation and campcraft, while those with a bit more experience might be tempted to extend their skills to winter walking or summer scrambling. Whatever your ambitions, once you've got the course covered nothing could be simpler than donning your boots and wandering off into the wild.

BULGARIA

BULGARIAN MOUNTAINS ADVENTURE
Kancho Shipkov, Kv. Dianabad bl 18 vh.A, 1172 Sofia
Phone: +359 2 620 688
Fax: N/A
Email: kancho@bglink.net
Website: http://pss.bglink.net/mysite/explorebg.html

Take a personal hike through Bulgaria

Bulgaria is one of the least explored hiking destinations in Europe, yet it has a superb choice of mountain ranges with routes to suit hikers of every standard. Bulgarian Mountains Adventure is a company based around members of the national mountain rescue service and they offer a personal, tailor-made guiding service. The options are almost limitless but some of the most popular peaks include the Pirin Mountains, with the highest peak being Vihren at 2,914 metres and no fewer than 176 lakes in the area. Another option is the Balkan Mountains, where Botev Vrah reaches 2,376 metres high and there are several steep canyons and waterfalls. The company can advise you of the best time to visit each range.

Activity prices: The trips are all tailor-made to suit your requirements and cost around US$50 per day or less, depending on what you do and where you go. The centre will advise you on the possibilities. The price also includes local transportation.

Accommodation: Food and lodging during the activity are included in the price and organised by the centre. Hotels and meals at he start and end of your trip are not included but the centre can help you arrange these.

Food: Food is included during the activity, but not at the start and end of your trip.

Equipment supplied: None.

What to take: Personal hiking and mountain clothing and suitable footwear.

When to go: Year round; the winter routes are particularly beautiful.

Established: 1997

Safety: At least one of the guides in every group is a qualified rescuer from the Bulgarian Mountain Rescue Service. They have plentiful experience and excellent local knowledge.

Insurance: Clients should arrange their own policy or the centre could arrange it on the spot.

Methods of payment: Bank transfer and cash.

Booking information: Advance booking is essential and a 30% deposit is payable. Cancellation penalties may apply.

Nearest airport: Sofia. Transfers can be arranged.

Nearest rail station: Sofia Central. Transfers can be arranged.

CORSICA

A MADUNINA EQUESTRIAN CENTRE OF TOURISM
Domaine de Croccano, Route de Granace km 3, F 20100 Sartene
Phone: +33 4 95 77 11 37
Fax: +33 4 95 73 42 89
Email: christain.perrier@wanadoo.fr
Website: www.corsenet.com/pub/m/madun/madun.html

Hiking in the mountains of Corsica
Of all Europe's wilderness areas, the mountains of Corsica must number among the most isolated and impressive. A Madunina organises seven-day walking holidays based in a restored Corsican house on the side of a mountain. Accompanied by a guide, groups of five to ten trekkers walk up to six hours a day, taking in some of the highlights of the surrounding landscape and countryside before returning to a traditional Corsican meal each night. Children aged from two to eight years can be looked after by your hostess Claudine, who is a state-registered educationalist, while eight- to twelve-year-olds can participate full- or part-time in any walk throughout the week.

Activity prices: FFr3,200 per person for a week-long guided trek, FFr1,900 for children under 12 years.
Accommodation: Included in the price.
Food: Full board is included in the price.
Equipment supplied: N/A.
What to take: Personal clothing for walking.
When to go: Year round except December. Accompanied treks are only available from January to March and October to November.
Established: 1977
Safety: All guides are highly experienced.
Insurance: Clients are responsible for arranging their own insurance, although insurance can be provided by the centre if required.
Methods of payment: VISA, Mastercard and cash.

Booking information: 30% deposit required for an advance booking. An optional cancellation policy is available.

Nearest airport: Figari or Ajaccio. Transfers to and from the airport cost an additional FF450 return.

Nearest rail station: N/A.

FRANCE

MOUNTAIN ACTIVITY EXPERIENCE
93 avenue Michel Croz, 74400 Chamonix
Phone: +33 4 50 55 80 80
Fax: +33 4 53 48 50
Email: M.A.X@wanadoo.fr
Website: montblanconeline.fr/max/max.htm

Hiking around Mont Blanc
Mountain Activity Experience's fully certified mountain leaders together share a wealth of information about the tracks and trails around Chamonix for those who prefer the horizontal to the vertical. Hidden lakes, trailside glaciers and a unique insight into the wildlife of the region are all experienced at a sedate, mountain-air pace. Half-day, full-day and five-day formulas are available with all abilities and aspirations carefully catered for, from average (two to five hours' walking per day) to serious (seven to eight hours per day). Prices include mountain leader fees and all transportation, but do depend on the number of people in the group. A classic, seven-day backpacking trek from hut to hut across the Italian, Swiss and French Alps costs from FFr3,000.

Activity prices: From FFr140 per person for a half day (4-12 people), FFr220 for a full day. Five-day courses from FFr1,000 per person (6-8 people) to FFr2,500 per person (2 people). Prices include mountain leader fees and transport but not lift passes.

Accommodation: Not included in the price.

Food: Not included.

Equipment supplied: None provided.

What to take: Personal hiking gear and suitable footwear (i.e. boots).

When to go: Summer only.

Established: 1997

Safety: All instructors are nationally qualified high mountain guides.

Insurance: Clients must provide their own insurance.

Methods of payment: Cheques and cash.

Booking information: A deposit is required to secure a booking. Cancellation within a month of the course forfeits the deposit.

Nearest airport: Geneva.

Nearest rail station: Chamonix.

ODYSSEE MONTAGNE

101 Les Marmottières, 74310 Les Houches
Phone: +33 (0)4 50 54 36 01
Fax: +33 (0)4 50 54 35 74
Email: odyssee@odyssee-montagne.fr
Website: http://odyssee-monatgne.fr

Hiking the classic Alpine routes

Hiking has always been the most popular activity in Chamonix, and for many there's no better way to experience summer in the Alps. The Tour du Mont Blanc, which passes through France, Italy and Switzerland, is arguably one of the top ten walks in the world, while Zermatt and Oberland are classics in their own right. With literally thousands of kilometres of trail to choose from, Odyssée Montagne offers six-day and week-long walking tours with a variety of options on accommodation, from basic route-side refuges to luxury mountain huts.

Activity prices: From FFr3,250 for six days and five nights.

Accommodation: Included.

Food: All food is included in the price.

Equipment supplied: No specialist equipment required.

What to take: Personal clothing for summer trekking.

When to go: June to September.

Established: 1993

Safety: All mountain guides are members of the *Ecole National de Ski et d'Alpinisme.*

Insurance: Comprehensive insurance can be provided at an additional 5% of the full price.

Methods of payment: travellers' cheques, VISA, Mastercard, SWIFT bank transfer, etc.

Booking information: A deposit of 30% is required at the time of booking.

Bookings will be accepted no later than 15 days before departure.

Nearest airport: Geneva. Airport collection available on request.

Nearest rail station: Saint Gervais.

SNOW SAFARI LIMITED

Chalet Savoy, 1351 route des Chavants, 74310 Les Houches
Phone: +33 (0)4 50 54 56 63;
UK bookings & information number: 01279 600 885
Fax: +33 (0)4 50 54 57 19
Email: Chalsavoy@aol.com
Website: www.chaletsavoy.com

Walking around the Mont Blanc Massif

Mont Blanc offers some of the finest walking in the world, from the spectacular Tour du Mont Blanc to the seriously steep Via Ferrata. There are over 300 km of walking trails in the Chamonix Valley alone, and staff at the Chalet Savoy will be happy to give advice on the best walks in the area. Accompanied walking trips are also available. Summer prices include half-board accommodation and free use of the Chalet sauna. B&B accommodation is also available at FFr140–195 per person, and airport transfers can be arranged at FFr370 per person.

Activity prices: Summer prices start from FFr140 per person for B&B, or FFr2,050 per person for seven days and seven nights.

Accommodation: Included in the price.

Food: Half board included in the price.

Equipment supplied: None.

What to take: Normal hiking clothes and good hiking boots.

When to go: May to December.

Established: 1987

Safety: All guides and leaders are fully qualified for the relevant activity.

Insurance: Clients must arrange their own insurance.

Methods of payment: VISA, Mastercard.

Booking information: Contact Snow Safari for booking form and full terms and conditions.

Nearest airport: Geneva.

Nearest rail station: Les Houches.

GREECE

CRETE UNLIMITED

Machis Kritis ,118GR 74100 Rethymnon, Crete

Phone: +30 831 53 328

Fax: +30 831 52 691

Email: info@hellasbike.com

Website: www.hellasbike.com

Hike the Crete Way

Michael Dirksen, who first came to the island in 1970 and eventually moved there in 1984, guides Crete Unlimited's hiking trips. He has excellent knowledge of the plants and animals on the island and has been guiding walks for the last seven years. He has also gathered wonderful insight into the Cretan people and their culture. The walks include impressive mountains, deep gorges, fertile plateaux and idyllic bays. He organises two week-long programmes of hikes, one for the springtime and one for autumn. The spring walks include visits to the Blue Lagoon, the only freshwater lake on Crete, and to the Samaria-Cretan National Park, a highly impressive gorge. The winter hikes include Vulture Gorge and Mount Ida, home to a holy cave. The one-week packages include five guided walks. Booking is done through Hellas Bike Travel.

Activity prices: A one-week package, including five guided walks and local transfers to/from your hotel, costs US$300.

Accommodation: Not included in price. The centre can help you arrange accommodation to suit your budget.

Food: Not included in price.

Equipment supplied: None.

What to take: Personal hiking and mountain clothing and suitable footwear, daypack, drink bottle and sun hat.

When to go: Late March to mid-October.

Established: 1992

Safety: Michael is a very experienced hiker and has excellent local knowledge.

Insurance: Third party insurance is included. Clients should arrange their own travel policy.

Methods of payment: Bank transfer prior to arrival only.

Booking information: Bank transfer should be credited to Hellas Bike Travel at least 14 days before arrival. Cancellation penalties apply on a sliding scale.

Nearest airport: Nicosia.

Nearest rail station: N/A.

IRELAND

CELTIC ADVENTURES
Caherdaniel, Co. Kerry
Phone: +353 (0)66 9475 277
Fax: +353 (0)66 9475 277
Email: info@activity-ireland.com
Website: www.activity-ireland.com

Hike it the Kerry way

Ireland's spectacular west coast is one of the most undisturbed areas of Europe and the Kerry Way circular walking trail, which twists through the coastal hills, is the country's longest way-marked trail. Over its 215 km the route follows old droving paths, 'butter roads' and paths used by the barons of Early Christian times. A highlight of the hike is the section through the Killarney National Park, where the views are simply wonderful. Throughout, you are accompanied by experienced and knowledgeable, European-qualified guides who can fill you in on the deep history of the region. When you get thirsty, there should be a cosy pub nearby where you can enjoy traditional music and famous Irish brews in front of a peat fire. Other shorter hikes in the south-west hills are also available.

Activity prices: Trips are tailor-made to suit clients' needs. Prices are based around I£20 per person per day from June to mid-August, I£18 otherwise. Discounts are available for students and school and scouting groups.

Accommodation: Hostel accommodation at I£8 or B&B at I£20, both per person/sharing basis. Availability depends on itinerary.

Food: Available at centre for approximately I£14 per day for all meals.

Equipment supplied: All specialist equipment provided.

What to take: Personal clothing and footwear.

When to go: Year round except December and January, depending on weather.

Established: 1988

Safety: All hiking guides hold European qualifications. Celtic Adventures is a member of the Irish Association of Adventure Sports and is promoted by the Irish Tourist Board, Bord Failte.

Insurance: Centre has insurance but it is recommended that clients arrange their own.

Methods of payment: VISA or personal cheque.

Booking information: Advance booking is recommended with payment requested at least 42 days in advance.

Nearest airport: Cork (2.5 hours) or Kerry (1.5 hours). Groups of clients travelling together can be collected from the airport.

Nearest rail station: Killarney (80 mins). Groups of clients travelling together can be collected from the station.

SPAIN

CASA DE LA MONTAÑA
33556 Asturias
Phone: +34 8 5844189
Fax: +34 8 5844189
Email: casamont@mundivia.es
Website: http://personales.mundivia.es/casamont

Hiking in the Picos de Europa

Spain's first National Park, Los Picos de Europa, is a spectacular and oft-overlooked mountain wilderness in the very north of Spain, with spectacular views out over the Atlantic Ocean. Casa de la Montaña (literally 'Mountain House') offers numerous trekking options in this fabulous region, from one day to one week. Guides, transport, refuge and centre accommodation and meals are all included in the price for added convenience. La Casa includes a TV and lecture room, a kitchen and restaurant, an information office for those who would prefer to make their own plans, a games lawn and mountain bike rental. Multi-activity options can also be included as part of the trekking itineraries, and include mountain biking, horse riding and canoeing.

Activity prices: A one-week trek costs around Pta59,000 per person (minimum six people), including transport, guided hiking and full board accommodation. Single days start from Pta4,000 per person, weekends Pta8,500 and multi-day trips Pta18,500, not including accommodation.

Accommodation: Full board mountain-refuge and centre accommodation is included in the price.

Food: All meals are included in the price.

Equipment supplied: None provided.

What to take: Personal hiking equipment including boots, rucksack, waterproofs, etc.

When to go: June to September.

Established: 1987

Safety: Mountain Guide Fernando Ruiz is a Professional Mountain Leader of the Asociacion Espagnola de Guias de Montaña (AEGM).

Insurance: Multi-activity insurance is available on request at an additional cost.

Methods of payment: Cash, VISA.

Booking information: A 30% deposit is required to secure a booking.

Nearest airport: Asturias & Santander (124 km). Pick-up from Santander Airport can be arranged for small groups at minimal cost.

Nearest rail station: Arriondas (22 km). Transfers can be arranged to and from the station.

HOTEL ELS FRARES
Avenida Pais Valencia NA 20, 038111 Quatretondeta, Alicante
Phone: +34 96 551 1234
Fax: +34 96 551 1200
Email: elsfrares@logiccontrol.es
Website: www.holidaybank.co.united Kingdom/elsfrares/

Guided mountain walking in the Costa Blanca Mountains
The classic limestone geology of Spain's Costa Blanca mountains is
typified by narrow ravines, knife-edge ridges and jagged peaks
towering more than 1,500 metres above sea level. Els Frares is based
in the small, traditional village of Quatretondeta, in the north-west of
Spain's most mountainous province. The hotel offers week-long
walking holidays, with guided tours of all the local mountains, as well
as trips further afield to the Rio Serpis Gorge and the ridge of Sierra
Mariola. Distances vary between 8 and 18 miles per day, and a good
head for heights is essential for some of the routes.

Activity prices: From £500 per week including air fares, collection from
Alicante Airport, full-board accommodation and all guided walks.
Accommodation: Quality hotel accommodation is included.
Food: Half board or full board available.
Equipment supplied: No equipment is provided.
What to take: A good pair of walking boots is essential.
When to go: September to June.
Established: 1992
Safety: Member of the Spanish Federation of Mountain Sports.
Insurance: Clients must take out relevant insurance for all activities.
Methods of payment: VISA, Mastercard, Amex, traveller's cheques and all
major credit cards.
Booking information: Contact Waymark Holidays Limited on
+44 (0)1753 516 477, fax +44 (0)1753 517 016.
Nearest airport: Collection from Alicante Airport is included in the price.
Nearest rail station: Alcoy.

ALPIN CENTER ZERMATT

Mountain Guides' Association, 3920 Zermatt
Phone: +41 (0)27 966 2460
Fax: +41 (0)27 966 2469
Email: alpincenter@zermatt.ch
Website: www.zermatt.ch/alpincenter

Hike the high route and Matterhorn

Zermatt has an enviable array of hiking routes surrounding it, including one around the much vaunted and seriously impressive looking Matterhorn. With the trails served by a well-established network of mountain huts, you can travel relatively lightweight to further enhance your enjoyment of the Alpine roses, edelweiss, marmots and ibex along the route. With glaciers, ragged peaks and sweeping meadows to see, the one-week long hikes will get you right away from your daily routine. For those wanting a bigger challenge, the Haute Route runs from Zermatt to Chamonix or to Verbier, taking in high Alpine trails. The one-week-long hike around the Matterhorn allows you to see all sides of this famous peak, including the treacherous North Face. The Alpin Center guides make wonderful hiking companions with their deep knowledge and obvious love of the area.

Activity prices: One-week hikes around the Zermatt area cost from SFr810; the Matterhorn hike costs SFr1180; the Haute Route to Verbier costs SFr920 and to Chamonix SFr1,190. Group size is between four and six.
Accommodation: A wide range of accommodation is available in the Zermatt area. The centre can assist with arranging it. Half-board accommodation is included on the hikes, in either hotels or mountain huts.
Food: Breakfast and dinner are included.
Equipment supplied: Specialist equipment is available to rent.
What to take: Specialist equipment (check with centre for recommended list). Personal mountain clothing and suitable footwear.

When to go: June to October (June to September for the Haute Route and the
Matterhorn).
Established: 1982
Safety: All the Alpin Center guides are fully licensed, qualified and highly
experienced.
Insurance: Clients must arrange their own personal accident insurance and it
is recommended that you also take out Rescue Insurance with Air Zermatt for
SFr20 per week or SFr30 per year. Forms available from the Alpin Center.
Methods of payment: VISA, cash or bank transfer.
Booking information: Advance booking is essential.
Nearest airport: Zurich.
Nearest rail station: Zermatt.

FOUR SEASONS GUIDES
Chalet L'Aurore, 1936 Verbier
Phone: +41 27 771 7683
Fax: +41 27 771 1603
Email: hans@verbier.ch
Website: www.swissguides.com

Freedom to Roam Swiss Hills
There are boundless opportunities for hiking in the Alps and Verbier
is a good base for accessing many of them. You could choose to
follow the Haute Route, traverse scenic valleys or do a five-day hike
to Arolla or Zermatt. Along the way, you may see ibex, marmot and
plenty of wild flowers. Of course, there are always hikes around the
classic Alpine summits of Mont Blanc, the Matterhorn and the
Eiger, but why not be different and head elsewhere to take in lesser-
known peaks, such as those found in the Valais region? Other less
well-known but still classic peaks include Grand Combin, Weisshorn
and Dent Blanche. The major advantage of having your own
personal guide is that you have limitless flexibility for arranging an
itinerary to suit your own abilities and wishes. The UIAGM guides
are renowned for their local knowledge and make excellent hiking
companions.

Activity pices: Guiding fees are SFr400 per day for one to two clients. For this, the guide will also arrange local travel and hotel bookings and the itinerary (clients pay directly to the hotel, bus company, etc).

Accommodation: Not included in the price. There is a large range of accommodation options in the area and the guide will help you to arrange it.

Food: Not included in the price, but there are plenty of eating options in the area too. While in the mountains, the client pays for his own food and that of the guide.

Equipment supplied: Specialist equipment can be hired in Verbier.

What to take: All specialist mountain clothing.

When to go: Year round; winter for ski-mountaineering options.

Established: 1990

Safety: All guides hold UIAGM qualifications.

Insurance: Clients are recommended to buy helicopter rescue insurance which costs SFr30 for one year.

Methods of payment: VISA, Mastercard, Amex, travellers' cheques and cash.

Booking information: Payment in full is required one week in advance. Full refunds are available for acceptable cancellation.

Nearest airport: Geneva. Transfers can be arranged.

Nearest rail station: Le Chable. Transfers can be arranged.

INTERNATIONAL SCHOOL OF MOUNTAINEERING, SWITZERLAND

Hafod Tan y Graig, Nant Gwynant, Gwynedd LL55 4NW, UK
Phone: +44 (0)1766 890441
Fax: +44 (0)1766 890599
Email: ism@dial.pipex.com
Website: http//:ds.dial.pipex.com/ism

Trekking around the highest mountain in Europe
ISM's summer Alpine trekking programme starts in mid-June and runs right through until late September. Multi-day treks cover every aspect of Alpine mountaineering and high-altitude trekking, and routes include a circuit of the Matterhorn, the Central Oberland Trek and the Swiss Haute Route. Courses include mountain hut accommodation and full board.

Activity prices: £615 to £645 for six-day treks.

Accommodation: All Alpine courses include hotel accommodation.

Food: Alpine courses include full board.

Equipment supplied: All specialist equipment is provided.

What to take: Personal clothing and footwear.

When to go: Year round.

Established: 1960

Safety: All guides hold the International Carnet, the highest qualification available in mountaineering.

Insurance: Relevant insurance required for all Alpine courses.

Methods of payment: All common payment methods accepted.

Booking information: Contact ISM for booking form and full terms and conditions.

Nearest airport: Geneva.

Nearest rail station: Leysin.

TURKEY

BITEZ YACHTING

Neyzen Tevfik Caddesi 142, 48400 Bodrum
Phone: +90 252 316 2139/2454
Fax: +90 252 316 3101
Email: ecomail@turk.net
Website: http://www.holidaybank.co.uk/bitezyachting

Trekking in Turkey

Lake Kocagol and the Gulf of Fethiye are the locations for Bitez's one-week trekking holidays, which combine some spectacular Mediterranean scenery with the very best in local culture and hospitality. The first few days are spent in a village home on the shores of Lake Kocagol, exploring the region on foot or by bike. A day is set aside for canoeing and fishing on the lake before heading for the Gulf of Fethiye, where you'll spend the days investigating the rarely visited ruins of Lissea and Lidea and the nights sleeping out under the stars. The final two days are spent on the Dalaman river as guests in a village home. Trekking can also be combined with sailing or diving if required.

Activity prices: From US$390 per week in the low season to US$435 per week in the high season.

Accommodation: Village guest-house and tented accommodation is included.

Food: Breakfast and lunch are included in the price.

Equipment supplied: All specialist equipment is provided.

What to take: Personal clothing and footwear suitable for the prevailing conditions; if in doubt, call ahead for advice.

When to go: May to October.

Established: 1986

Safety: All English-/Dutch-speaking guides are highly experienced.

Insurance: Clients are responsible for arranging their own insurance.

Methods of payment: Cash and/or bank transfer.

Booking information: A 25% deposit is required to confirm a booking, with the balance paid on arrival. There is a 5% charge for a cancellation within two weeks of the departure date.

Nearest airport: Dalaman and Bodrum. Tranfers to and from the airport are included in the price.

Nearest rail station: N/A.

UNITED KINGDOM

ACORN ACTIVITIES
PO Box 120, Hereford HR4 8YB
Phone: +44 (0)1432 830083
Fax: +44 (0)1432 830110
Email: sales@acornactivities.co.uk
Website: www.acornactivities.co.uk

Scrambling in Scotland, Snowdonia and the Lake District
The UK's mountainous regions provide some of the most challenging hiking in the world for walkers willing to test their nerve, confidence and skill. An exciting day of ascent and descent consists of scrambling over boulders, walking along exposed ridges and through spectacular gullies and crags. Moving un-roped over steep, awkward terrain is not for the faint of foot, but approaching the summit from a unseen scramble adds a whole new perspective to a day in the hills.

Activity prices: £40 for a full mountain adventure day (minimum booking four people, although individuals may join groups).

Accommodation: Not included in the price.

Food: Not included.

Equipment supplied: All specialist equipment is provided.

What to take: Warm, windproof and waterproof clothing, depending on conditions.

When to go: Year round, weather permitting.

Established: 1990

Safety: All the guides are qualified with the relevant national associations.

Insurance: Insurance is required, although this can be arranged through Acorn Activities.

Methods of payment: VISA, Mastercard, cheque and cash.

Booking information: Late bookings are welcomed. A non-refundable deposit of £10 per day is required. Cancellation charges apply on a sliding scale from 80% for over 43 days before departure to 100% for up to 14 days.

Nearest airport: Depends on tour.

Nearest rail station: Depends on the itinerary.

ALAN KIMBER

Calluna, Heathercroft, Fort William PH33 6RE
Phone: +44 (0)1397 700 451
Fax: +44 (0)1397 700 489
Email: mountain@guide.u-net.com
Website: www.guide.u-net.com

Take a hike in the Scottish Highlands

There are few better places in the UK to hike than the awe-inspiring Scottish Highlands and Alan Kimber is based right in among them. His five-day summer courses visit some of the most beautiful rugged peaks of the region and there is a Lochaber Munro Round trip that visits the Mamores, Grey Corries, the Aonachs, Glen Coe and Ben Nevis. While on the trail, you learn about map reading, compass work and mountain safety skills. There will also be ample time for photography and there is an option of doing some snow work in courses during April and May. For the more adventurous, try the scrambling course which takes you on to steeper ground.

Activity prices: The Lochaber Munro Round course costs £210 for instruction only. Accommodation: On-site self-catering accommodation is available in the beautifully located and homely Calluna Lodge. Various room options. Hotel accommodation can be arranged.

Equipment supplied: None.

What to take: Personal clothing, footwear, raingear and other items. Full list sent on booking.

When to go: April to November.

Established: 1972

Safety: All instructors are MLTB qualified. The centre is approved by the Mountaineering Council of Scotland and the British Mountaineering Council. Insurance: Insurance is available from the centre and costs £10.70 for seven days.

Methods of payment: VISA, Mastercard, cheque, cash (3.5% surcharge on credit card payments).

Booking information: Advance booking is essential. A non-refundable 50% deposit is payable on booking. Balance paid on arrival. Cancellation within four weeks of course start date forfeits the whole course price unless replacement client is found.

Nearest airport: Glasgow.

Nearest rail station: Fort William.

BLACK MOUNTAIN ACTIVITIES
PO Box 5, Hay on Wye, Hereford HR3 5YB
Phone: +44 (0)1497 847 897
Fax: +44 (0)1497 847 897
Email: enquiries@blackmountain.co.uk
Website: www.blackmountain.co.uk

Explore the hills of the Brecon Beacons

The wonderful Brecon Beacons National Park has a wonderful selection of hiking routes to suit all levels of ability. It is also an ideal place for testing your navigational skills as the hilltops are quite featureless, meaning navigation is more challenging. The Black Mountain Activities guides will teach you mountain safety techniques and the basics of navigating in high and varied terrain. If you wish to extend your trip then you can book an overnight trip where you spend a night out under canvas.

Activity prices: £30 per day or £20 for a half-day trip.

Accommodation: Not included in the price. There is a range of accommodation available locally and the centre will advise you.

Food: Not included. Packed lunches can be arranged.

Equipment supplied: All specialist equipment is supplied.

What to take: Personal clothing, swimsuit, suitable footwear.

When to go: Year round.

Established: 1992

Safety: All the centre's staff are fully qualified in their respective sports, hold first aid qualifications and are highly professional. All equipment used meets national safety standards. The centre is licensed by the AALA and the Welsh Tourist Board.

Insurance: The centre is insured though clients may wish to take out separate insurance too.

Methods of payment: Personal cheque and cash.

Booking information: Advance booking is recommended though late bookings may be possible.

Nearest airport: Depends on tour. Cardiff and Bristol are nearest to the centre.

Nearest rail station: Depends on the itinerary. Hereford and Abergavenny are nearest to the centre.

COMPASS HOLIDAYS

48 Shurdington Road, Cheltenham, Gloucestershire GL53 0JE
Phone: +44 (0)1242 250 642
Fax: +44 (0)1242 529 730
Email: compass.holidays@bigfoot.com
Website: http://dialspace.dial.pipex.com/town/road/xdt51/index.htm

Footsteps through the Heart of England
Hiking around the historic sites and beautiful countryside of the Cotswolds, the UK's largest Area of Outstanding Natural Beauty, is one of the most relaxing and rewarding holidays you could choose.

Compass Holidays offer a range of guided and self-guided tours, ranging from short breaks to eight-day circular routes. Some of the highlights include tours from the ancient Roman capital of Cirencester that visit the source of the River Thames; stays in Bilbury, described by William Morris as 'the prettiest village in England'; and the wildlife along the Windrush Valley. Daily walking distances range between 6 and 12 miles, giving plenty of time for stopping to enjoy the scenery, and group size is between six and fourteen.

Activity prices: There are a large number of tours available at varying prices, starting from £66 per person for a one day/two night break in B&B accommodation.

Accommodation: Included in the price. Ranges from pubs and B&B to farmhouses and luxury hotels.

Food: Breakfast is included, all other meals are optional.

Equipment supplied: Maps, route directions.

What to take: Personal hiking clothing, small backpack, suitable footwear.

When to go: Year round. Guided tours run from April to October.

Established: 1990

Safety: Qualified guides lead Guided tours. Compass Holidays is a member of the Heart of England Tourist Board and the West Country Tourist Board.

Insurance: Clients need to arrange their own insurance.

Methods of payment: VISA, Mastercard, personal cheque, cash.

Booking information: Advance booking is advised. Payment is due eight weeks prior to departure. A deposit of £50 per person is required with booking.

Cancellation charges apply, ranging from 75% with 27 days' or more notice to 100% for less than 27 days.

Nearest airport: Depends on tour.

Nearest rail station: Depends on tour.

CUILLIN GUIDES

Stac Lee, Glenbrittle, Isle of Skye, Inverness-shire IV47 8TA
Phone: +44 (0)1478 640 289
Fax: N/A
Email: Not available. Booking form on website.
Website: www.w-o-w.com/clients/cuillin

Skye high Scottish hiking

There are few places in the UK that can match the Isle of Skye off Scotland's west coast for beautiful and dramatic wilderness scenery. And the ridge walks of the Black Cuillin are some of the finest on Skye. The Cuillin Guides have over twenty-seven years' experience of experience of guiding clients on hikes across Skye, including all the Munro peaks. They can tailor a trip to suit your own requirements. Examples include a Knoydart area trek taking in Ladhar Bheinn, Sgurr Na Ciche and Sgurr Mhor; or they could take you to the Kintial or Torridon areas. Their intimate knowledge of the area will enlighten your time there.

Activity prices: The trips are tailor-made so the prices vary, but a trip lasting from Sunday to Friday like those mentioned above would cost around £175.

Accommodation: Included in the price. Accommodation is in bothies or bunkhouses in the mountains.

Food: Not included.

Equipment supplied: None.

What to take: A full equipment list is supplied on booking.

When to go: Year round, except the stalking season 11 August to 20 October.

Established: 1972

Safety: All the guides are qualified mountain leaders.

Insurance: Clients need to arrange their own insurance.

Methods of payment: Personal cheque, cash.

Booking information: Advance booking is essential. A deposit of £20 is payable.

Nearest airport: Glasgow.

Nearest rail station: Kyle of Lochalsh.

HIGH TREK SNOWDONIA

Tal y Waen, Deiniolen, Caernarfon, Gwynedd LL55 3NA
Phone: +44 (0)1286 871 232
Fax: +44 (0)1286 870 576
Email: high.trek@virgin.net
Website: www.hightrek.co.uk

Hike the high routes of Wales

Snowdonia is the highest mountain range in Wales and High Trek specialise in exploring the most magnificent parts of it. In addition to three-day guided hikes into secluded cwms and along alternative summit routes, the company offers a challenging weekend hike that takes you to the summit of all fourteen 3,000 feet high mountains in Wales. This is a classic walk following ridges, though there are a few big descents and ascents to contend with as well. At the end of each day, you can relax and refuel your muscles with a drink and hearty food in front of a roaring log fire. You can also join trips that take in just parts of the longer route, such as the three summits of Snowdon, including the notorious knife-edge ridge of Crib Goch, or the Carneddau range. High Trek also offer winter walking courses, where you are taught how to use a walking axe and crampons and how to read winter weather conditions and avalanche potential.

Activity prices: For three days and three nights, the all-inclusive price is £205. The winter course lasts three days and three nights and costs £225.

Accommodation: Included in the price. You stay at the homely Tal y Waen farmhouse in bunk-bed accommodation.

Food: Included in price. You get full board including wine with dinner and a packed lunch.

Equipment supplied: Everything except personal clothing and boots is provided.

What to take: Personal clothing, suitable footwear.

When to go: April to October.

Established: 1985

Safety: All the centre's hiking guides hold the Mountain Leader Certificate and a first aid qualification. The centre is approved by the Association of Mountaineering Instructors and the Wales Tourist Board.

Methods of payment: VISA, Mastercard, Switch, cheques, cash.

Booking information: Advance booking is recommended though late bookings may be possible. A £75 deposit is payable and full payment is due four weeks in advance. Sliding scale for cancellation depends on time of cancellation.

Nearest airport: Manchester.

Nearest rail station: Bangor.

KEVIN WALKER MOUNTAIN ACTIVITIES

74 Beacons Park, Brecon, Powys LD3 9BQ
Phone: +44 (0)1874 625111
Fax: +44 (0)1874 625111
Email: kevin@mountain-acts.freeserve.co.uk
Website: http://www.mountain-acts.freeserve.co.uk

Hill walking in north and south Wales

Kevin Walker has been leading courses in the Welsh mountains for more than 20 years and for many of these has been extensively involved with Mountain Leader Training Board (MLTB) courses, the most recognised mountain leadership courses in the UK. There are two courses that fit under the broad banner of hiking. The five-day Hill Walkers' Confidence Course provides the sort of skills needed to strike out into remote and adventurous countryside with confidence. Navigation, safety, first aid and moving safely across steep ground are all covered, as are route planning and selection. And all of this on the uncrowded slopes of the Brecon Beacons. A maximum of six clients per instructor ensures individual attention and enjoyment. Also relevant is the two-day Mountain Navigation course, which covers map interpretation, compass skills, estimating time and distance, poor visibility navigation and relocation. No previous knowledge is required, although some hill-walking experience would be beneficial. Participants must be over 18 years of age and in reasonably good physical condition.

Activity prices: From £95 for a two-day course to £225 for a five-day course.
Accommodation: Not included in the price, although a good range of accommodation is available locally – see the brochure for recommendations.
Food: Clients to arrange their own.
Equipment supplied: All specialist equipment is provided.
What to take: Outdoor clothing and footwear suitable for the prevailing conditions (available for hire if necessary); if in doubt, call ahead for advice.
When to go: Year round.
Established: 1979
Safety: Kevin Walker Mountain Activities is an MLTB recognised centre, and all instructors are MLTB qualified.

Cycling along quiet backroads is a good way to keep fit,
both physically and mentally.

White water kayaking normally requires two hands, but dare to be different.

Sea kayaking is a perfect way to explore coastlines, for a day, a week or a month.

Coasteering requires a head for heights and a good dose of courage.

Hand holds are not always easy to come by when rock climbing.

Seeing a hot air balloon take off can inspire desperate action
from those unlucky enough to be left behind.

Canyoning is not the sport for aquaphobics.

I feel the need, the need for speed:
snowboarding is a great way to zip down the slopes.

Canadian canoes offer a more tranquil way of paddling on water.

Kayaking wild white water rivers requires a bit of advance planning.

A hike in winter means more equipment to carry but fewer people on the hills.

Insurance: The centre carries indemnity insurance for all activities and can advise on personal accident insurance if required.

Methods of payment: Cash, cheques from British banks and sterling travellers' cheques.

Booking information: Reservations essential. A 20% deposit secures a booking, with the balance due three weeks prior to the course. Cancellation four to six weeks before the course forfeits 30% of the fee, two to four weeks before 50% and less than two weeks before 100%.

Nearest airport: Cardiff (South Wales) or Manchester (North Wales), depending on the course.

Nearest rail station: Abergavenny (South Wales) or Betws-y-Coed (North Wales).

PEAK ACTIVITIES

Rock Lea Activity Training Centre, Station Road, Hathersage, Hope Valley, Derbyshire S32 1DD
Phone: +44 (0)1433 650 345
Fax: +44 (0)1433 650 342
Email: admin@iain.co.uk
Website: www.iain.co.uk

Hopeful hiking in Derbyshire

Trek over high, scenic crags, wander through woodlands or follow the beautiful rivers around Hope Valley in the Peak District National Park, located virtually on the doorsteps of Peak Activities' Hathersage centre. The guided walks can be either linear or circular and are arranged to suit the group's preferences; distances vary between 10 and 14 miles per day. Alternatively, head for the trackless plateau of Kinder Scout and Bleaklow to experience the wildness of England's uplands with a well-qualified mountain guide.

Activity prices: Two full days of guided walking with minibus support cost £59 per person.

Accommodation: Not included in the tour price. There is a large range of options within easy reach of the centre, ranging from hostels and B&B to farmhouses and hotels.

Food: Not included in tour price but there are plenty of local eateries to suit all budgets.

Equipment supplied: All specialist equipment and bad weather gear if necessary.

What to take: Personal clothing and suitable footwear. Full list supplied on booking.

When to go: Year round.

Established: 1979

Safety: All the guides used by Peak Activities are nationally qualified and have first aid qualifications. Staff carry radios and first aid kits. The company is licensed by the AALA and is a member of the Heart of England Tourist Board. Supplied specialist equipment is of a high standard and regularly maintained and replaced.

Insurance: All Peak Activity tours are fully insured for public and third party liability. Optional additional insurance can be taken out to guard against cancellation, illness, loss of property, etc.

Methods of payment: VISA, Mastercard, Eurocard, personal cheques.

Booking information: A 50% deposit is requested with all bookings.

Nearest airport: Leeds (45 mins), Manchester (45 mins), Birmingham (90 mins) or Sheffield (12 mins). Transfers can be arranged.

Nearest rail station: Hathersage. Transfers can be arranged.

PLAS Y BRENIN

National Mountain Centre, Capel Curig, Conwy LL24 0ET
Phone: +44 (0)1690 720 214
Fax: +44 (0)1690 720 394
Email: info@pyb.co.uk
Website: www.pyb.co.uk

Enjoy Snowdonia's classic heights

The rugged and dramatic peaks of north Wales offer some of the UK's best opportunities for hikers of all abilities. The range of courses provided by Plas y Brenin are designed to give you the skills to enhance both your enjoyment and personal safety. For novices, the Introduction to Navigation course covers the basics of route planning from using a compass to more effective map reading. The Hillwalking Skills course takes you into Snowdonia to learn about mountain environment, emergency procedures and navigation too. For those with previous experience, there are longer courses that teach the necessary techniques for multi-day hikes, including basic ropework, and scrambling courses for hikers who wish to explore more exposed terrain.

Activity prices: A two-day Navigation Skills course costs £110, the Hillwalking Skills course costs £295 and the various longer courses range from £295 to £320.

Accommodation: Prices include shared accommodation.

Food: Course prices include full board.

Equipment supplied: All specialist equipment and clothing is provided.

What to take: Personal clothing and your own equipment if you prefer to use it.

When to go: Year round for Navigation Skills, March/April to October/November for other courses.

Established: 1954

Safety: All instructors hold nationally recognised qualifications and only the most capable and experienced are employed. The centre is licensed by the AALA. Great emphasis is placed on safety and the high quality equipment used is regularly checked and replaced.

Insurance: The centre carries public liability insurance for all activities and recommends that clients take out independent insurance against curtailment and cancellation of their course (available from the centre) and a personal accident policy.

Methods of payment: VISA, Mastercard, Access, personal cheque, cash.

Booking information: Reservations must be made in advance and a deposit is required.

Nearest airport: Manchester.

Nearest rail station: Llandudno. Free transfer available by prior arrangement.

ROCK AND ICE

Birch Tree House, Shirley, nr Ashbourne, Derbyshire DE6 3AS
Phone: +44 (0)1335 360 490
Fax: N/A
Email: rock.ice@bigfoot.com
Website: www.rockandice.demon.co.uk

Explore the Peaks of the Derbyshire Dales
Rock and Ice are located in the Peak District National Park, home to some of the country's most delightful walking country. Rock and Ice offer courses and holidays ranging from one day to two weeks in duration. A typical course involves navigation, including route choice and leadership skills, advice on wild camping and an introduction to scrambling. The scrambling element allows you to explore less-visited, more exposed areas of the mountains and may include some simple ropework. Large groups are also catered for.

Activity prices: Prices are based around £80 per day for one to one tuition and £50 per person on a one instructor to two clients basis.

Accommodation: Not included in the tour price. The centre will help you to arrange accommodation in the local area.

Food: Not included in price but there are local places to suit all budgets.

Equipment supplied: Specialist equipment for scrambling is provided.

What to take: Personal mountain clothing and suitable footwear. Suggested list supplied on booking.

When to go: Year round, depending on weather.

Established: 1987

Safety: The instructors employed by Rock and Ice are all qualified by the national governing bodies.

Insurance: The centre recommends outdoor pursuits travel insurance that starts at £12.50 for up to four days.

Methods of payment: Personal cheques and cash.

Booking information: A 50% deposit is requested with all bookings. Balance is due 28 days before course. Cancellation penalties are applied.

Nearest airport: Manchester.

Nearest rail station: Derby. Transfers can be arranged.

HORSE RIDING

Saddling up a horse and striking off across country along quiet tracks and back roads is one of the most enlivening adventures you can have. If you pick the right horse to match your own personality and riding aspirations then you can in an instant convert from a gentle walk to an exhilarating gallop. And it would take a wooden-hearted rider indeed to not develop some kind of affection for your steed during even the shortest of rides. It is lovely to see the horse's ears prick up the moment you start to talk to it. However, riding horses demands great skill and learning the techniques should not be taken lightly. Horses have their own minds and if they decide to take off, you want to learn to be confident enough to stay with them. Thankfully, the vast majority of horses used by riding centres are superbly trained and are very responsive to even the most unskilled rider. If they aren't then you would not even be on them as a beginner. There are many possible ways to develop your interest should you wish to, with show jumping, eventing, polo and dressage just some of the options. So, mount up, take hold of the reins and ride off into the sunset.

CORSICA

A MADUNINA EQUESTRIAN CENTRE OF TOURISM
Domaine de Croccano, Route de Granace km 3, F 20100 Sartene
Phone: +33 4 95 77 11 37
Fax: +33 4 95 73 42 89
Email: christain.perrier@wanadoo.fr
Website: www.corsenet.com/pub/m/madun/madun.html

Horse riding in the mountains of Corsica

An oft-neglected gem adrift in the azure waters of the Mediterranean Sea, Corsica boasts some of the most dramatic mountain scenery in Europe. A Madunina offers week-long riding courses at their base in Sartene for beginners and experts alike. For more proficient riders, they also organise a number of multi-day, guided horse treks to suit a variety of passions and pockets. De luxe treks include hotel accommodation and a gastronomic evening meal, with a luggage vehicle on hand twice a day. Comfort treks include accommodation in a simple guesthouse, with traditional Corsican fare at a nearby country inn. Lastly, bivouac treks involve a picnic lunch, a campfire dinner and accommodation in mother nature's bosom. Routes vary from rugged coastline to soaring mountains and each group consists of five to twelve riders, plus a guide. Saddle bags are kept to a strict minimum, but might include a pair of walking boots (November to April) or trainers, a fleece, swimsuit and towel, sun cream, torch, knife and waterproofs.

Activity prices: From FFr3,300 to FFr7,000 for a week-long trek depending on the itinerary/route. Courses from FFr3,600 to FFr4,300 per week.

Accommodation: Treks include accommodation in hotels, guest houses and tents depending on the level of comfort chosen. For courses, twin bedroom accommodation at the centre is included in the price.

Food: Full board is included in the price.

Equipment supplied: All tackle and riding hats.

What to take: Personal clothing.

When to go: Year round except December.

Established: 1977

Safety: All instructors are Accompagnateurs de Tourisme Equestre (ATE) qualified and the centre is a member of the Fédération Française d'Equitation.

Insurance: Clients are responsible for arranging their own insurance, although insurance can be provided by the centre if required.

Methods of payment: VISA, Mastercard and cash.

Booking information: 30% deposit required for an advance booking. An optional cancellation policy is available.

Nearest airport: Figari or Ajaccio. Transfers to and from the airport cost an additional FFr450 return.

Nearest rail station: N/A.

JIM'S WILDERNESS ADVENTURES LIMITED
Wolfbay Lodge, Rajaniementie 39, 93999 Kuusamo
Phone: +358 400 258 669
Fax: +358 8 856 101
Email: jwa.ltd@koillismaa.fi
Website: www.koillismaa.fi/wolfbay

Horse trekking in Finland
Oulanka National Park in Kuusamo stretches over an area of 270 sq km and is located just south of the Arctic Circle on the border with Russia, where untouched wilderness still abounds. The park's policy of low impact travel means horses are the only alternative to travelling on foot. Jim's Wilderness Adventures offers a week-long trekking expedition through virgin forest, across idyllic streams and past roaring rapids. Eagles, hawks, reindeer and elk abound, and bears and wolverines can sometimes be spotted along the trail. In the evenings riders will cook over a camp fire and sleep in a laavu, a traditional Finnish lean-to. The route covers 25–35 km per day, but the Finnish horses are easy to handle and only a basic knowledge of riding techniques is required.

Activity prices: FM5,200 for a week-long expedition.
Accommodation: Private cabins with sauna at Wolfbay Lodge and more basic cabins on the expedition.
Food: All meals included.
Equipment supplied: All specialist equipment provided.
What to take: Riding boots, wet weather gear and warm clothing for chilly evenings.
When to go: June to October.
Established: 1995
Safety: An experienced local guide called Jorma guides all expeditions.
Insurance: Relevant insurance is provided.
Methods of payment: VISA, Mastercard and SWIFT bank transfers.
Booking information: No deposit required, but payment must be made at least one month before arrival. Cancellation within the final month will forfeit 50% of the full activity prices.

Nearest airport: Kuusamo.
Nearest rail station: N/A.

ICELAND

ĪSHESTAR ICELANDIC RIDING TOURS
Bæjarhraun 2, 220 Hafnarfjörour
Phone: +354 565 3044
Fax: +354 565 2113
Email: info@ishestar.is
Website: www.ishestar.is

Gallop the lava fields
Explosive geysers, isolated beaches and wild mountain landscapes
form the backdrop to horse riding in Iceland. Ishestar offer a large
number of tours, from two to three hours to sixteen days, to suit riders
of all experience levels. For the novice there are shorter trips around
the lava fields of Hejomark Nature Park, while more capable riders,
for example, can take on a nine-day tour to the waterfalls of Lake
Myatvin. The ultimate trip is the 16-day Northern Exposure tour that
takes you along the famous Löngufjörur beaches, over mountain
passes in the north of Iceland and to the mysterious lakes at
Arnarvatnsheioi. Ishestar has been established since 1982 and is the
leading horse-riding operator in the country. Longer tours include all
food and accommodation.

Activity prices: Short tour prices range from £26 for the two- to three-hour
Lava Tour to £69 for the one-day Viking Tour. Longer tours range from £391
for the four-day Leirubakki Volcano Tour to £1,897 for the 16-day Northern
Exposure Tour. Tours are available at most prices in between.
Accommodation: All accommodation is included during riding tours and, on
longer tours, a night before and after the tour in a guesthouse.
Food: Full board (Icelandic breakfast, picnic lunch and dinner) is included on
longer tours. Lunch is included on one-day tours.
Equipment supplied: Good rain clothes, a riding helmet, saddle bag and
sleeping bag in addition to horse equipment.

What to take: Riding boots (rubber is better due to the number of river crossings), riding trousers, warm personal clothing and swimsuit.

When to go: Shorter tours all year round, longer tours June to September.

Established: 1982

Safety: All the riding guides are very experienced horse riders and the company is a member of SAF{?}.

Insurance: Centre has full liability insurance but clients must arrange their own travel/riding insurance.

Methods of payment: VISA, Mastercard, personal cheque or travellers' cheques.

Booking information: Advance booking at least nine weeks before is recommended. Cancellation charges apply on a sliding scale (10% for more than six weeks' notice up to 100% for less than one week's notice).

Nearest airport: Keflavík (30 mins). Transfer is included in tour price.

Nearest rail station: N/A.

IRELAND

DRUMGOOLAND HOUSE
29 Dunnanew Road, Seaforde, Downpatrick, Co. Down,
Northern Ireland BT30 8PJ
Phone: +44 (0)1396 811 956
Fax: +44 (0)1396 811 265
Email: frank.mc_leigh@virgin.net
Website: www.horsetrek-ireland.com

Saddle up in the Mountains of Mourne
Drumgooland is a 100-year-old country house set in 60 acres and has its own adjoining equestrian centre. Nearby are the magnificent Mountains of Mourne, which are full of potential for riders of all abilities. The equestrian centre offers a comprehensive range of riding options. If you just want a short holiday, the Riding Break packages give you two nights of accommodation and six hours of riding, including one hour of tuition, through forests and along beaches. If you wish to venture further afield, then the three and six-day Trail Riding packages offer circular routes that take in ancient castles, nature reserves, beaches, lakes and mountains. Accommodation en route is included.

For the more committed rider, the centre runs an excellent six-day course with tuition in show jumping, dressage, cross-country and horse care. During the course you also take off on the surrounding trails.

Activity prices: The two-night Riding Breaks cost £170, including B&B accommodation and snack lunches. The Trail Riding holidays are available on guesthouse B&B basis, costing £307 for three days and £539 for six days. For country house, full-board packages the prices are £399 for the three-day and £725 for the six-day holiday.

Accommodation: Included in price, see above, either at Drumgooland House or private hotels and guesthouses en route.

Food: Some or all food is included depending on the package.

Equipment supplied: Horse equipment and safety helmets.

What to take: Riding boots, riding trousers, personal outdoor clothing, including waterproof gear.

When to go: Year round.

Established: 1994

Safety: All the staff are fully trained and experienced. The equestrian centre is approved by the Northern Ireland and British Horse Society and the Department of Agriculture. All the guides carry mobile phones.

Insurance: Clients should arrange their own personal accident insurance or take out the policy offered by the centre.

Methods of payment: VISA, Mastercard, Amex, cheque or bank transfer.

Booking information: Advance booking is essential.

Nearest airport: Belfast. Transfers are available at £25 per person return. Transfers also possible from Dublin at £40.

Nearest rail station: N/A.

ITALY

RIFUGIO PRATEGIANO

Loc. Prategiano 45, I-58026 Montieri
Phone: +39 (0)566 997 700
Fax: +39 (0)566 997 891
Email: prategiano@bigfoot.com
Website: http://prategiano.heimatseite.com/holidaysvacations.html

A medieval ride in Tuscany

Set in the heart of the Alta Maremma, the most unspoiled and deserted region of Tuscany, the family-owned Rifugio Prategiano is a wonderful retreat for riders looking to combine trail action with true relaxation. With 20 Maremma horses to choose from, you are sure to find one that suits and then you can head off on a selection of half-day, full-day or up to six-day-long rides. The rides can take you to medieval villages, sweeping meadows, clear rivers, white sand beaches and hot springs. Even on the six-day rides, you are transported back to the Rifugio Prategiano (the horses stay at the stop point) so you can relax in the swimming pool and enjoy the panoramic views, regional wines and Tuscan cuisine. Bliss!

Activity prices: Accommodation and food costs from 332 to 592 euros, depending on season and food package. Rides cost from 158 to 189 euros for approximately 15 hours in the saddle per week on Satellite Rides, 305 to 379 euros for 30 hours per week (six full days).

Accommodation: Included in price. You stay at the 20-bed Rifugio Prategiano Hotel. You can also stay in the basic stable quarters for lower cost.

Food: Full-board and half-board packages are available.

Equipment supplied: Horse equipment, saddle bags, helmets.

What to take: Riding boots, riding trousers, personal clothing and swimsuit.

When to go: Shorter satellite rides run from March to November, longer rides from April to October. Swimming pool open from June to August.

Established: 1971

Safety: All guides have vocational 'guida ambiente equestre' qualifications issued by the Tuscan authorities. The centre is a member of ANTE{?}.

Insurance: The centre has liability insurance. Clients should arrange their own travel insurance.

Methods of payment: Travellers' cheques and cash are preferred.

Booking information: Advance booking is recommended, though late booking is accepted. Horse riding should be booked a few months ahead. A 40% deposit is required with all bookings.

Nearest airport: Pisa or possibly Florence.

Nearest rail station: Via Florence to Follonica.

SPAIN

HURRICANE HOTEL
CN 340 Km 78, Tarifa, Cádiz
Phone: +34 956 684 919
Fax: +34 956 684508
Email: hurricane@redestb.es
Website: www.andalucia.com/hurricane

On drovers' trails from Tarifa to Ronda
Riding an Andalucian throughbred, famed for their beauty, grace and speed, is exciting at the best of times, but if you fancy a really memorable holiday then try the Hurricane Hotel's wonderful Tarifa to Ronda riding tour. It follows beautiful white sand beaches and old bull-drovers' trails, passing through ancient cork oak forests and tiny whitewashed Spanish villages. Overnight, you stay in lovely inns, country houses and a 17th-century restored convent. En route, you will see the Moorish fortress village of Castellar de la Frontera. The tour ends in the old Arab town of Ronda, dramatically perched above the narrow gorge of Guadalevin. The town is home to Spain's oldest bullring. You spend around six to seven hours per day in the saddle on this eight-day long ride to remember.

Activity prices: Prices for 2000 were not available at time of writing. Contact the centre for the latest information.

Accommodation: Included in price. See information above.

Food: Full board is included in the price.

Equipment supplied: All the horse equipment is provided.

What to take: Your own riding clothes and boots. Helmets are available at the centre.

When to go: Only two trips per year, going from Tarifa to Ronda in May and from Ronda to Tarifa in September. Check with hotel for actual dates.

Established: 1984

Safety: Horse riding guides are qualified and very experienced.

Insurance: Clients must arrange their own insurance.

Methods of payment: VISA, Mastercard, travellers' cheques and cash.
Booking information: Advance booking is essential due to limited availability of this trip.
Nearest airport: Malaga.
Nearest rail station: N/A.

SWITZERLAND

ALPIN RAFT
Postfach 78, 3800 Matten
Phone: +41 33 823 4100
Fax: +41 33 823 4101
Email: mail@alpinraft.ch
Website: www.alpinraft.ch

Horse riding in the Swiss Alps
If you prefer four legs to two, exploring the Jungfrau region on horseback offers a truly unique experience away from the well-trodden tourist trails. Whether you're a complete beginner or a champion show-jumper, there are routes and rides to suit everyone.

Activity prices: From SFr75 for two hours.
Accommodation: Backpacker accommodation available at the centre.
Food: Not included.
Equipment supplied: All specialist equipment is provided.
What to take: Normal hiking clothes.
When to go: April to October.
Established: 1988
Safety: All teachers are fully qualified and experienced.
Insurance: Clients must arrange their own insurance.
Methods of payment: All common methods of payment accepted.
Booking information: Book by phone or email. Full payment is charged for cancellation on the day of trip.
Nearest airport: Bern.
Nearest rail station: Interlaken.

UNITED KINGDOM

ACORN ACTIVITIES

PO Box 120, Hereford, HR4 8YB
Phone: +44 (0)1432 830083
Fax: +44 (0)1432 830110
Email: sales@acornactivities.co.uk
Website: www.acornactivities.co.uk

Horse riding in the Welsh Borders
While Acorn Activities offers over 20 different activities in locations up and down the country, horse riding is particularly well catered for. For those with no previous experience, half and full-day pony trekking provides a taster in some of the most spectacular scenery in Scotland, England and Wales. Two and five-day courses take you through the basics of tacking up, stable management, grooming and all the other practical skills that are needed to get you started in handling and riding horses. But it's not all work and no play. You will have plenty of riding instruction, and the chance to go for a short hack with walking and trotting. Those on the five-day course are likely to improve considerably with more adventurous rides. Riders with two or more years' experience can enjoy the thrill of trail rides over open moorland. But for the full monty, it's difficult to beat the Trans Wales Trail Ride, a 110-mile, multi-day trip from Abergavenny to Aberdovey through the Black Mountains and the Elan Valley. Riders must have a minimum of five years' experience and be fit enough to ride for up to six hours a day.

Activity prices: £25 for a half-day pony trekking, £40 for a full day. Riding instruction £20 per hour. Introductory riding courses cost £100 for two days and £250 for five days. For more experienced riders, trail riding costs £45 for a full day, or £150 for a two-day break. The seven-day ride across Wales costs £775 per person, including all accommodation, meals (special diets are not catered for), guides and transport.

Accommodation: Not included, except for the seven-day ride. A two-day break with two nights' farmhouse accommodation costs £140.

Food: Breakfast and dinner are included in the two-day break (see above).

Equipment supplied: All equipment is provided, including hard hats.

What to take: Warm, windproof and waterproof clothing, depending on conditions.

When to go: Year round.

Established: 1990

Safety: All mounts and escorts are highly skilled and experienced.

Insurance: Insurance is required, although this can be arranged through Acorn Activities.

Methods of payment: VISA, Mastercard, cheques and cash.

Booking information: Late bookings are welcomed. A non-refundable deposit of £10 per day is required. Cancellation charges apply on a sliding scale from 80% for over 43 days before departure to 100% for up to 14 days.

Nearest airport: Cardiff or Birmingham International.

Nearest rail station: Depends on the itinerary.

CAE IAGO RIDING CENTRE

Ffarmers, Llanwrda, Carmarthenshire SA19 8LZ
Phone: +44 (0)1558 650 303
Fax: N/A
Email: riding@caeiago.co.uk
Website: www.caeiago.co.uk

Welsh riding at its best

Cae Iago has been running horse riding trips for more than 30 years and is acknowledged as one of the leading centres in Wales. They are located on the edge of the magnificent Cambrian Mountains where there are excellent trails and wildlife. The routes follow old Roman roads and drovers' tracks. The centre has a wide range of willing horses and Welsh cobs to suit all ages and abilities. The rides last for around four to five hours per day. There is plenty of home-cooked food as well as cosy local pubs to enjoy in the evenings and the accommodation is in a Victorian farmhouse.

Activity prices: Weekend breaks including two full days of riding cost £110 while a week-long stay with five days of riding costs £290. Midweek breaks start from £100. Daily rides cost £27 for a full day and £13.50 for a half-day.

Accommodation: Prices include full board in the Victorian farmhouse.

Food: All meals are included in the price.

Equipment supplied: Riding hats can be provided.

What to take: Personal clothing, riding boots and hat.

When to go: Year round.

Established: 1969

Safety: The guides all meet national qualification standards. The centre is approved by the British Horse Society, the Wales Tourist Board, the Wales Riding and Trekking Association and Carmarthenshire County Council.

Insurance: Insurance should be organised by the client.

Methods of payment: Cheque and cash.

Booking information: Advance booking is essential. A non-refundable deposit of £40 per person is required on booking.

Nearest airport: Cardiff.

Nearest rail station: Llandovery. Transfers are included if required.

IN THE SADDLE

Laurel Cottage, Ramsdell, Tadley, Hampshire RG26 5SH
Phone: +44 (0)1256 851665
Fax: +44 (0)1256 851667
Email: rides@inthesaddle.com
Website: www.inthesaddle.com

Exploring Europe's wilderness on horseback

In the Saddle specialises in exploring the lesser-known parts of Europe on horseback, from Lapland in Finland to the Sierra Nevada in southern Spain. Rides last one to two weeks and there are a variety of routes suitable for beginners as well as more experienced riders. Travelling in small groups, riders can choose from a list of destinations, including France, Italy, Portugal, Ireland, Wales and Iceland. Experienced riders will cover 15–25 miles per day, while beginners may cover less than half that distance. In some areas, unguided rides are available for competent and adventurous riders, with trails providing six to twelve days of secluded coastline, rugged mountains and forest landscapes.

Activity prices: From £485 for a week's riding.
Accommodation: Prices include full board, ranging from basic camping to small country inns, depending on the itinerary.
Food: All meals are included in the price.
Equipment supplied: Horses and all non-personal equipment.
What to take: Personal clothing, riding boots and hat.
When to go: Year round.
Established: 1995
Safety: Guides must meet local qualification requirements.
Insurance: Insurance is mandatory and can be arranged if required.
Methods of payment: Cash, cheque or bank transfer.
Booking information: Advance booking is essential and a deposit of £150 is required, with the balance payable eight weeks prior to departure.
Nearest airport: Depends on location.
Nearest rail station: Depends on location.

ROOKIN HOUSE EQUESTRIAN AND ACTIVITY CENTRE
Troutbeck, nr Penrith, Cumbria, CA11 0SS
Phone: +44 (0)17684 83561
Fax: +44 (0)17684 83276
Email: deborah@rookinhouse.freeserve.co.uk
Website: www.rookinhouse.freeserve.co.uk

Riding away in the English Lakes
There can be few better ways to enjoy the stunning scenery of the English Lake District than on horseback. Rookin House caters for all riding abilities from complete novice to the most experienced. The rides follow bridleways and quiet country lanes or, if the weather is OK, across the fells and through forests. The rides are led by experienced, qualified escorts and take in the country surrounding Ullswater. If you are looking for some variety to your stay, Rookin House offers a range of other adventure activities, including go-karting, tank driving, archery and human bowling.

Activity prices: Prices for short trail rides start from £10 per hour, with three hours costing £24. A full-day fell ride costs £40. An all-inclusive riding weekend for experienced riders starts from £140 per person.

Accommodation: Only included in the all-inclusive weekend rides when accommodation is provided at a local hotel. Clients on other courses need to make their own arrangements. For groups, Rookin House has a wonderful 18th-century converted barn that sleeps up to 20 people in comfort. Call the centre for prices and availability.

Food: Only included in the all-inclusive riding weekends. The centre's café is open during school holidays and weekends only. Outside of this, catering can be arranged with prior booking.

Equipment supplied: Helmets and overalls are provided.

What to take: Warm clothing, a waterproof jacket, hat and gloves.

When to go: Year round.

Established: 1984

Safety: All the Rookin House instructors have recognised governing body qualifications while the centre is approved by the ABRS and is a member of the Cumbria Tourist Board.

Insurance: Rookin House has public liability insurance but clients are advised to arrange their own personal accident insurance.

Methods of payment: VISA, Delta, Switch, personal cheques, cash.

Booking information: Prior booking is strongly recommended. A 30% non-refundable deposit is required with booking and full payment is due 21 days before the course.

Nearest airport: Newcastle.

Nearest rail station: Penrith.

WELLINGTON RIDING

Heckfield, Hook, Hampshire RG27 0LJ
Phone: +44 (0)118 932 6308
Fax: +44 (0)118 932 6661
Email: welly@riding.demon.co.uk
Website: www.wellington-riding.co.uk

British riding at its best

Wellington Riding is one the UK's leading riding centres and caters for riders from beginner level to the very top riders in the country. They have over 100 horses and ponies, many riding courses and all the indoor and outdoor facilities you would expect at such a well-established centre. An example of their many courses is the weekday adult riding course that gives three hours of mounted instruction plus lectures and practice in stable management. A five-day course allows even more time for progress and there is the option of riders being filmed for subsequent playback and instruction by video. These courses are only available during the week. The centre also offers courses leading to recognised national qualifications, including NVQs.

Activity prices: The one-day course costs £87 and the five-day course costs £347. Enquire to centre regarding the many other options.

Accommodation: Not included in price. Accommodation is available at local inns or hotels costing around £20–90 per night for B&B.

Food: Not included in price. Food is available at the centre or locally.

Equipment supplied: All specialist equipment can be arranged.

What to take: Personal clothing, riding boots and hat (if you have them).

When to go: Year round.

Established: 1974

Safety: The centre is approved by the British Horse Society to teach and train all the way up to top instructor level.

Insurance: Insurance to be arranged by client.

Methods of payment: VISA, JCB, Mastercard, Delta, Switch, cheques and cash.

Booking information: Advance booking is essential and full payment is made at time of booking. At least 24 hours' notice of cancellation must be given for booked hours to be transferred to a different day.

Nearest airport: London Heathrow.

Nearest rail station: Reading.

HYDROSPEEDING

Up until recently, running rapids has been the preserve of rafters, kayakers and canoeists, but a new kid on the block has taken the excitement of white water to its logical extreme.

Hydrospeeding, or boogie-boarding as it is sometimes called, involves floating down the river on a buoyant 'sled' barely bigger than a swimming float. Holding handles on either side of the board and clad only in a neoprene wetsuit, a helmet and flippers, participants have to negotiate rocks, drops and holes on their way down the river. While this might seem similar to rafting and kayaking, the difference is one of degree: while a rafter might be as much as four feet off the surface and the kayaker as much as three, your average hydrospeeder is going to be getting a face-full of action barely three inches away. And when you're ploughing through a fifteen-foot wave train, that's a whole lot of inches above you!

An Amazon adventure

Mike Horn, a South African member of the renowned Sector No Limits team of adventurers, spent 171 days hydrospeeding the whole length of the Amazon river, a meaty 6,500 km long. To get to the start, he walked the 600 kilometres too for good measure (of course, he carried the hydrospeed on his back the whole way and a paraglider so that he could speed up the hike by flying off hills). En route down river, he was taken prisoner by Ashaninca Indians, got caught for thirty minutes in a whirlpool and encountered anacondas and piranhas. Crazy? Of course, but someone had to be the first to do it.

Not unlike canyoning, hydrospeeding has really caught on in the Alps and is gradually gaining acceptance in other European countries. There are numerous centres that offer everything from a half-day taster of family fun to a full-day blast down the biggest rapids in the region – all you need is a towel, a swimsuit and a passion for white water!

FRANCE

SNOW SAFARI LIMITED

Chalet Savoy, 1351 route des Chavants, 74310 Les Houches
Phone: +33 (0)4 50 54 56 63;
UK bookings & information number +44 (0)1279 600 885
Fax: +33 (0)4 50 54 57 19
Email: Chalsavoy@aol.com
Website: www.chaletsavoy.com

Hydrospeeding down the Chamonix Valley
The latest and arguably the most exciting method of negotiating white water rapids, hydrospeeding has become extremely popular in the Chamonix region. The Chalet Savoy offers a two-hour introductory course that involves 5 km of relatively easy Grade II rapids. For those who are already at home in the water, there's an hour-long descent of the Arveyron rapids, from the Mer de Glacé glacier to the confluence with the Arve river just above Chamonix. All transport, equipment and instruction are included in the price.

Activity prices: From FFr250 for a one-hour introduction to FFr280 for a more advanced river course.
Accommodation: Available at the Chalet Savoy. Summer prices start from FFr140 per person for B&B or FFr2,050 per person for seven days and seven nights.
Food: Included in the accommodation price.
Equipment supplied: All necessary equipment is provided.
What to take: Swimsuit, towel and a warm change of clothes.
When to go: May to September.
Established: 1987

Safety: All guides and leaders are fully qualified for the relevant activity.

Insurance: Clients must arrange their own insurance.

Methods of payment: VISA, Mastercard.

Booking information: Contact Snow Safari for booking form and full terms and conditions.

Nearest airport: Geneva.

Nearest rail station: Les Houches.

ITALY

CENTRO CANOA RAFTING DIMARO

Val Di Sole, Via Gole 105 – 38025 Dimaro, Trentino
Phone: +39 (0)463 974 332/973 278
Fax: +39 (0)463 973 200
Email: rafting@tin.it
Website: www.raftingcenter.it

Alone down the River Noce

The fast-flowing River Noce twists through the stunning Val Di Sole region in northern Italy. One of the most exciting ways to experience the power of the water is to go it alone in a hydrospeed. This exciting new sport is offered as a day trip, a five-day course or as part of a five-day multi-sport course at Alessandro Mariani's Canoeing and Rafting Centre. You can test your wits and endurance at two different levels. Beginners complete a theory lesson before tackling a 4 km descent while more experienced hydrospeeders take on a 6 km course that promises plenty of thrills. After a hard day dealing with the rapids, you can relax in the campsite swimming pool, play tennis or simply build up your energy levels for the next day by eating pizza in the restaurant.

Activity prices: One-day descents cost L68,000 for introductory level and L85,000 for advanced. A five-day hydrospeed course costs L370,000. The multi-sport course (which includes rafting, kayaking and mountain biking) costs L360,000 for five days or L160,000 for a weekend. Camping and equipment are included in the weekend and five-day course prices.

Accommodation: Four-star camping is available at the centre and is free for clients booking weekend or one-week courses. Local hotel accommodation can also be arranged by the centre.

Food: Special prices are available for clients at the campsite restaurant.

Equipment supplied: All specialist equipment is supplied.

What to take: Swimsuit, trainers, t-shirt.

When to go: May to September.

Established: 1984

Safety: All hydrospeed guides are qualified teachers with AIRAF{?}.

Insurance: Cover is included in the course price.

Methods of payment: VISA, travellers' cheques, cash.

Booking information: A minimum of two weeks' advance booking is recommended. A deposit of 20% is required.

Nearest airport: Verona Villafranca. Clients can be picked up from the airport on request.

Nearest rail station: Trento–Trento Malè

SLOVENIA

TOP EXTREME
TOP d.o.o., Vojkova 9, 5000 Nova Gorica
Phone: +38 (0)66 522 006
Fax: +38 (0)66 522 006
Email: info@top.si
Website: www.top.si

One by one down the River Soča

If you have grown weary of team adventure sports and want to try something more personally challenging, then go to Slovenia's River Soča and head down on a hydrospeed. After a briefing session on the basic techniques of using the equipment, you and your Top Extreme guide will plunge into the rapids for the ride of a lifetime. No previous experience is necessary though you should be able to swim. The Soča river in Slovenia was host to the 1991 World Kayak Championship, so you are guaranteed a thrilling descent as the standard hydrospeed course takes you along the same route.

Activity prices: Hiring the hydrospeed costs DM33 for a half-day or DM49 for a full day. The guide will cost you DM65 per half-day per person.

Accommodation: Not included. Available locally.

Food: Not included. Available locally.

Equipment supplied: Special wetsuits, neoprene shoes, fins, helmet, lifejacket.

What to take: Swimsuit, t-shirt and towel.

When to go: April to November.

Established: 1993

Safety: The centre's hydrospeed staff are all qualified instructors.

Insurance: Accident insurance is included in the price. The company also has liability insurance.

Methods of payment: Eurocard, Mastercard and cash.

Booking information: Advance booking is essential.

Nearest airport: Ljubljana (100 km).

Nearest rail station: Most na Soci (30 km).

SWITZERLAND

ALPIN RAFT
Postfach 78, 3800 Matten
Phone: +41 33 823 4100
Fax: +41 33 823 4101
Email: mail@alpinraft.ch
Website: www.alpinraft.ch

Hydrospeeding in the Swiss Alps
The latest craze in running rapids, hydrospeeding brings you closer than any other activity to the thrill and excitement of pounding white water. Swimming head-first down the river on a floating boogie-board and wearing only a wetsuit, a helmet and a buoyancy aid for protection, hydrospeeding is fast, furious and very, very wet. No experience is necessary as full instruction will be given, and all guides are fully qualified in river rescue and first aid.

Activity prices: From SFr99.

Accommodation: Backpacker accommodation available at the centre.

Food: Lunch is included.

Equipment supplied: Wetsuit, booties, helmet and buoyancy aid.

What to take: Swimsuit and towel.

When to go: May to October.

Established: 1988

Safety: All guides are fully qualified in white water rescue and first aid.

Insurance: Clients must arrange their own insurance.

Methods of payment: All common methods of payment accepted.

Booking information: Book by phone or email. Full payment is charged for cancellation on the day of trip.

Nearest airport: Bern.

Nearest rail station: Interlaken.

ICE CLIMBING

The line between winter mountaineering and ice climbing is at best hazy, although it's probably safe to say that many of the basic skills of the former are prerequisites for getting started in the latter. In many ways ice climbing is the logical extension of winter mountaineering, in that it encompasses steeper climbs, icier slopes and more technical skills. In fact there is almost no limit to how steep or icy the slope can be in a sport that is not unlike rock climbing on ice.

Because of the inherent dangers involved in scrambling about on ice-covered rock, not to mention the cost of specialised equipment to get you there in the first place, the best way to get started is by taking an introductory course. As well as front-pointing with crampons and climbing with ice axes, you'll be taught essential ropework and safety procedures that'll set you on the path to striking out on your own.

At this point it's probably worth pointing out that ice climbing is a million miles away from rafting. While it's not unusual for rafters to paddle a grade V on their first day, it would take most mountaineers years to reach the equivalent grade on snow or ice. Ice climbing is all about experience, practice and patience – perhaps in no other adventure sport are the watchwords 'slowly, slowly, catchee monkey' more appropriate. Summer walkers and rock climbers without any experience would be well advised to acquire the more basic winter mountaineering skills before getting stuck into ice.

FRANCE

INTERNATIONAL SCHOOL OF MOUNTAINEERING, SWITZERLAND

Hafod Tan y Graig, Nant Gwynant, Gwynedd LL55 4N, UK

Phone: +44 (0)1766 890441
Fax: +44 (0)1766 890599
Email: ism@dial.pipex.com
Website: http//:ds.dial.pipex.com/ism

Ice climbing classic routes in the French Alps
ISM's Winter Ice programme is ideal for people who want guaranteed, top quality ice climbing during precious winter holidays. Temperatures in the Alps remain low and relatively stable throughout the winter, and the dramatic ice falls that form in many Alpine valleys offer some of the best ice climbing in the world. Five and six-day courses are offered at two levels according to the grade/steepness of the routes to be tackled. Winter Ice Level 1 covers climbs at grade III standard and is aimed at gaining technical skills and coping with all aspects of the winter Alpine environment. Winter Ice Level II progresses to grade IV and V routes, often with some strenuous vertical sections, for the more experienced climber. Some previous experience is desirable even for the first level course. The courses are based in Chamonix and accommodation in mountain resort hotels is included in the price.

Activity prices: From £695 to £1,085 for a six-day course or ascent of an Alpine summit.
Accommodation: All Alpine courses include hotel accommodation.
Food: Alpine courses include full board.
Equipment supplied: All specialist equipment is provided.
What to take: Personal climbing clothing and footwear.
When to go: Year round.
Established: 1960
Safety: All guides hold the International Carnet, the highest qualification available in mountaineering.
Insurance: Relevant insurance is required for all Alpine courses.
Methods of payment: All common payment methods accepted.
Booking information: Contact ISM for booking form and full terms and conditions.
Nearest airport: Geneva.
Nearest rail station: Leysin.

MOUNTAIN ACTIVITY EXPERIENCE
93 avenue Michel Croz, 74400 Chamonix
Phone: +33 4 50 55 80 80
Fax: +33 4 53 48 50
Email: M.A.X@wanadoo.fr
Website: montblanconeline.fr/max/max.htm

Ice climbing on Mont Blanc
Ice climbing practically began on Mont Blanc, so what better place to sharpen your teeth and get to grips with the ice? Mountain Activity Experience offers private lessons from a half-day to a full day tailored to individual requirements. With a maximum group size of three (prices are per lesson, not per person), individual attention is guaranteed, making progress fast but safe. Ice falls are particularly impressive in the Chamonix area, and the highly experienced mountain guides will be happy to take you to the latest cool spot. Mountain boots, crampons and ice axes are not included in the price, but can be rented for an additional fee.

Activity prices: Private tuition (one to three people) costs from FFr690 for a half-day and FFr1450 for a full day.
Accommodation: Not included in the price.
Food: Not included.
Equipment supplied: Technical group equipment such as ropes and climbing hardware is provided.
What to take: Mountain boots, crampons and ice axes are not included, but can be rented at the centre.
When to go: Year round, depending on experience and conditions.
Established: 1997
Safety: All instructors are nationally qualified high mountain guides.
Insurance: Clients must provide their own insurance.
Methods of payment: Cheques and cash.
Booking information: A deposit is required to secure a booking. Cancellation within a month of the course forfeits the deposit.
Nearest airport: Geneva.
Nearest rail station: Chamonix.

ODYSSEE MONTAGNE
101 Les Marmottières, 74310 Les Houches
Phone: +33 (0)4 50 54 36 01
Fax: +33 (0)4 50 54 35 74
Email: odyssee@odyssee-montagne.fr
Website: http://odyssee-monatgne.fr

Ice climbing classic Alpine routes
Mont Blanc is the birthplace of technical Alpine climbing, and has long
held a special place in the fast-beating hearts of ice climbers the world
over. Not so long ago winter ascents were the domain of the committed
few, fighting heroic battles against steep couloirs in extreme conditions.
Today, however, thanks to decisive progress in both protective clothing
and technical equipment, winter climbing has become increasingly safe
and accessible: steep faces, vertiginous couloirs, snow and rock faces
and even frozen waterfalls have become fair game, and the Mont Blanc
region offers all these options in abundance. Odyssee Montagne's
strong team of guides offers a number of winter climbing options, from
a six-day initiation for beginners to a week-long course tackling couloirs
and gullies of the world-renowned Mont Blanc massif.

Activity prices: From FFr4,200 for six days and five nights.

Accommodation: Mountain hut accommodation included.

Food: All food is included in the price.

Equipment supplied: All technical equipment including ropes and ice axes is
included.

What to take: Personal climbing equipment, including harness, boots and
crampons.

When to go: December to April.

Established: 1993

Safety: All mountain guides are members of the Ecole National de Ski et
d'Alpinisme.

Insurance: Comprehensive insurance can be provided at an additional cost of
5% of the full price.

Methods of payment: Travellers' cheques, VISA, Mastercard, Swift bank
transfer, etc.

Booking information: A deposit of 30% is required at the time of booking.
Bookings will be accepted no later than 15 days before departure.
Nearest airport: Geneva. Airport collection available on request.
Nearest rail station: Saint Gervais.

SWITZERLAND

ALPIN CENTER ZERMATT
Mountain Guides' Association, 3920 Zermatt
Phone: +41 (0)27 966 2460
Fax: +41 (0)27 966 2469
Email: alpincenter@zermatt.ch
Website: www.zermatt.ch/alpincenter

The cream of Swiss ice
Take the plunge into the wild and weird world of ice climbing with a
course in Zermatt. The Alpin Center offers a complete range of
courses and guided climbs to test people of all abilities. Beginners can
choose between one-day, three-day and one-week long courses that
cover basic climbing skills, belaying methods and the development of
movement techniques on ice. For those with previous experience, you
can try your axe and crampons out on a myriad of ice routes in the
area all under the expert guidance of an Alpin Center guide.

Activity prices: One-day course costs SFr120; three-day course costs SFr720
(including half-board); one-week course costs SFr830. Advanced climbing
courses cost SFr180 per day with a maximum group size of two per instructor.
Accommodation: A wide range of accommodation is available in the Zermatt
area. The centre can assist with arranging it. Half-board accommodation is
included on some of the courses.
Food: Included on some of the courses. There are plenty of eating options in
Zermatt.
Equipment supplied: Specialist equipment is available.
What to take: Specialist equipment that you own. Check with centre for
recommended list. Personal mountain clothing and suitable footwear.
When to go: June to October.

Established: 1982

Safety: All the Alpin Center guides are fully licensed, qualified and highly experienced. You are in very safe hands.

Insurance: Clients must arrange their own personal accident insurance and it is recommended that you also take out Rescue Insurance with Air Zermatt for SFr20 per week or SFr30 per year. Forms available from the Alpin Center.

Methods of payment: VISA, cash or bank transfer.

Booking information: Advance booking is essential.

Nearest airport: Zurich.

Nearest rail station: Zermatt.

FOUR SEASONS GUIDES
Chalet L'Aurore, 1936 Verbier
Phone: +41 27 771 7683
Fax: +41 27 771 1603
Email: hans@verbier.ch
Website: www.swissguides.com

Up ice and personal

A private guide offers you almost limitless flexibility when it comes to where and how you spend your adventure holiday. And guides don't come much more credible than those qualified through the UIAGM. Verbier is ideally located in the Val de Bagnes with its many waterfalls that become classic ice routes in winter. Most of the climbs are from three to six pitches in length and are 'in season' from December to late March. For beginners, there is the wonderful artificial ice climbing wall at the centre (the first of its kind in the country) where you can practise your techniques before heading for the real stuff. All with the personal touch of your own instructor.

Activity prices: Guiding fees are SFr400 per day for one to two clients. For this, the guide will also arrange local travel and hotel bookings and the itinerary (clients pay directly to the hotel, bus company etc.).

Accommodation: Not included in the price. There is a large range of accommodation options in the area and the guide will help you to arrange it.

Food: Not included in the price, but there are plenty of eating options in the area too. While in the mountains, the client pays for his own food and that of the guide.

Equipment supplied: Specialist equipment can be hired in Verbier.

What to take: All specialist mountain clothing.

When to go: December to late March for the waterfalls. Year round for high Alpine routes.

Established: 1990

Safety: All guides hold UIAGM qualifications.

Insurance: Clients are recommended to buy helicopter rescue insurance which costs SFr30 for one year.

Methods of payment: VISA, Mastercard, Amex, travellers' cheques and cash.

Booking information: Payment in full is required one week in advance. Full refunds are available for acceptable cancellation.

Nearest airport: Geneva. Transfers can be arranged.

Nearest rail station: Le Chable. Transfers can be arranged.

UNITED KINGDOM

ALAN KIMBER

Calluna, Heathercroft, Fort William PH33 6RE
Phone: +44 (0)1397 700 451
Fax: +44 (0)1397 700 489
Email: mountain@guide.u-net.com
Website: www.guide.u-net.com

An icy Scottish tower scoop

Alan Kimber is one of the most experienced mountain guides in the country, having climbed extensively around the world. He chooses to live in Fort William, a good indicator of just how impressive the winter climbing is in this region. There are several courses offered to suit people of all abilities, including complete beginners. The courses are run with small numbers to ensure personal attention. Alan's Introduction course covers climbing routes between grades I and III, so it is also suitable for clients with a little winter experience. Courses are tailored to suit you, but this course may include essential skills, snow belays, snow cave shelters and moving together while roped up.

After tackling some simple gullies, you will move on to steeper ice climbs before having the chance to lead a climb yourself under supervision. Locations used include Ben Nevis Tower Scoop and Curved Ridge in Glen Coe.

Activity prices: The seven-day introduction course costs £325 for the course only, £375 with six nights self-catering accommodation or £541 in a hotel. Advanced courses cost around £550 (course only).

Accommodation: On-site self-catering accommodation is available in the beautifully located and homely Calluna Lodge. Various room options. Hotel accommodation can be arranged.

Food: Not included in the price. Accommodation is self-catering. It is just a ten-minute walk to the centre of Fort William.

Equipment supplied: Technical climbing equipment is supplied.

What to take: Personal clothing, footwear and other items. Full list sent on booking.

When to go: January to April.

Established: 1972

Safety: All instructors are MLTB qualified. The centre is approved by the Mountaineering Council of Scotland and the British Mountaineering Council.

Insurance: Mountaineering insurance is available from the centre and costs £10.70 for seven days.

Methods of payment: VISA, Mastercard, cheque, cash (3.5% surcharge on credit card payments).

Booking information: Advance booking is essential. A non-refundable 50% deposit is payable on booking. Balance paid on arrival. Cancellation within four weeks of course start date forfeits whole course price unless replacement client is found.

Nearest airport: Glasgow.

Nearest rail station: Fort William.

CUILLIN GUIDES
Stac Lee, Glenbrittle. Isle of Skye, Inverness-shire IV47 8TA
Phone: +44 (0)1478 640 289
Fax: N/A
Email: Not available. Booking form on website.
Website: www.w-o-w.com/clients/cuillin

An icy Skye

The Isle of Skye off Scotland's west coast is renowned for its dramatic wilderness scenery and the ice climbing potential is impressive. The instructors from Cuillin Guides have excellent knowledge of the area and always know where the best ice conditions are. They offer personal tuition tailored to your needs or a snow and ice climbing course. The course is designed for those with winter hill walking experience and basic climbing ropework techniques and covers step-cutting, ice axe and ice tool techniques with practical experience on the ridges and gullies of the Cuillin area. There are minimum fitness standards for clients wishing to take this course as it is physically demanding.

Activity prices: The snow and ice climbing course costs £275.

Accommodation: Included in the price. Accommodation is in bothies or bunkhouses in the mountains.

Food: Not included.

Equipment supplied: Crampons and ice axes and technical equipment.

What to take: A full equipment list is supplied on booking.

When to go: January to March.

Established: 1972

Safety: All the guides are qualified mountain leaders.

Insurance: Clients need to arrange their own insurance.

Methods of payment: Personal cheque, cash.

Booking information: Advance booking is essential. A deposit of £20 is payable.

Nearest airport: Glasgow.

Nearest rail station: Kyle of Lochalsh.

MOUNTAIN CRAFT

Glennfinnan, Fort William PH37 4LT
Phone: +44 (0)1397 722213
Fax: +44 (0)1397 722213
Email: mail@mountaincraft.co.uk
Website: www.mountaincraft.co.uk

Ice climbing in Scotland

The area around Fort William is one of Scotland's finest mountain areas, with almost 2,000 square miles of spectacular scenery, while Ben Nevis – Britain's highest mountain – has long been a mecca for serious snow and ice climbers from all over the world. As well as introductory courses to winter mountaineering, Mountain Craft also offers more advanced snow and ice climbing courses for those who already have some winter experience. Advanced Winter Mountain-craft includes more demanding terrain and ropework without progressing on to steep ice, while the snow and ice climbing courses include such subjects as belay selection, rope management and more advanced techniques for climbing both ice and mixed ground.

Activity prices: From £350 for a five-day ice climbing course. Private instruc-tion and guiding are also available.

Accommodation: Not included in the price, but can be arranged locally at a budget to suit.

Food: Not included in the price.

Equipment supplied: All technical climbing equipment is supplied.

What to take: Personal climbing clothing and boots.

When to go: January to April.

Established: 1996

Safety: All instructors are MLTB qualified.

Insurance: Insurance can be arranged directly through Mountain Craft.

Methods of payment: VISA, Mastercard and cheque.

Booking information: Advanced booking and £75 deposit required.

Nearest airport: Glasgow.

Nearest rail station: Fort William.

PLAS Y BRENIN

National Mountain Centre, Capel Curig Conwy LL24 0ET
Phone: +44 (0)1690 720 214
Fax: +44 (0)1690 720 394
Email: info@pyb.co.uk
Website: www.pyb.co.uk

An icy Scottish blast

Making the transition from rock climbing to ice climbing can be a daunting prospect as new skills and tools are needed to cope with the white stuff. Plas y Brenin offers a progression of courses to help you make the leap. Winters in Highland Scotland provide conditions and challenges that rival those in the Alps. The centre's five-day Scottish Snow and Ice Climbing course will teach you the basic winter techniques, including avalanche evaluation, ice axe and crampon use, and more advanced skills such as front pointing and buttress climbing. With only two students to each instructor, you are guaranteed personal attention to maximise your improvement. Some previous experience with ropework and winter hill walking is necessary. A shorter course in Wales is also available. Once you are confident on ice, you can head off on the centre's ten-day Alpine Climbing course where you further enhance your skills climbing in the highest mountain ranges of Europe.

Activity prices: The Scottish five-day course, based at Alltshellach, costs £440, the two-day Welsh course costs £250 and the ten-day Alpine course costs £530.

Accommodation: Prices for most courses include shared accommodation. The Alpine course price does not include accommodation and food for two nights in mountain huts.

Food: Most course prices include full board.

Equipment supplied: All specialist equipment and clothing is provided.

What to take: Personal clothing and your own equipment if you prefer to use it.

When to go: January to March for the UK and April for the Alpine course.

Established: 1954

Safety: All instructors hold nationally recognised qualifications and only the most capable and experienced are employed. The centre is licensed by the AALA. Great emphasis is placed on safety and the high quality equipment used is regularly checked and replaced.

Insurance: The centre carries public liability insurance for all activities and recommends that clients take out independent insurance against curtailment and cancellation of their course (available from the centre) and a personal accident policy.

Methods of payment: VISA, Mastercard, Access, personal cheque, cash.

Booking information: Reservations must be made in advance and a deposit is required.

Nearest airport: Depends on tour.

Nearest rail station: Depends on tour.

KAYAKING

Pioneered by Canada's Inuit Eskimos, kayaking is often mistakenly referred to as canoeing. While a canoe has an open cockpit and single-bladed paddle, a kayak has a closed cockpit and a double-bladed paddle. Usually designed for just one person, kayaks are arguably more versatile than canoes by virtue of the fact that they won't fill up with water, making them ideally suited to running white water.

White water grades

International grading of white water uses the following approximate guidelines:

Grade I – Some small waves, but basically little more than a bob.

Grade II – Slightly bigger waves and a few obstacles, but nothing that cannot be anticipated well in advance.

Grade III – Heavier white water with numerous obstacles, through which an obvious line can be negotiated.

Grade IV – Usually much more powerful and continuous – a safe line may only be apparent after inspection from the bank.

Grade V – As for IV, but often bigger and more technically demanding – even after inspection, the safest line is not obvious. This is the highest grade that can be commercially rafted.

Grade VI – The limit of possibility, and runnable only at particular water levels – awareness, anticipation and reactive skills must be completely reliable.

When most people think of kayaking, they picture long, thin boats slicing through the waves and weaving in and out of slalom gates trying to avoid the worst of the water, but that's far from the full story. Today's short, plastic kayaks are quite capable of bouncing down rock-strewn rapids and waterfalls with disdain, and with practice they are easy to roll back up in the event of a capsize (Canadian canoes can be paddled on white water, but they are more prone to filling with water and are much more difficult, if not impossible, to roll).

Severn river surfers

The Severn Bore wave that funnels up the River Severn near Gloucester in the United Kingdom is one of the largest surfable waves in the world. On certain spring tides, the wave surges up the river at speeds of around 17 kph and reaches heights of up to 3 metres, though it is usually only up to about head height. On the biggest waves of the year, at equinoxes and one to three days after full and new moons, the competition to get a ride in a kayak or on a surfboard is intense and only the clever and the quick manage to get a decent surf. Many newcomers simply freeze as the roar of the oncoming water is heard moments before the wave pounds around the bend ripping at the trees on the bank. However, in 1988, David Partington rode the wave for two and a half miles – a world record for any wave.

Kayaks can also be used for touring rivers and inland waterways where a great deal of equipment doesn't need to be carried, and are ideally suited to surfing, either on breaking waves generated by the sea or on 'standing' waves formed by rocks beneath the surface of a river. With a bit of practice it's even possible to perform cartwheels, flat-spins and all manner of moves and tricks that were unheard of ten years ago. If you're willing to get wet and are prepared to persevere, there's almost no limit to what you can do.

AUSTRIA

SPORTSCHULE FANKHAUSER – TIROL RAFTING

Dorfstrasse 17, A-6382 Kirchdorf, Tirol
Phone: +43 5352 62233
Fax: +43 5352 62587
Email: fanky@netwing.at
Website: www.tirolrafting.com

A Tirol rafting extravaganza
The kayaking potential in the Tirol region of Austria is some of the best in Europe and Sportschule Fankhauser are ideally placed to take advantage of the most exciting white water possibilities. The centre runs a range of one-day kayaking trips in the Kirchdorf area, mainly on the Tiroller Ache, which takes in the spectacular Entenloch Gorge. Experienced kayaking guides will accompany you and brief you on relevant paddling skills and on safety and rescue techniques before you enter the water. Then you face the rapids, though the guides are always close at hand to advise you further.

Activity prices: The kayaking and canoeing trips cost Sch480 per person.
Accommodation: Available at centre, either camping or in a bunkhouse, or in private hotel.
Food: Breakfast and half-board packages are available at the centre.
Equipment supplied: All specialist rafting equipment is supplied, including wetsuits, neoprene shoes, helmets and lifejackets.
What to take: Swimsuit.
When to go: Year round, daily.
Established: 1985
Safety: All the kayaking guides hold national qualifications. The centre is approved by the Austrian Tourist Office.
Insurance: The centre has liability insurance but clients should arrange their own accident policy.
Methods of payment: VISA, Mastercard, Eurocard, travellers' cheques and cash.

Booking information: Advance booking is essential at least one day ahead. No deposit is required and there are no cancellation penalties.

Nearest airport: Innsbruck, Salzburg or Munich. Transfers can be arranged.

Nearest rail station: St Johann in the Tirol. Transfers can be arranged.

BULGARIA

BULGARIAN MOUNTAINS ADVENTURE
Kancho Shipkov, Kv. Dianabad bl 18 vh.A, 1172 Sofia
Phone: +359 2 620 688
Fax: N/A
Email: kancho@bglink.net
Website: http://pss.bglink.net/mysite/explorebg.html

Tailor-made Bulgarian paddle
If you are looking for something new or different to spice up your European adventure then head for the relatively unexplored rivers and lakes of Bulgaria. Surrounded by majestic mountains and attractive forests, the Bulgarian lakes are ideal places to learn the basics of paddling. For more experienced canoeists, the Arda river in Southern Bulgaria is an enthralling run; or there are the Kamica, Roporamo and Veleka rivers that flow into the Black Sea. They can be explored up or downstream depending on your ability, and on some you get to see wild turtles. At night you can pull in to the bank and enjoy a meal around the campfire. Bulgarian Mountains Adventure is a company based around members of the national mountain rescue service. They offer personal and tailor-made guiding services in a variety of adventure sports.

Activity prices: The trips are all tailor-made to suit your requirements and cost around US$50 per day, or less, depending on what you do and where you go. The centre will advise you on the possibilities. The price also includes local transportation.

Accommodation: Food and lodging during the activity are included in the price and organised by the centre. Hotels and meals at the start and end of your trip are not included but the centre can help you arrange these.

Food: Food is included during the activity, but not at the start and end of your trip.

Equipment supplied: All specialist equipment is supplied.

What to take: Personal clothing, suitable footwear, swimsuit and towel.

When to go: Year round, though winter is only for the crazy!

Established: 1997

Safety: At least one of the guides in every group is a qualified rescuer from the Bulgarian Mountain Rescue Service. They have plentiful experience and excellent local knowledge.

Insurance: Clients should arrange their own policy, or the centre can arrange it on the spot.

Methods of payment: Bank transfer and cash.

Booking information: Advance booking is essential and a 30% deposit is payable. Cancellation penalties may apply.

Nearest airport: Sofia. Transfers can be arranged.

Nearest rail station: Sofia Central. Transfers can be arranged.

ITALY

CENTRO CANOA RAFTING DIMARO
Val Di Sole
Via Gole 105 – 38025 Dimaro
Trentino
Italy
Phone: +39 (0)463 974 332/973 278
Fax: +39 (0)463 973 200
Email: rafting@tin.it
Website: www.raftingcenter.it

Kayaking the River Noce
Based in the beautiful Val Di Sole region of northern Italy, this centre offers kayaking trips for all levels of ability on the fast flowing River Noce. Five-day courses for beginners include theory lessons and plenty of practice time, while higher level courses teach you how to slalom and eskimo roll. The price includes use of buoyancy jackets, helmets and wetsuits as well as the necessary hardware to get you

safely down the river. Shorter courses are also available. After a hard day paddling, you can relax in the campsite swimming pool, play tennis or simply build up your energy levels for the next day by having pizza-eating competitions in the restaurant.

Activity prices: A five-day kayaking course including camping and equipment costs L415,000. Shorter courses are also offered starting at L45,000.

Accommodation: Four-star camping is available at the centre and is free for clients booking weekend or one-week courses. Local hotel accommodation can also be arranged by the centre.

Food: Special prices are available for clients at the campsite restaurant.

Equipment supplied: All specialist equipment is supplied.

What to take: Swimsuit, trainers, t-shirt.

When to go: May to September.

Established: 1984

Safety: All river kayaking guides are qualified teachers with FICK.{?}

Insurance: Cover is included in the course price.

Methods of payment: VISA, Travellers' cheques, cash.

Booking information: A minimum of two weeks' advance booking is recommended. A deposit of 20% is required.

Nearest airport: Verona Villafranca. Clients can be picked up from the airport on request.

Nearest rail station: Trento – Trento Malè

SLOVENIA

TOP EXTREME
TOP d.o.o., Vojkova 9, 5000 Nova Gorica
Phone: +38 (0)66 522 006
Fax: +38 (0)66 522 006
Email: info@top.si
Website: www.top.si

Paddle a world championship descent
The Soča river in Slovenia was host to the 1991 World Kayak Championship, so you are guaranteed an exciting descent. However,

the river is not just for expert paddlers. Top Extreme run a whole range of kayaking courses to cater for all levels of ability, including complete novices. The course prices include all gear and members of the Slovenia national kayaking team will guide you. A one-day course gives you four hours on the river, a weekend course eight hours and a five-day course allows 18 hours of paddling. There are also eskimo and slalom courses available.

Activity prices: Two-day courses cost DM110. A five-day course for beginners costs DM220 and for advanced DM230.
Accommodation: Not included. Available locally.
Food: Not included. Available locally.
Equipment supplied: Wetsuits, shoes, helmet, lifejacket and waterproof jacket.
What to take: shorts, t-shirt and towel.
When to go: June to August for beginners, April to November for advanced.
Established: 1993
Safety: The centre's kayaking staff are all qualified instructors and very experienced.
Insurance: Accident insurance is included in the price. The company also has liability insurance.
Methods of payment: Eurocard, Mastercard and cash.
Booking information: Advance booking is essential.
Nearest airport: Ljubljana (100 km).
Nearest rail station: Most na Soci (30 km).

SWEDEN

NORDMARKENS CANOE CENTER
NKTC Inc, Box 24, 672 21 Arjang
Phone: +46 573 38060
Fax: +46 573 38095
Email: canoes@swipnet.se
Website: www.nordkanot.se

A Swedish dream paddle

Based on the Swedish–Norwegian border about 200 km north of the port city of Gothenburg, the Nordmarkens Canoe Center must be one of the longest surviving adventure sport operators in Europe. They have been operating, under the same manager, Preben Mortensen, for over 43 years, as sure a sign as you will ever get that their trips are deservedly popular. With beautiful lakes and stunning wilderness mountain scenery all around the centre, you will certainly be able to relax as you paddle either Canadian canoes or sea kayaks on your journey between secluded waterside camps. The centre will tailor-make trips to suit your requirements or you can join a group. Although the centre has a long history, you will be paddling with the latest, high quality equipment.

Activity prices: There is a whole range of prices as the trips are tailor-made, so contact the centre to discuss your requirements. The prices are very reasonable.

Accommodation: You spend the nights during the trip camping in anything from two-man mountain tents to huge army-style tents or even teepees.

Food: Food is available from the centre or you can take your own.

Equipment supplied: All specialist canoeing gear is supplied.

What to take: Personal outdoor clothing and suitable footwear.

When to go: Year round.

Established: 1956

Safety: The centre's guides and instructors are qualified having spent one year in guide school. The centre is approved by the Swedish Canoe Federation.

Insurance: The guides have liability insurance but clients should arrange their own accident and travel policy.

Methods of payment: All major credit cards and cash.

Booking information: Advance booking is recommended. No deposit is required.

Nearest airport: Karlstad (Sweden) or Gardermoen (Norway), both about 110 km away.

Nearest rail station: Karlstad.

UNITED KINGDOM

ACORN ACTIVITIES
PO Box 120, Hereford HR4 8YB
Phone: +44 (0)1432 830083
Fax: +44 (0)1432 830110
Email: sales@acornactivities.co.uk
Website: www.acornactivities.co.uk

Canoeing in South Wales
The highlight of Acorn Activities' canoeing ventures is a multi-day trip on the River Wye. The trip from the highest navigable point near Hay on Wye down to the tidal estuary at Chepstow takes six days, and is the perfect 'source-to-sea' for those with some white water experience. Shorter trips are also possible and Acorn Activities will be happy to advise. Paddlers can choose between open canoes and one-man kayaks, and are also provided with a laminated map, detailed route guide, waterproof barrel for storing dry clothes and provisions, and of course a helmet and a buoyancy aid. All the equipment will be transported back to the start point for your journey home. Campsite or B&B accommodation is included in the price. For those who like the idea of someone else taking responsibility, half-day and full-day kayak and canoe instruction is also available.

Activity prices: Kayak instruction £25 for a half-day, £40 for a full day. Multi-day canoe trips on the River Wye start from £105 for two days to £305 for six days. Kayaks can be hired by those with previous experience for £12 per half-day and £20 per day, with a £15 charge for pick-up at the end of the day if required. Two-seater open canoes can be hired for £20 per half-day and £35 per day.
Accommodation: Camping is included in the price of the multi-day trips only. B&B accommodation with evening meal costs extra.
Food: Breakfast and dinner are only included in the multi-day B&B option.
Equipment supplied: Paddles, buoyancy aids and helmets are included in the price.

What to take: Contact Acorn Activities for a list of suitable clothing appropriate to the length of activity.

When to go: Year round.

Established: 1990

Safety: All instructors are British Canoe Union qualified.

Insurance: Insurance is required, although this can be arranged through Acorn Activities.

Methods of payment: VISA, Mastercard, cheque and cash.

Booking information: Late bookings are welcomed. A non-refundable deposit of £10 per day is required. Cancellation charges apply on a sliding scale from 80% for over 43 days before departure to 100% for up to 14 days.

Nearest airport: Depends on river location.

Nearest rail station: Depends on the itinerary.

AVALON ADVENTURE

The Mill House, Dulford, Cullompton, Devon EX15 2ED
Phone: +44 (0) 9220 1717
Fax: +44 (0) 9220 1717
Email: avalon-adventure@dial.pipex.com
Website: http://dialspace.dial.pipex.com/avalon.adventure/

A paddle in the cream of Devon

All of Avalon Adventure's kayaking courses emphasise learning while having fun in the safest possible conditions. The centre has a whole range of courses to take you from complete beginner to skilled white water paddler. The Canoe Fun course is aimed at novices looking for a taste of kayaking on calm water while learning the basic skills. The BCU 2 and 3 star course pushes your paddling skills on further while the 4 star course is for people confident enough to paddle on grade II white water. The Introduction to White Water course will provide the bridge between calm water paddling and the wilder stuff, where you learn ferry gliding, breaking in and out, reading moving water and basic rescue techniques. More advanced white water courses are also available, including sea surfing.

Activity prices: The Canoe Fun course costs £25, the 2/3 star course £60 and the 4 star course £70. Introduction to White Water costs between £60 and £80.

Accommodation: Not included in the price. The centre will help you arrange accommodation to suit your budget

Food: Not included.

Equipment supplied: All specialist equipment is supplied.

What to take: Personal clothing, swimsuit, suitable footwear.

When to go: Canoe Fun courses run from April to September, other courses generally from March to December.

Established: 1992

Safety: All the instructors are fully BCU qualified and hold first aid qualifications. The centre is licensed by the AALA.

Insurance: The centre is insured though clients may wish to take out separate insurance too.

Methods of payment: VISA, Mastercard, cheques and cash.

Booking information: Advance booking is essential.

Nearest airport: Exeter. Transfers can be arranged.

Nearest rail station: Exeter. Transfers can be arranged.

BLACK MOUNTAIN ACTIVITIES

PO Box 5, Hay on Wye, Hereford HR3 5YB
Phone: +44 (0)1497 847 897
Fax: +44 (0)1497 847 897
Email: enquiries@blackmountain.co.uk
Website: www.blackmountain.co.uk

Paddle Welsh white water

The key to becoming a good paddler is to build your skills on a firm base. Black Mountain Activities have instructors who can gradually teach you techniques that will serve you well in your future kayak adventures. Starting with the kayaking taster days, you paddle on the flat water at Glasbury, developing paddle strokes and safety routines before putting them into practice on a trip down river. Once you have the confidence, you can try a white water course, which involves grade II and III river sections. You will learn how to read white water, positioning of your boat and paddling skills.

Activity prices: For taster courses it costs £30 per day or £20 for a half-day trip. White water courses cost £70 for two days.

Accommodation: Not included in the price. There is a range of accommodation available locally and the centre will advise you.

Food: Not included. Packed lunches can be arranged.

Equipment supplied: All specialist equipment is supplied.

What to take: Personal clothing, swimsuit, suitable footwear.

When to go: Year round for taster course, November to March for white water courses.

Established: 1992

Safety: All the centre's staff are fully qualified in their respective sports, hold first aid qualifications and are highly professional. All equipment used meets national safety standards. The centre is licensed by the AALA and the Welsh Tourist Board.

Insurance: The centre is insured though clients may wish to take out separate insurance too.

Methods of payment: Personal cheque and cash.

Booking information: Advance booking is recommended though late bookings may be possible.

Nearest airport: Depends on tour. Cardiff and Bristol are nearest to the centre.

Nearest rail station: Depends on the itinerary. Hereford and Abergavenny are nearest to the centre.

CROFT-NA-CABER

Kenmore, Loch Tay, Perthshire
Phone: +44 (0)1887 830 236
Fax: +44 (0)1887 830 649
Email: info@croftnacaber.co.uk
Website: www.croftnacaber.co.uk

Riding Scottish white rivers

The River Tay is one of Scotland's most exciting and most popular rivers for kayaking. Croft-na-Caber's half-day trips take in one or more of three different sections, including the Grandtully, a very challenging ride that has been used in the British white-water kayaking championships. There are gentler sections more suited to beginners, such as the one around Cat's Hole. The half-day course lasts for about three hours including travelling time while the full day course runs for around seven hours. The Tay is a beautiful river, too – if you ever get the chance to look up and take a breather from the thrilling action.

Activity prices: The half-day kayaking course costs £32 per person and the full-day course costs £58.

Accommodation: Self-catering log cabins or hotel accommodation is available at the centre.

Food: Hotel restaurant and bar at centre.

Equipment supplied: All specialist equipment is supplied.

What to take: Personal clothing, swimsuit, suitable footwear.

When to go: Year round.

Established: 1974

Safety: All the centre's staff are fully qualified in their respective sports, hold first aid qualifications and are highly professional. All equipment used meets national safety standards. The centre is licensed by the AALA.

Insurance: The centre is insured up to £6 million for liability but clients may wish to take out separate insurance for accidents/cancellation too.

Methods of payment: VISA, Mastercard, cheques and cash.

Booking information: Advance booking is essential. Payment of 20% deposit is required. Tour must be confirmed or cancelled at least seven days in advance.

Nearest airport: Edinburgh. Transfers can be arranged.

Nearest rail station: Perth or Pitlochry. Transfers can be arranged.

HOVE LAGOON WATERSPORTS

Hove Lagoon, Kingsway, Hove BN3 4LX
Phone: +44 (0)1273 424842
Fax: +44 (0)1273 421919
Email: windsurf@hovelagoon.co.uk
Website: www.hovelagoon.co.uk

Learn to canoe on England's south coast
For those with little or no experience of canoeing, a good way to start is to take the BCU 1-star course. In the safe environment of Hove

Lagoon, potential paddlers will be taken through the basic strokes, safety and equipment. Weekend courses run from March to November: the first day is generally dedicated to training and games in the lagoon, while the second day tends to involve a day trip to another location to get some experience of moving water. By the end of the second day, you will be able to paddle forwards and backwards, turn with ease and capsize with complete confidence! Competent paddlers who aren't interested in completing a qualification can go straight on to a day trip, which usually involves a scenic coastal route or river, with a pub lunch along the way.

Activity prices: From £20 for two hours to £120 for a full weekend, including all instruction and specialist equipment. Guided day trips for competent paddlers from £60. Private tuition, nationally recognised certification and group discounts also available.

Accommodation: Local B&B and hotel accommodation can be arranged from £15 per night, but is not included in the price.

Food: Catering facilities and a licensed bar are available, but are not included in the price.

Equipment supplied: All specialist equipment is supplied.

What to take: Personal clothing, swimsuit, towel and a pair of shoes that can get wet.

When to go: March to November.

Established: 1994

Safety: All instructors have qualifications recognised by the national governing body for the appropriate activity (e.g. Royal Yachting Association, British Canoe Union etc.)

Insurance: The centre is insured for all licensed activities.

Methods of payment: All common methods of payment are accepted.

Booking information: Advance booking required by phone, post or email. A 50% deposit is required to secure a booking.

Nearest airport: London Gatwick.

Nearest rail station: Hove.

Getting there: Pick-up can be arranged for groups.

PLAS Y BRENIN

National Mountain Centre, Capel Curig, Conwy LL24 0ET
Phone: +44 (0)1690 720 214
Fax: +44 (0)1690 720 394
Email: info@pyb.co.uk
Website: www.pyb.co.uk

Indulge in Snowdonia's watery delights
Plas y Brenin is an ideal location for sampling all the canoeing
disciplines on the endless variety of water on offer in Snowdonia,
including fast rivers, challenging white water and complex coastal sea
tides. The centre has its own lake and grade II section of white water
right on its doorstep plus a heated indoor pool for practising your
rolling techniques. If you are unsure of which type of canoeing to take
up, then try the five-day Introduction to Canoe Sport course that gives
you a taste of sea kayaking, open canoeing and white water kayaking.
For a really fun course opt for the White Water Sea and Surf course
where you will learn to surf waves, bounce down rapids and run a tide
race. The Introduction to Kayaking course covers clothing and
equipment, paddling skills and rescue techniques. Advanced courses
are also on offer for those looking to polish their performance.

Activity prices: The Introduction to Canoe Sport course and the Sea and Surf
course cost £295 each, while the weekend Introduction to Kayaking course
costs £99.
Accommodation: Prices include shared accommodation.
Food: Course prices include full board.
Equipment supplied: All specialist equipment and clothing is provided.
What to take: Personal clothing and your own equipment if you prefer to use it.
When to go: April to September for beginners' courses and January to
November for advanced courses.
Established: 1954
Safety: All instructors hold nationally recognised qualifications and only the
most capable and experienced are employed. The centre is licensed by the
AALA. Great emphasis is placed on safety and the high quality equipment
used is regularly checked and replaced.

Insurance: The centre carries public liability insurance for all activities and recommends that clients take out independent insurance against curtailment and cancellation of their course (available from the centre) and a personal accident policy.

Methods of payment: VISA, Mastercard, Access, personal cheque, cash.

Booking information: Reservations must be made in advance and a deposit is required.

Nearest airport: Manchester.

Nearest rail station: Llandudno. Free transfer available by prior arrangement.

TWR-Y-FELIN NO LIMITS

The TYF Group, 1 High Street, St Davids, Pembrokeshire SA62 6QS
Phone: +44 (0)1437 721 611
Fax: +44 (0)1437 721 692
Email: info@tyf.com
Website: www.tyf.com

Kayak in West Wales

The TYF No Limits centre is based in Britain's smallest city but the surrounding scenery is big on excitement. There is some of the best white water in the country here and the centre is recognised by the WCA as being a Centre of Excellence. Their Introduction to Kayaking course covers all of the basic strokes, forward and reverse paddling, turning, support strokes, safety and rescue techniques. The theory side covers tides, weather and equipment. You start in sheltered waters before trying a few short trips. At the end of it you should be able to pass the BCU 1-star course. The Improver Kayak course lets those with a little bit of experience learn rolling and more advanced techniques.

Activity prices: The Introduction to Kayaking course costs from £89 if you camp up to £160 full board. The Improver course costs the same.

Accommodation: Included in price. You can either camp or have B&B, half board or full board accommodation in the Twr-y-Felin Hotel, a beautiful converted 18th-century windmill.

Food: Included in hotel-based course prices (see above).

Equipment supplied: All specialist equipment and clothing is provided.

What to take: Personal clothing and your own equipment if you prefer to use it.

When to go: April to October for Introduction courses and May to September for Improvers.

Established: 1986

Safety: All instructors hold BCU qualifications and are very experienced.

Insurance: The centre has liability insurance but recommends that clients take out independent insurance against curtailment and cancellation of their course (available from the centre) and a personal accident policy.

Methods of payment: VISA, Mastercard, Switch, cheque and cash.

Booking information: Advance booking is required.

Nearest airport: Cardiff.

Nearest rail station: Haverfordwest. Transfers may be arranged.

LAND YACHTING

It seems hard to believe that the world speed record for land yachting is over the national speed limits for most European countries. In fact, at over 100 mph, you'd be forgiven for thinking that sailing on sand was a sport best left to the certifiably insane. But of course there's more to it than that, and a few hours going through the basics will soon see you flying along quite happily at 30 mph, without a second thought to the fact you're barely three inches off the ground.

A land yacht is basically a grown-up go-kart, with three wheels, a sail and a low-slung hull to lie in. By positioning the yacht across the wind, all you have to do to get going is pull in the sail. The more you pull in the sail and the stronger the wind, the faster you sail. If all this gets a bit out of hand, stopping is simply a matter of turning into the wind and spilling the sail. There's some small mercy in the fact that the hull is so close to the ground that the low centre of gravity makes land yachts very difficult to flip. By the same token, turns can be tight and fast without any chance of going mast over boom.

Not surprisingly, some sailing experience is an advantage when it comes to understanding the basic principles, but because there are so few moving parts, it'll only be a matter of minutes before you're well on your way to breaking your own speed limit.

UNITED KINGDOM

KIRRAWEE LAND YACHTS
10 Lyndhurst Road, Dymchurch, Kent, TN29 0TE
Phone: +44 (0)1303 874 673
Fax: N/A

Email: kirrawee@landyachting.co.uk
Website: www.landyachting.co.uk

Fly along Kent's beaches
Land yachting is the fastest wind powered sport available in the UK
and Roger Gosbee's Kirrawee Land Yachting take advantage of the
wonderful Greatstone beach in Kent. A qualified instructor takes you
through the basic steering skills needed to drive a modern land yacht.
It is a sport that is easy to get started in but a real challenge to master,
so you may well get hooked! The beach is within easy reach of
London, the south-east and northern France, so get yachting!

Activity prices: Half-day sessions cost £35 and full-day sessions cost £58.
Accommodation: Not included in price. Advice is given on local places.
Food: Client to arrange own. There are pubs and shops nearby.
Equipment supplied: All safety equipment, helmets, gloves.
What to take: Wear old clothing and plenty of layers for warmth.
When to go: Year round except July and August.
Established: 1998
Safety: Roger Gosbee, the centre's owner, has been land yachting since he
was eight years old and is a registered instructor. All his instructors are
BFSLYC{?} registered. The centre is also linked to BFSLYC.
Insurance: Third party insurance is included. Clients should arrange their own
personal accident policy.
Methods of payment: Cash or personal cheque.
Booking information: Advance booking is essential and a £10 deposit is
required. Cancellation by client is not subject to penalty if notice is given. If
course is cancelled due to weather, a 90% refund is given.
Nearest airport: Lydd.
Nearest rail station: Ashford (Kent).

WINDSPORT INTERNATIONAL
Mylor Yacht Harbour, Falmouth, Cornwall TR11 5UF
Phone: +44 (0)1326 376 191/363
Fax: +44 (0)1326 376 192

Email: windsport.international@btinternet.com
Website: www.windsport-int.com

A sail out of Cornish water
Windsport International use the excellent dragonfly land yachts that can have you whizzing over the sand at up to 45 mph. On their introductory course, you will learn the basic skills for handling the yacht before moving on to more advanced manoeuvres in the afternoon. The centre also has a special group day where you can get up to higher speeds and further enhance your driving ability. With the group days, they set up a race session for you and your friends to go head to head. Courses can be tailored to meet your requirements.

Activity prices: The one-day introductory course costs £54 and a two-hour lesson costs £20.
Accommodation: Clients to arrange own. There are plenty of options in Falmouth.
Food: Client to arrange own.
Equipment supplied: All safety equipment and clothing.
What to take: Suitable footwear.
When to go: Year round.
Established: 1985
Safety: All instructors are RYA qualified and the centre is licensed by the AALA and recognised by the RYA.
Insurance: Insurance is required and a scheme is offered by the centre
Methods of payment: VISA, Mastercard, Switch, Delta, cheque with bank card and banker's drafts.
Booking information: Advance booking is preferred, though tuition and boat hire are available on the day. A 25% deposit is required and cancellation policy may be applied.
Nearest airport: Newquay. Connections to London airports.
Nearest rail station: Truro.

MICROLIGHTING

This is what happens when adventurers get restless and look for new ways to develop their sport. Microlighting sprang into life in the 1970s when hang glider pilots who were rather bored with just soaring along ridges decided that they wanted to travel further and needed an engine. They raided their garden sheds, broke their lawnmowers and the rest, as they say, is history. Unfortunately, so are quite a few of those early pilots! It certainly was a maverick sport when it started, but gradually national associations developed and regulations were introduced to govern both pilot training and microlight construction. The result was a significant increase in safety and a boom in the number of people learning to fly this way. It holds great attractions for people who want to fly but cannot afford to learn to fly aircraft. Microlights are simpler to fly and cost much less to buy (and they are more fun too!). There are two types of microlight design. Those with more traditional aircraft wing design and enclosed cockpit are called three axis, while the more well known delta-shaped wing style is called a flex-wing. The dual taster flights allow you to feel the excitement of flying without the responsibility while the pilot training courses can take you to solo flying level. As one instructor said to me, 'It is like flying a Harley Davidson across the sky.'

Around the world in eighty days

During 1998, in one of the most remarkable and possibly romantic around the world adventures of recent decades, Brian Milton took just 80 flying days to fly his microlight round the globe. In his BT Global Flyer, Milton tried to retrace the path taken by fictional character

Phileas Fogg in Jules Verne's classic story. From London, he flew over Europe, the Middle East, China, Japan and into Russia. He then crossed to Alaska and travelled down via Canada to the USA. His return leg took him over Greenland, Iceland and Scotland before he arrived back in London. The epic story is retold in his own book, Global Flyer: Around the World in 80 Flying Days.

UNITED KINGDOM

ACORN ACTIVITIES
PO Box 120, Hereford HR4 8YB
Phone: +44 (0)1432 830083
Fax: +44 (0)1432 830110
Email: sales@acornactivities.co.uk
Website: www.acornactivities.co.uk

Microlighting throughout the UK
As one of the UK's biggest adventure sports operators, Acorn Activities has access to a number of airfields and microlight schools all over the country, meaning you won't have to travel far to reach for the sky. With no cockpit these tiny aircraft are open to the mercy of the wind, providing a 360 degree panoramic buzz on take-off. Trial lessons last 25–30 minutes, which is plenty of time to drink in the view . . . in every direction. The minimum age for microlighting is 14 years, and the maximum weight is 14 stones.

Activity prices: £60 for a 30 minute trial flight lesson.
Accommodation: Not included.
Food: Not included.
Equipment supplied: All specialised equipment is provided.
What to take: Warm clothing and sturdy shoes.
When to go: Year round, weather permitting.
Established: 1990
Safety: All instructors are CAA qualified.
Insurance: Insurance is required, although this can be arranged through Acorn Activities.

Methods of payment: VISA, Mastercard, cheque and cash.

Booking information: Late bookings are welcomed. A non-refundable deposit of £10 per day is required. Cancellation charges apply on a sliding scale from 80% for over 43 days before departure to 100% for up to 14 days.

Nearest airport: Depends on flight location.

Nearest rail station: Depends on the itinerary.

FREEDOM SPORTS AVIATION

4 Catholme Lane, Barton under Needwood, Burton on Trent, Staffs DE13 8DA

Phone: +44 (0)1283 716265

Fax: N/A

Email: s.baker@virgin.net

Website: http://freespace.virgin.net/s.baker

Microlighting in the Peak District

Although Freedom Sports Aviation is based in Burton on Trent, flights can also be arranged from two additional sites near Ashbourne in the Peak District and Church Stretton in Shropshire. Flights are in two-seat microlight aircraft with a qualified instructor, who will explain and demonstrate the controls. Actually taking control of the aircraft is possible if weather conditions are suitable. A 20-minute taster flight costs £35, while a full hour in the air will set you back £75.

Activity prices: Trial flight vouchers from £35 for 20 minutes, £55 for 40 minutes and £75 for one hour. Lessons are £69 per hour and flying courses to obtain a licence start at £515.

Accommodation: Facilities on site suitable for camping and caravans.

Food: Coffee and tea available, and a bar.

Equipment supplied: All specialist equipment is supplied, including two-seater microlight, flying suit, helmet, intercom and air chart.

What to take: Personal clothing and gloves.

When to go: Year round.

Established: 1996

Safety: All instructors are CAA qualified.

Insurance: Passenger liability insurance is mandatory and is included in the price.

Methods of payment: Cash or cheque only.

Booking information: Trial flight vouchers are valid for one year. In the event of cancellation due to unsuitable weather, flights can be rearranged.

Nearest airport: East Midlands Airport.

Nearest rail station: Burton on Trent.

SABRE AIR SPORTS

Shobdon Airfield, Shobdon, nr Leominster, Herefordshire HR6 9NR
Phone: +44 (0)1568 708 168
Fax: +44 (0)1568 708 553
Email: sabre@microlight.kc3ltd.co.uk
Website: www.kc3ltd.co.uk/local/sabre.html

Fly at old World War II airfield

The Welsh border country around Hereford makes a stunning backdrop for taking to the air in a microlight. Sabre Air Sports is based at Shobdon airfield which saw action during the Second World War, so there is plenty of atmosphere there. Steve Jones, Sabre's owner, offers the full range of microlight courses to take you from complete novice to qualified pilot. The taster sessions are a great way to get hooked: you get to experience the thrill without the worry as your qualified pilot flies the machine while you take in the experience. The centre can help you to arrange buying an aircraft should you wish to become a pilot, or they can teach you on the centre's aircraft. There is a restaurant and bar on site so you can swap flying tales over a beer at the end of the day.

Activity prices: A 30-minute trial lesson costs £45 and a one-hour session costs £73. Full training for a PPL licence costs £70 per hour on dual control aircraft.

Accommodation: Camping is available at £2 per night. There are hotels nearby costing from £15 per night per person.

Food: Not included. There is a canteen/restaurant at the airfield.

Equipment supplied: All specialised equipment is provided.

What to take: Warm clothing.

When to go: Year round, except Mondays and Tuesdays. Open all bank holidays.

Established: 1993

Safety: All flying instructors are BMAA and CAA approved.

Insurance: Clients need to arrange their own insurance and they must sign a disclaimer before flying.

Methods of payment: Cash or personal cheque (with banker's card) only.

Booking information: Advance bookings are essential and a deposit may be required.

Nearest airport: Birmingham International.

Nearest rail station: Leominster.

MOUNTAIN BIKING

Mountain biking began in California's Marin County in the late 1970s and has since evolved to become one of the success stories of the 1990s. Today, mountain biking is bigger than ever and still growing fast. Whether you're a Sunday afternoon rider or a demon downhill racer, there's bound to be a bike and a bump to suit your style.

The best thing about mountain biking is its accessibility – anyone can do it, and even disillusioned city-dwellers don't have to travel far to find the nearest trail. At its most simple, mountain biking requires little more than a bike, but if you're going further from home or exploring an unknown area, a map might help. After that, the options for off-road excitement are almost limitless. For many, the thought of a long haul uphill is as unpleasant as it is daunting, but once you've made the effort, the rewards are worth the wait.

A number of companies throughout Europe offer a variety of mountain biking options, from one-day bike hire to multi-day, cross-country expeditions. If you're unfamiliar with an area and want to get the most out of the mountains, then going with a guide is an ideal way to build up knowledge and confidence. On longer trips, luggage and camping equipment are often transported on ahead, allowing you to make the most of the trails and tracks on offer. Always check that the bike is the right size for you and the saddle is at the right height (your leg should be only slightly bent when the ball of your foot's on the bottom pedal) – nothing will put you off mountain biking quicker than struggling along with your knees up around your chest. And one final word of warning: few trails are designated specifically for mountain bikers, so give way to walkers and horse riders.

Fully suspended or not

Over the last decade there has been monumental progress in mountain bike technology and design. Probably the most obvious change is the introduction of front and rear suspension units. They are designed to make the whole mountain biking experience a more comfortable and controllable affair. However, the new designs are not necessarily suitable for everyone. Full suspension bikes are really only suited to downhill riding and quite extreme downhill riding at that. The benefits of full suspension would be lost on most riders out for a ride around their local forestry tracks. On uphills, these bikes are positively a disadvantage as the flex in the suspension units absorbs the energy you are putting into going up the slope. Hills are hard enough as it is. Non-suspension bikes are still around and they are far more responsive on climbs. If you are looking to buy a bike and fancy suspension, then why not just try a front suspension model first and see how you go with that?

AUSTRIA

SPORTSCHULE FANKHAUSER – TIROL RAFTING
Dorfstrasse 17, A-6382 Kirchdorf, Tirol
Phone: +43 5352 62233
Fax: +43 5352 62587
Email: fanky@netwing.at
Website: www.tirolrafting.com

A Tirol biking downhill treat
The Kirchdorf area of Austria's Tirol region has some superb mountain biking possibilities and Sportschule Fankhauser are ideally placed to take advantage of the most exciting routes. They offer a variety of half-day biking trips, including the amazing downhill route from the Steinplatte. The trips are guided by fully qualified and experienced guides and only run on Thursdays and Fridays.

Activity prices: The biking downhill trips cost Sch450 per person.

Accommodation: Available at centre, either camping or in a bunkhouse, or in a private hotel.

Food: Breakfast and half-board packages are available at the centre.

Equipment supplied: Good quality mountain bikes and helmets are provided.

What to take: Personal biking clothing and suitable footwear.

When to go: Year round, Thursdays and Fridays only.

Established: 1985

Safety: All the biking guides hold national qualifications. The centre is approved by the Austrian Tourist Office and the Austrian Rafting Association.

Insurance: The centre has liability insurance but clients should arrange their own accident policy.

Methods of payment: VISA, Mastercard, Eurocard, Traveller's cheques and cash.

Booking information: Advance booking is essential at least one day ahead. No deposit is required and there are no cancellation penalties.

Nearest airport: Innsbruck, Salzburg or Munich. Transfers can be arranged.

Nearest rail station: St Johann in the Tirol. Transfers can be arranged.

BULGARIA

BULGARIAN MOUNTAINS ADVENTURE

Kancho Shipkov, Kv. Dianabad bl 18 vh.A, 1172 Sofia
Phone: +359 2 620 688
Fax: N/A
Email: kancho@bglink.net
Website: http://pss.bglink.net/mysite/explorebg.html

A Bulgarian pedal party

If you fancy something a little different from the norm then head for the dramatic mountains of Bulgaria, where there are plenty of relatively unexplored biking trails to keep everyone happy. Bulgarian Mountains Adventure is a company based around members of the national mountain rescue service. They offer personal and tailor-made guiding services and can organise rides to suit bikers of varying standards. Some of the best routes for less experienced riders are found in the Rhodopi Mountains, where the trails are wide and soft, and there is a network of mountain roads too. Other locations with decent trails include Eastern Rila and the Sredna Gora Mountains. There are also plenty of tough routes for challenge junkies.

Activity prices: The trips are all tailor-made to suit your requirements and cost around US$50 per day, or less, depending on what you do and where you go. The centre will advise you on the possibilities. The price also includes local transportation.

Accommodation: Food and lodging during the activity are included in the price and organised by the centre. Hotels and meals at the start and end of your trip are not included but the centre can help you arrange them.

Food: Food is included during the activity, but not at the start and end of your trip.

Equipment supplied: All specialist equipment is supplied; though you can take your own bike if you have it.

What to take: Personal biking clothing and suitable footwear.

When to go: Year round, though winter is only for the crazy!

Established: 1997

Safety: At least one of the guides in every group is a qualified rescuer from the Bulgarian Mountain Rescue Service. They have plentiful experience and excellent local knowledge.

Insurance: Clients should arrange their own policy, or the centre can arrange it on the spot.

Methods of payment: Bank transfer and cash.

Booking information: Advance booking is essential and a 30% deposit is payable. Cancellation penalties may apply.

Nearest airport: Sofia. Transfers can be arranged.

Nearest rail station: Sofia Central. Transfers can be arranged.

CYPRUS

CYPRUS BIKE TRAVEL
Machis Kritis , 118GR 74100 Rethymnon, Crete, Greece
Phone: +30 831 53 328
Fax: +30 831 52 691

Email: info@hellasbike.com
Website: www.hellasbike.com

A mountain challenge in Cyprus

Cyprus Bike Travel is linked to Hellas Bike Travel, which operates in Greece. They provide similar mountain biking packages and all booking is done through the Crete office. The Level 2 Cyprus rides aim to show you some of the more offbeat parts of the country using easy tracks and quiet back roads. The Level 3 tours are for very fit and experienced bikers who have good bike handling skills. The trails used are narrow and physically demanding. The supplied bikes are all high quality Scott bikes. Tours last from six to eight hours with breaks.

Activity prices: A one-week Level 2 or 3 course, including five guided tours, costs US$290 and includes the Scott hire bike, a permanent support vehicle, transfers to and from your hotel, guiding and third party insurance. You also get a free t-shirt and water bottle to keep. Cycle hire is available separately too.
Accommodation: Not included in price. The centre can help you arrange accommodation to suit your budget.
Food: Not included in price. The tours pass by typical Cypriot taverns where home-cooked foods may be sampled.
Equipment supplied: Scott mountain bike and helmet.
What to take: Personal cycling clothing and footwear.
When to go: Mid-March to mid-November.
Established: 1988
Safety: All the guides have bike mechanic training or substantial experience in the field. They have first aid qualifications and speak German and English well. All guides are skilled at dealing with clients of all abilities and have good local knowledge.
Insurance: Third party insurance and accident insurance is included. Clients should arrange their own travel policy.
Methods of payment: Bank transfer prior to arrival only.
Booking information: Bank transfer should be credited to Cyprus Bike Travel at least 14 days before arrival. Cancellation penalties apply on a sliding scale.
Nearest airport: Paphos.
Nearest rail station: N/A.

FRANCE

SNOW SAFARI LIMITED
Chalet Savoy, 1351 route des Chavants. 74310 Les Houches
Phone: +33 (0)4 50 54 56 63;
UK bookings & information number 01279 600 885
Fax: +33 (0)4 50 54 57 19
Email: Chalsavoy@aol.com
Website: www.chaletsavoy.com

Mountain biking around Mont Blanc
Outdoor pursuits are the bread and butter of Chamonix, and
mountain biking is no exception. Most of the lifts in the valley accept
mountain bikes, making it easy to access the biking trails as far away
as Les Contamines and Megève. One of the most spectacular routes
crosses the Possette pass into Switzerland. The staff at Chalet Savoy
are happy to give advice on the best trails in the area. On certain
dates accompanied rides are also available.

Activity prices: Bikes can be hired for FFr100 per day.
Accommodation: Available at the Chalet. Summer prices from FFr140 per
person for B&B or FFr2,050 per person for seven days and seven nights.
Food: Included in the accommodation price.
Equipment supplied: Bikes and helmets are available.
What to take: Personal hiking/biking clothing.
When to go: May to September.
Established: 1987
Safety: All guides and leaders are fully qualified for the relevant activity.
Insurance: Clients must arrange their own insurance policy.
Methods of payment: VISA, Mastercard.
Booking information: Contact Snow Safari for booking form and full terms and
conditions.
Nearest airport: Geneva.
Nearest rail station: Les Houches

GREECE

HELLAS BIKE TRAVEL
Machis Kritis 118, GR 74100 Rethymnon, Crete
Phone: +30 831 53 328
Fax: +30 831 52 691
Email: info@hellasbike.com
Website: www.hellasbike.com

A multi-island Greek extravaganza
Hellas Bike Travel offers mountain biking tours on no fewer than five of the most dramatically beautiful Greek islands. They have mountain bike centres on Corfu, claimed as 'my island of magic' by empress Sissi in Homer's *Odyssey*, and Halkidiki, with its wide beaches, and secluded bays surrounded by pine forests and gentle hills. Or you can go to Rhodes, the sunniest island in Greece with its old Byzantine ruins; Paros, the 'princess of the Cyclades'; or Crete. With its unique character, mountains and wonderful beaches, Crete has it all for bikers looking for a thrill. The centre has two levels of mountain biking tours. Level 2 tours require good physical condition and include some cross-country biking on moderately steep gradients. Level 3 'Extreme Biking' is suitable for bike 'freaks' with outstanding bike control skills and very good sporting condition. Not for wimps, this one!

Activity prices: Both Level 2 and 3 one-week courses, including five guided tours, cost US$300 each. This includes the Scott hire bike, a permanent support vehicle, transfers to and from your hotel, guiding and third party insurance. You also get a free t-shirt and water bottle to keep. Bike hire is available separately.
Accommodation: Not included in price. The centre can help you arrange accommodation to suit your budget.
Food: Not included in price.
Equipment supplied: Scott mountain bike and helmet.
What to take: Personal cycling clothing and footwear.

When to go: Mid-March to mid-November.

Established: 1988

Safety: All guides are experienced at dealing with clients of all abilities and have good local knowledge. They also have mechanical knowledge and first aid qualifications. The tours are mainly conducted in German and English. The Crete centre only runs English tours or French on request.

Insurance: Third party insurance and accident insurance is included. Clients should arrange their own travel policy.

Methods of payment: Bank transfer prior to arrival only.

Booking information: Bank transfer should be credited to Hellas Bike Travel at least 14 days before arrival. Cancellation penalties apply on a sliding scale.

Nearest airport: Depends on the island chosen.

Nearest rail station: Depends on the island chosen.

ITALY

RIFUGIO PRATEGIANO

Loc. Prategiano 45, I-58026 Montieri

Phone: +39 (0)566 997 700

Fax: +39 (0)566 997 891

Email: prategiano@bigfoot.com

Website: http://prategiano.heimatseite.com/holidaysvacations.html

Rough beauty in Tuscany

The family-owned Rifugio Prategiano is located at the very heart of Alta Maremma, the most unspoiled and under-populated region of Tuscany, and it provides bikers with an ideal base for discovering great secluded trails by day and relaxing in style at night. You can bring your own bike or hire one of the good quality bikes at the hotel and head off on of four organised, full-day, circular trails. The 30 km long Monte di Prata trail involves a long uphill climb followed by a short steep section that rewards you with views over all of Maremma. What goes up must come down, and the ride back is thrilling. The 35 km long Chiusdino Trail takes you along narrow forest trails to the medieval village of Chiusdino. A steep downhill leads to the River

Merse for a cool-off before the long climb back to the hotel. Or ride the web of trails around the Natural Park Bandite Di Scarlino. Tours can be customised.

Activity prices: Accommodation and food costs from 332 to 592 euros, depending on season and food package. Biking tours cost around 50 euros for a full day with guide and hire bike, 15 euros less with your own bike. A six-day package with guide and hire bike costs from 258 to 284 euros. The hotel swimming pool is open from June to August.

Accommodation: Accommodation is included at the 20-bed Rifugio Prategiano Hotel. You can also stay in the basic stable quarters at lower cost.

Food: Full board and half-board packages are available.

Equipment supplied: Bikes are available for hire.

What to take: Your own bike if desired, helmet, cycling clothing, footwear.

When to go: March to November.

Established: 1971

Safety: All guides have vocational 'guida ambiente equestre' training certificates issued by the Tuscan authorities. The centre is a member of ANTE.

Insurance: The Centre has liability insurance. Clients need to arrange their own travel and accident insurance.

Methods of payment: Cheques are preferred.

Booking information: Advance booking is recommended though late bookings are accepted. A 40% deposit is required with all bookings.

Nearest airport: Pisa or possibly Florence. Transfers are available.

Nearest rail station: Via Florence to Follonica. Transfers are available.

SPAIN

ESPAÑA BIKE TRAVEL

Avenida de Tirajana 25, Lokal 8, 35100 Playa del Ingles, Gran Canaria, Spain

Phone: +34 609 549 324

Fax: +34 928 773317

Email: jose@sas-sports.de OR sasmax@arrakis.es

Website: www.espanabike.com

Rough riding the Canaries

España Bike Travel is based on the stunning island of Gran Canaria in the Canary Islands. It is linked to the company that owns Hellas Bike Travel in Greece and offers a similar high level of service in its mountain biking packages. Gran Canaria has a plethora of off-road trails and EBT has access to the best of them. The Level 2 tours are designed for casual bikers and those more advanced bikers looking for something challenging without being eyeballs out. The Level 3 tours are only for advanced riders and involve narrow, sometimes exposed trails where you need to be the master of the bike and not the other way around. The centre has excellent quality Scott mountain bikes for the tours. The rides last from about six to eight hours per day, including breaks for lunch and drinks.

Activity prices: A one-week Level 2 or Level 3 course, including five guided tours, costs US$300 and includes the Scott hire bike, a permanent support vehicle, transfers to and from your hotel, guiding and third party insurance. You also get a free t-shirt and water bottle to keep. Cycle hire is available separately too, as are shorter biking packages.

Accommodation: Not included in price. The centre can help you arrange accommodation to suit your budget.

Food: Not included in price, except a picnic on the tours.

Equipment supplied: Scott mountain bike and helmet.

What to take: Personal cycling clothing and footwear.

When to go: Year round.

Established: 1996

Safety: All the guides have experience in the field and first aid qualifications.

Insurance: Third party insurance and accident insurance is included. Clients should arrange their own travel policy.

Methods of payment: VISA or bank transfer.

Booking information: Bank transfer should be credited to España Bike Travel at least fourteen days before arrival. Cancellation penalties apply on a sliding scale.

Nearest airport: Las Palmas (32 km).

Nearest rail station: N/A.

SIERRA CYCLING HOLIDAYS

Urb. Pueblo Castillo No 7, Fuengirola, Malaga 29640
Phone: +34 95 247 1720
Fax: +34 95 247 1720
Email: sierracyc@arrakis.es
Website: www.mercuryin.es/sierracycling

Guided mountain biking in Andalucia

Andalucia's climate is among the best in Europe, with over 300 days of sunshine every year. What's more, the mountains of the Sierra de Ronda and the Sierra Nevada provide some of the best off-road biking in Spain. Based in the lively town of Fuengirola, Sierra Cycling Holidays is only minutes from the scenery and solitude of the mountains. Cyclists typically stay for a week, with a different guided ride every day. Routes include 20–30 km of cycling per day and usually last three to four hours at a leisurely pace, allowing plenty of time to lie back and soak up the scenery. Transportation to and from every ride is included in the price, as is B&B accommodation in spacious beach-houses and afternoon tea and cakes after every ride. No experience is necessary and bikes can be hired for those who don't wish to bring their own.

Activity prices: £275 per week, including all guided rides, beach-front B&B, swimming pool, afternoon tea and transport to and from the airport.

Accommodation: Seafront accommodation included in the price.

Food: Breakfast and afternoon tea included in the price.

Equipment supplied: Bike hire is not included and costs an additional £55 per week.

What to take: Personal cycling clothing.

When to go: Year round.

Established: 1992

Safety: All guides are qualified in first aid and bike maintenance.

Insurance: Clients must provide their own insurance.

Methods of payment: Traveller's cheques and cash.

Booking information: £50 per person deposit required at the time of booking, which will be forfeited in the event of cancellation.

Nearest airport: Malaga. Clients arriving from abroad will be met at Malaga airport.

Nearest rail station: Fuengirola. Transfers can be arranged.

SWITZERLAND

ADVENTURE'S BEST
PO Box 9, Via Basilea 28, CH-6903 Lugano
Phone: +41 91 966 11 14
Fax: +41 91 966 12 13
Email: info@asbest.ch
Website: www.asbest.ch

Trail riding in southern Switzerland
Established in 1994, Adventure's Best is ideally situated in Ticino, the southernmost state of Switzerland and an area characterised by placid lakes, white water rivers and rugged mountain ranges. Mountain biking is available year round, with hundreds of kilometres of routes and trails to choose from, whether you're a downhill demon or an easy rider. Accommodation is not included in the price but can be arranged at the centre, from dormitory rooms to a double room with en suite bath and shower.

Activity prices: Contact the centre for latest prices.

Accommodation: Not included in the price, but is available at the centre. Shared dorms cost an additional SFr20 per person, a double room SFr40 per person, a double room with en suite bath/shower SFr50 per person and a single room with en suite bath/shower SFr60 per person.

Food: Not included in the price, but is available at the centre. Buffet breakfast costs SFr15 per person.

Equipment supplied: All specialist equipment is provided.

What to take: Personal clothing.

When to go: Year round.

Established: 1994

Safety: All instructors hold recognised qualifications from the relevant national or international governing body.

Insurance: Clients are responsible for arranging their own insurance.

Methods of payment: VISA, Mastercard, Amex, travellers' cheques and cash.

Booking information: No deposit required.

Nearest airport: Lugano-Agno (5 km).

Nearest rail station: Lugano (200 metres).

ALPIN RAFT

Postfach 78, 3800 Matten
Phone: +41 33 823 4100
Fax: +41 33 823 4101
Email: mail@alpinraft.ch
Website: www.alpinraft.ch

Mountain biking in the Swiss Alps

The region around Interlaken and the Brienzer See offers a haven of outdoor opportunities, and mountain biking is particularly well catered for. The options for off-road biking are almost limitless and there's no better way to explore the mountains if you're short of time. Whether you're after fast and steep or slow and easy, there are tracks and trails to suit every ability, and if you're not sure where to go, Alpin Raft will point you in the right direction.

Activity prices: From SFr25 for a half-day to SFr35 for a full day. Rental from SFr 25.

Accommodation: Backpacker accommodation available at the centre.

Food: None provided.

Equipment supplied: Mountain bikes and helmets are available.

What to take: Biking clothes and a good pair of biking or hiking style shoes.

When to go: May to October.

Established: 1988

Safety: All mountain bikes are well maintained and checked on a regular basis.

Insurance: Clients must arrange their own insurance.

Methods of payment: All common methods of payment accepted.

Booking information: Book by phone or email. Full payment is charged for cancellation on the day of trip.

Nearest airport: Bern.

Nearest rail station: Interlaken.

ANDIAMO ADVENTOURS
Läagernstrasse 5, 8200 Schaffhausen
Phone: +41 (0)52 624 9336
Fax: +41 (0)52 624 9336
Email: mike_gomes@andiamoadventours.com
Website: www.andiamoadventours.com

Bike to the max in the Swiss Alps
Andiamo Adventours offer three Swiss off-road trips that will thrill riders
at moderate and advanced level. To get you started in this exciting
sport, they also offer an introduction weekend in the Appenzell region.
European certified instructor Hans Peter Geier will guide you through
some of Switzerland's most scenic Alpine routes. There are theory
lessons and technique classes to build your confidence on the rough
stuff and the trails get progressively more challenging. More competent
riders can dive straight into the six-day Grindelwald Vertical tour where
you tackle moderate trails around the famous Eiger Mountain. For more
advanced riders, the five-day tour through central Switzerland is the
ideal challenge. You spend all five days in a small village and tackle the
varied and stunningly beautiful trails around Lake Luzern.

Activity prices: The introduction weekend includes three nights accommoda-
tion, transfers, bike and helmet, breakfast and lunch, a fondue dinner, two
guided tours and a support van for US$695. The Grindelwald tour on a similar
basis costs US$1,000 and the central Switzerland tour costs from US$1,100.
Accommodation: Ranges from hostels to three-star hotels/chalets.
Food: Breakfast and lunches are included and a fondue dinner.
Equipment supplied: Bikes, helmets, handlebar bags, water bottles, repair kits.
What to take: Personal cycling clothing and footwear, cycling gloves,
sunscreen.
When to go: June to August on specific dates.
Established: 1992
Safety: All mountain bikes are well maintained and checked on a regular basis.
The guides are very experienced and hold guiding qualifications.
Insurance: Clients must arrange their own insurance.
Methods of payment: VISA, Mastercard, cheques, cash.

Booking information: Advance booking is essential. Book by phone or email. A US$400 deposit is payable and final payment is due 60 days before departure.
Nearest airport: Geneva.
Nearest rail station: Depends on tour.

UNITED KINGDOM

ACORN ACTIVITIES
PO Box 120, Hereford HR4 8YB
Phone: +44 (0)1432 830083
Fax: +44 (0)1432 830110
Email: sales@acornactivities.co.uk
Website: www.acornactivities.co.uk

Mountain biking in the Welsh Borders
Some of the very best mountain biking country in the UK can be found in Wales, Herefordshire and Shropshire, and Acorn Activities have a variety of packages to suit all tastes and abilities. If you simply want to spend a day or two cycling as part of an activity break, bikes can be hired, routes can be recommended and everything picked up from your accommodation at the end of the day. If, on the other hand, you want a fully saddled mountain bike holiday, look no further than a two-day mountain bike break. Riding 21-gear aluminium mountain bikes, you will be staying at either the Greyhound Hotel or the Pencraig Gardens Hotel in Builth Wells, which will be your base for the weekend. A variety of circular routes is available, each bringing you back to tea, coffee and en suite showers every evening. All equipment is included and no previous experience is necessary.

Activity prices: £150 for any two nights. Mountain bike hire from £25 per day including puncture repair kit, locks, stuff-sacks and detailed route maps. Bikes can be delivered to and collected from local accommodation for an additional charge.
Accommodation: Included in the price. Ranges from pubs and B&Bs to farmhouses and hotels.
Food: Dinner, packed lunch and breakfast included.

Equipment supplied: Map, selected routes, helmet, repair kit, saddlebag and waterproof if required.

What to take: Personal cycling clothing.

When to go: Year round.

Established: 1990

Safety: There are a variety of routes to suite all abilities.

Insurance: Insurance is required, although this can be arranged through Acorn Activities.

Methods of payment: VISA, Mastercard, cheque and cash.

Booking information: Late bookings are welcomed. A non-refundable deposit of £10 per day is required. Cancellation charges apply on a sliding scale from 80% for over 43 days before departure to 100% for up to 14 days.

Nearest airport: Cardiff or Birmingham International.

Nearest rail station: Depends on the itinerary.

ADVENTURE SPORTS

Carnkie Farmhouse, Carnkie, Redruth, Cornwall TR16 6RZ
Phone: +44 (0)1209 218 962
Fax: +44 (0)1209 314 118
Email: holidays@adventure-sports.co.uk
Website: www.adventure-sports.co.uk

On the Cornish pastie trail

Cornwall is one of the UK's most scenic regions with its dramatic coastline, open hills and tiny old villages. It is criss-crossed by numerous trails and quiet back roads that make it a wonderful destination for mountain biking. Adventure Sports' experienced biking guides have thorough knowledge of the possible rides and can tailor your route to suit your ability. They can also advise you on riding techniques. The courses are always great social affairs, so keep a little bit of energy for the evening too. You can mix biking with some of the other sports on offer at the centre.

Activity prices: A three-day camping stay with two days of activities costs from £76 (low season) to £100 (high season) and prices go up to £329 for a seven night/seven activity days course.

Accommodation: Included in price. You have a choice of camping, self-catering chalets or a converted self-catering farmhouse. There are many social options nearby or on the site.

Food: Not included.

Equipment supplied: Bikes, helmets.

What to take: Personal clothing and suitable footwear.

When to go: Summer months only.

Established: 1982

Safety: All of the centre's biking guides hold nationally recognised qualifications and are very experienced. The centre is a member of the West Country Tourist Board.

Insurance: Insurance is required. Policies are offered by the centre.

Methods of payment: VISA, cheque and cash.

Booking information: Advance booking is required. A £50 deposit is payable.

Nearest airport: Newquay.

Nearest rail station: Redruth. Transfers can be arranged.

BIKE RIDES

Bremhill, Calne, Wiltshire SN11 9LA
Phone: +44 (0)7000 560 749
Fax: +44 (0)7000 560 749
Email: tours@bike-rides.co.uk
Website: www.bike-rides.co.uk

Riding top UK trails

Bike Rides is at the forefront of organised mountain biking tours in the UK and Europe. They provide tours to suit every level of ability from beginners to very experienced in some of the most attractive parts of the country. Their popular guided weekend tours in the UK include the North Downs, the Welsh Borders, the Yorkshire Dales, the Quantocks and the famous Sustrans Coast to Coast route from Whitehaven to Sunderland. The rides are always great social occasions too. The weekends also serve as good practice times for riders wishing to take on one of the longer European tours offered. These include rides through Cathar country in the French Pyrenean foothills, the volcanic lands of the French Auvergne and the Minho region of Portugal. Riding distance is normally 15–30 miles a day with a back-up support vehicle for those wanting to rest. Accommodation is chosen for its location and charm so you can really relax after the day's ride and enjoy the wine and food.

Activity prices: The weekend trips cost between £85 and £95, including accommodation and food. The four-day Coast to Coast tour costs £195. Overseas tours range from £285 to £435.

Accommodation: Included in the price. Ranges from hotels and B&B to farmstays and camping.

Food: Some tours are full board, others half board. Wine is included on some tours.

Equipment supplied: Bikes (suspension or normal) and helmets are available for hire; route plans are provided, and guides carry repair kits.

What to take: Your own bike and helmet if you have one, personal cycling clothing, cycling gloves and shoes.

When to go: Selected departure dates all year round.

Established: 1992

Safety: Experienced guides are used on all tours.

Insurance: For overseas tours, clients can take out the Bike Rides insurance policy or arrange their own. Clients need to arrange their own insurance for UK trips.

Methods of payment: VISA, Mastercard, Delta, Switch, personal cheque, cash.

Booking information: Advance booking is advised. Payment is due eight weeks prior to departure. A deposit of £35 per person is required for UK rides and £75 for overseas. Cancellation charges apply.

Nearest airport: Depends on tour.

Nearest rail station: Depends on tour.

BLACK MOUNTAIN ACTIVITIES
PO Box 5, Hay on Wye, Hereford HR3 5YB
Phone: +44 (0)1497 847 897
Fax: +44 (0)1497 847 897
Email: enquiries@blackmountain.co.uk
Website: www.blackmountain.co.uk

Beacon biking

The Brecon Beacons has some of the UK's best mountain biking routes with plenty of remote tracks and some hair-raising descents. You can either hire a bike from the centre or bring your own and learn new techniques from the Black Mountain Activities leaders for coping with the rough stuff. There is also a wide choice of quiet back roads for those looking for a gentler experience. The course price includes a helmet, repair kit, pump and maps.

Activity prices: Guided biking courses (including bike hire) cost £30 per day or £20 for a half-day trip. Bike hire only costs £16 per day, £9 per half-day.

Accommodation: Not included in the price. There is a range of accommodation available locally and the centre will advise you.

Food: Not included.

Equipment supplied: Bikes and helmets are available.

What to take: Personal biking clothing and suitable footwear.

When to go: Year round.

Established: 1992

Safety: All the centre's staff are fully qualified in their respective sports, hold first aid qualifications and are highly professional. All equipment used meets national safety standards. The centre is licensed by the AALA and the Welsh Tourist Board.

Insurance: The centre is insured though clients may wish to take out separate insurance too.

Methods of payment: Personal cheque and cash.

Booking information: Advance booking is recommended though late bookings may be possible.

Nearest airport: Depends on tour. Cardiff and Bristol are nearest to the centre.

Nearest rail station: Depends on the itinerary. Hereford and Abergavenny are nearest to the centre.

COMPASS HOLIDAYS
48 Shurdington Road, Cheltenham, Gloucestershire GL53 0JE
Phone: +44 (0)1242 250 642
Fax: +44 (0)1242 529 730

Email: compass.holidays@bigfoot.com
Website: http://dialspace.dial.pipex.com/town/road/xdt51/index.htm

Biking through the Heart of England
With some of Britain's prettiest countryside as a backdrop and the easy accessibility from the M4 and M5 motorways, the Cotswolds and Wiltshire are perfect places for a short break on your mountain bike. Compass Holidays offer a wide range of tour options, from one day to one week, that take you over the mud tracks and quiet back roads of the area. Some are guided, though most are self-guided. For riders just starting out in mountain biking, there are several tuition courses on offer that teach you the proper techniques for dealing with the rough stuff. At the end of it all, you can relax in your hotel and recharge the batteries for the next day's challenge.

Activity prices: There are a huge number of tours available at varying prices, but they start from £66 per person for a one day/two night break in B&B accommodation.
Accommodation: Included in the price. Ranges from pubs and B&B to farmhouses and luxury hotels.
Equipment supplied: Bikes (suspension or normal), helmets, locks, water bottles, maps, route directions.
What to take: Personal clothing, cycling gloves and shoes.
When to go: Year round.
Food: Breakfast is included, all other meals are optional.
Established: 1990
Safety: Qualified guides lead guided tours. Compass Holidays is a member of the Heart of England Tourist Board and the West Country Tourist Board.
Insurance: Clients need to arrange their own insurance. The bikes are insured by Compass.
Methods of payment: VISA, Mastercard, personal cheque, cash.
Booking information: Advance booking is advised. Payment is due eight weeks prior to departure. A deposit of £50 per person is required with booking.
Cancellation charges apply, from 75% with 27 days' or more notice to 100% for less than 27 days.
Nearest airport: Depends on tour.
Nearest rail station: Depends on tour.

CYCLING ADVENTURE TOURS LTD
Flat 4, 74 Lexham Gardens, Kensington, London W8 5JB
Phone: +44 (0)207 835 0288
Fax: +44 (0) 207 835 0288
Email: cycling@venturetours.co.uk
Website: www.venturetours.co.uk

Mountain biking throughout the UK
From the South Downs Way to the southern Cotswolds, England
offers some of the finest mountain biking in Europe. Cycling
Adventure Tours provides a huge variety of rides from weekend
wanders to multi-day mountain rides. Rides are graded from A
(complete beginner) to F (an experienced rider with a high level of
fitness). One of the highlights on offer is a seven-day C2C (or 'Sea to
Sea') across the Lake District and the Pennines for £413, which
includes a guide, all accommodation and food, luggage transfer, and
rail travel to and from London. Another classic is a four-day route
along the excellent trails of the South Downs for just £209 – because
of the chalk bedrock, they rarely, if ever, get muddy, providing ideal
riding conditions all year round.

Activity prices: Guided weekend trips start from £58 with an early booking
discount of £20. A two-week trip costs around £770, with an early booking
discount of £30. Self-led trips start at £58 for a weekend and £530 for a two-
week trip.
Accommodation: B&B accommodation is included in the price on all trips.
Food: Breakfast and packed lunches are included in the price and evening
meals are usually taken in pubs near to the accommodation.
What to take: A suitable mountain bike. A rack and panniers are also
recommended to carry luggage.
When to go: Year round.
Equipment supplied: None provided, but bike hire can be arranged on request.
Established: 1998
Safety: No formal qualifications, just four years' experience.
Insurance: Travel insurance is recommended but is not provided.
Methods of payment: Cash, cheques, travellers' cheques, electronic transfer,

Transcash and Eurogiro. Foreign currency transactions may attract additional charges.

Booking information: A 5% deposit is required to secure a booking.

Nearest airport: Depends on the itinerary.

Nearest rail station: Depends on the itinerary. Travel can be arranged from any UK station to the start point of a trip.

PEAK ACTIVITIES

Rock Lea Activity Training Centre, Station Road, Hathersage,
Hope Valley, Derbyshire S32 1DD
Phone: +44 (0)1433 650 345
Fax: +44 (0)1433 650 342
Email: admin@iain.co.uk
Website: www.iain.co.uk

Peak pedalling

With its base in the heart of the delightfully scenic Derbyshire Peak District, Peak Activities is perfectly located for exploring the trails and byways of the national park. The trails run alongside pine-fringed reservoirs, such as Derwent and Howden, and through dramatic mountain landscapes. With your experienced guides to show you the route, you can just relax and enjoy the biking. The guides will also fill you in on the history and the wildlife that you encounter along the way. Routes can be as tough or as easy as you desire, though most rides last around three to four hours per day. The supplied mountain bikes are well maintained and feature 15, 18 or 21 speed gears.

Activity prices: A two-day weekend mountain biking tour costs £85 per person, including bike, helmet, mechanic, guide and support vehicle.

Accommodation: Not included in the tour price. There is a large range of options within easy reach of the centre, ranging from hostels and B&B to farmhouses and hotels.

Food: Not included in tour price but there are plenty of local eateries to suit all budgets.

Equipment supplied: Bikes, helmets, repair kits, bad weather clothing if necessary.

What to take: Personal cycling clothing, gloves and shoes.

When to go: Year round.

Established: 1979

Safety: All the guides and instructors used by Peak Activities are qualified in their relevant fields and have first aid qualifications too. Staff carry radios and first aid kits. The company is licensed by the AALA to run biking tours year round in the UK and is a member of the Heart of England Tourist Board. Supplied specialist equipment is of a high standard and regularly maintained and replaced.

Insurance: All Peak Activity tours are fully insured for public and third party liability. Optional additional insurance can be taken out to guard against cancellation, illness, loss of property etc.

Methods of payment: VISA, Mastercard, Eurocard, personal cheques.

Booking information: A 50% deposit is requested with all bookings.

Nearest airport: Leeds (45 mins), Manchester (45 mins), Birmingham (90 mins) or Sheffield (12 mins). Transfers can be arranged.

Nearest rail station: Hathersage. Transfers can be arranged.

MOUNTAINEERING

Often difficult to define, mountaineering can perhaps best be described as the skills of walking, climbing and navigation all rolled into one. Typically it refers to these activities in winter conditions, when the potential for danger is far greater and the necessary skills for safe participation more specialised.

Matterhorn – the fourth dimension

The gnarly and daunting Matterhorn is one of the best-known mountains in the world and to climb it just once in your lifetime would be a feat worthy of champagne. On 19 August 1992, Hans Kammerlander and guide Diego Wellig descended back down off the Matterhorn for the fourth time . . . in just one day! Leaving at midnight on the 18th, the two were already starting their second ascent by 7 a.m. and had made it back to the summit for the third time by 4 p.m. and the fourth time by 9 p.m. At 11.26 p.m., they were back at the Hornli Refuge and celebrating a new record of 23 hours and 26 minutes. Go on, you can surely do it at least once!

Skills to be mastered include use of crampons and ice axes, avalanche avoidance, mountain first aid and basic ropework, not to mention pinpoint navigation – in a whiteout, the last thing you want to do is wander too close to a hidden gully. If all that sounds a bit melodramatic, then rest assured the rewards are worth the extra effort. Mountain landscapes are transformed in winter, and even in bad weather they can offer cold, crisp mountain air and challenges that don't even exist in summer. Many of these skills are simply part and parcel of climbing mountains, of which more technical ice climbing can be a vital component, but for many it's simply a way of extending hill walking into the winter months.

Winter climbing grades

Grade I – Uncomplicated average angled snow climbs, having no pitches under adequate snow conditions. These routes can on occasions present cornice difficulties or have dangerous outruns in the event of a fall.

Grade II – Gullies containing either individual or minor pitches or high angle snow with difficult cornice exits. The easier buttresses that under winter snow cover provide more continuous difficulty. Probably equates to the technical standard of Very Difficult.

Grade III – Serious climbs which should only be attempted by parties experienced in winter ascents. Probably equates to the technical standard of Severe.

Grade IV – Routes that are of sustained difficulty yet too short to be included in the highest grade.

Grade V – Routes of sustained difficulty that provide serious expeditions only to be climbed when conditions are favourable.

FRANCE

INTERNATIONAL SCHOOL OF MOUNTAINEERING, SWITZERLAND

Hafod Tan y Graig, Nant Gwynant, Gwynedd LL55 4NW, UK
Phone: +44 (0)1766 890441
Fax: +44 (0)1766 890599
Email: ism@dial.pipex.com
Website: http//:ds.dial.pipex.com/ism

Explore the Mont Blanc Massif

From the Mont Blanc Special to the Matterhorn Ascent, ISM offers a chance to climb the classics in a safe and supervised environment. For those who aren't prepared to go out on a limb, Softer Summits is a course designed for people with little or no experience. Mountain hotels and hot showers are the order of the day, and the course offers climbing at two levels. Level 1 covers the basic techniques and ropework needed for a day's climbing, while the Level 2 course includes an ascent of a high Alpine summit. At the other extreme, the Oberland Giants is a multi-day course that aims to climb the Eiger, Monch and Jungfrau. If you fall somewhere in between, Classic 4000m Peaks might be more your bag.

Activity prices: From £345 to £1,085 for a six-day course.

Accommodation: All Alpine courses include hotel accommodation.

Food: Alpine courses include full board.

Equipment supplied: All specialist equipment is provided.

What to take: Personal climbing clothing and footwear.

When to go: Year round.

Established: 1960

Safety: All guides hold the International Carnet, the highest qualification available in mountaineering.

Insurance: Relevant insurance is required for all Alpine courses.

Methods of payment: All common payment methods accepted.

Booking information: Contact ISM for booking form and full terms and conditions.

Nearest airport: Geneva.

Nearest rail station: Leysin.

MOUNTAIN ACTIVITY EXPERIENCE

93 avenue Michel Croz, 74400 Chamonix
Phone: +33 4 50 55 80 80
Fax: +33 4 53 48 50
Email: M.A.X@wanadoo.fr
Website: montblanconeline.fr/max/max.htm

Mountaineering in the Chamonix Valley

As the spiritual home of Alpine mountaineering, Chamonix and the satellite summits of the Mont Blanc range can be a little daunting, but even celebrated climbers had to start somewhere. Basic ice climbing courses and glacier touring from one to five days are available for the uninitiated, while refresher courses are offered for those who want to acquire autonomy and security in their skills. Weather permitting, days are very much geared to individual requirements, so you can choose between granite, ice and ridge routes – or leave all the decision-making up to the guides! Ascents of Mont Blanc, multi-day routes around the mountain and hut-to-hut itineraries are also possible. Personal climbing gear (harness, climbing boots, helmet, ice axes) is not included on any of the courses, but can be rented for a nominal fee.

Activity prices: Private tuition costs FFr1,350 per day, FFr750 per half-day. Group rates (four to six people) are FFr340 per person for a full day and FFr190 for a half-day. Initiation and one-day outings costs from FFr500 per person. A two-day ascent of Mont Blanc costs FFr2,650 per person. An introductory five-day course costs from FFr3,350 per person (six people) to FFr4,230 per person (two people). Five-day improvement courses cost FFr3,400 per person for three people and FFr8,000 for private guiding.

Accommodation: Not included in the price.

Food: Picnic and half-board are included only on longer courses (five days or more).

Equipment supplied: Technical group equipment such as ropes and climbing hardware.

What to take: Helmets, harnesses, ice axes and crampons are not included, but can be rented at the centre.

When to go: Year round, depending on experience.

Established: 1997

Safety: All instructors are nationally qualified high mountain guides.

Insurance: Clients must provide their own insurance.

Methods of payment: Cheques and cash.

Booking information: A deposit is required to secure a booking. Cancellation within a month of the course forfeits the deposit.

Nearest airport: Geneva.

Nearest rail station: Chamonix.

ODYSSEE MONTAGNE
101 Les Marmottières, 74310 Les Houches
Phone: +33 (0)4 50 54 36 01
Fax: +33 (0)4 50 54 35 74
Email: odyssee@odyssee-montagne.fr
Website: http://odyssee-monatgne.fr

Up at the mountaineering mecca
Chamonix is a mecca for mountaineers, and many of the classic routes in the surrounding mountains are available through Odyssée Montagne, which offers two and six-day courses for all the main summits, including Mont Blanc and the Matterhorn. The longer the course, the higher the chances of getting to the top, but success also depends on fitness levels, experience and weather conditions. Mont Blanc via the traditional route is not considered a technically difficult climb, but it does require determination, fitness and appropriate acclimatisation. The Barre des Ecrins, the Alps' southernmost summit, is another long, relatively gentle climb that offers plenty of opportunity to drink in the view. Guiding for all the main summits is also available.

Activity prices: Courses from FFr3,950 for six days and five nights. Guiding for one or two-day ascents from FFr2,350 to FFr4,850 for up to four clients, depending on the difficulty of the climb.
Accommodation: Mountain hut accommodation included.
Food: All food is included in the price.
Equipment supplied: All technical equipment such as rope, crabs, etc. is supplied.
What to take: Personal equipment such as rucksack, boots, harness and ice axe.
When to go: June to September.
Established: 1993
Safety: All mountain guides are members of the Ecole National de Ski et d'Alpinisme.
Insurance: Comprehensive insurance can be provided at an additional cost of 5% of the full price.

Methods of payment: Travellers' cheques, VISA, Mastercard, SWIFT bank transfer, etc.

Booking information: A deposit of 30% is required at the time of booking. Bookings will be accepted no later than 15 days before departure.

Nearest airport: Geneva. Airport collection available on request.

Nearest rail station: Saint Gervais.

SWITZERLAND

ADVENTURE'S BEST

PO Box 9, Via Basilea 28, CH-6903 Lugano
Phone: +41 91 966 11 14
Fax: +41 91 966 12 13
Email: info@asbest.ch
Website: www.asbest.ch

Scaling the heights of southern Switzerland

Based in Ticino, the southernmost state of Switzerland, Adventure's Best has been running mountaineering courses in the region for five years. The region is characterised year-round by Alpine lakes, roaring rivers and glacier-capped mountains rising up to 3,400 metres. All courses and climbs are led by a nationally qualified Alpine mountain guide. Accommodation is not included in the price but can be arranged at the centre at a budget to suit.

Activity prices: Contact the centre for the latest prices.

Accommodation: Not included in the price, but is available at the centre. Shared dorms cost an additional SFr20 per person, a double room SFr40 per person, a double room with en suite bath/shower SFr50 per person and a single room with en suite bath/shower SFr60 per person.

Food: Not included in the price, but is available at the centre. Buffet breakfast costs SFr15 per person.

Equipment supplied: All specialist equipment is provided.

What to take: Personal clothing.

When to go: Year round.

Established: 1994

Safety: All instructors hold recognised qualifications from the relevant
national or international governing body.

Insurance: Clients are responsible for arranging their own insurance.

Methods of payment: VISA, Mastercard, Amex, travellers' cheques and cash.

Booking information: No deposit required.

Nearest airport: Lugano-Agno (5 km).

Nearest rail station: Lugano (200 metres).

ALPIN CENTER ZERMATT

Mountain Guides' Association, 3920 Zermatt
Phone: +41 (0)27 966 2460
Fax: +41 (0)27 966 2469
Email: alpincenter@zermatt.ch
Website: www.zermatt.ch/alpincenter

Climb the Matterhorn

Over the past few years the Matterhorn has become almost fashion-
able, yet it remains a very serious undertaking for experienced
mountaineers. However, there are plenty of other peaks surrounding
it that can provide ideal training for eventually taking on the big one.
The Alpin Center runs a whole range of mountaineering courses,
many of which summit on peaks over 4,000 metres high, to suit every
ability level. One of the easiest high peaks that offers superb views is
the 4,164 metre high Breithorn. It can be climbed in a day and is ideal
for mountain enthusiasts. Climbing Riffelhorn is deemed to be the
best place to prepare for climbing the Matterhorn as it offers a variety
of climbs at all degrees of difficulty. Whichever peak you choose, you
won't have time to get bored!

Activity prices: Day ascents cost from SFr120 (e.g. Breithorn) up to SFr250.
The Riffelhorn costs SFr180. The Matterhorn is only available on a 1:1
guide:client ratio and costs from SFr710 depending on the route.

Accommodation: A wide range of accommodation is available in the Zermatt
area. The centre can assist with arranging it. Half-board accommodation is
included on some of the courses.

Food: Food is included on some of the courses. There are plenty of eating options in Zermatt.

Equipment supplied: Specialist equipment is available.

What to take: Specialist equipment that you own. Check with centre for recommended list. Personal mountain clothing and suitable footwear.

When to go: Generally June to October with a few local variations on some peaks.

Established: 1982

Safety: All the Alpin Center guides are fully licensed, qualified and highly experienced. You are in very safe hands.

Insurance: Clients must arrange their own personal accident insurance and it is recommended that you also take out Rescue Insurance with Air Zermatt for SFr20 per week or SFr30 per year. Forms available from the Alpin Center.

Methods of payment: VISA, cash or bank transfer.

Booking information: Advance booking is essential (at least two weeks for the Matterhorn).

Nearest airport: Zurich.

Nearest rail station: Zermatt.

FOUR SEASONS GUIDES

Chalet L'Aurore, 1936 Verbier
Phone: +41 27 771 7683
Fax: +41 27 771 1603
Email: hans@verbier.ch
Website: www.swissguides.com

A personal Swiss peak

Verbier is ideally located for attempting to summit on a host of 3,000 and 4,000 metre high summits, some famous, such as Mont Blanc and the Eiger, others not so well known but still magnificent adventures in themselves. Hiring a private guide gives you the flexibility to design your own programme of acclimatisation and summit bagging, so you can do it as quickly or slowly as your abilities and desires dictate. The UIAGM qualified guides have extensive experience and some of the best safety practices around. If you fancy mixing things a bit, you could try climbing a peak in the Pinennine Alps and then skiing back down again.

Activity prices: Guiding fees are SFr400 per day for one to two clients. For this, the guide will also arrange local travel and hotel bookings and the itinerary (clients pay directly to the hotel, bus company, etc.).

Accommodation: Not included in the price. There is a large range of accommodation options in the area and the guide will help you to arrange it.

Food: Not included in the price, but there are plenty of eating options in the area. While in the mountains, the client pays for his own food and that of the guide.

Equipment supplied: Specialist equipment can be hired in Verbier.

What to take: All specialist mountain clothing.

When to go: Year round; winter for ski-mountaineering options.

Established: 1990

Safety: All guides hold UIAGM qualifications.

Insurance: Clients are recommended to buy helicopter rescue insurance which costs SFr30 for one year.

Methods of payment: VISA, Mastercard, Amex, travellers' cheques and cash.

Booking information: Payment in full is required one week in advance. Full refunds are available for acceptable cancellation.

Nearest airport: Geneva. Transfers can be arranged.

Nearest rail station: Le Chable. Transfers can be arranged.

UNITED KINGDOM

ALAN KIMBER

Calluna, Heathercroft, Fort William PH33 6RE
Phone: +44 (0)1397 700 451
Fax: +44 (0)1397 700 489
Email: mountain@guide.u-net.com
Website: www.guide.u-net.com

Snowy route to adventure

Having climbed in many of the world's greatest mountain ranges, Alan Kimber is one of the most experienced mountain guides in the UK. He offers both weekend and five-day mountaineering courses in the Scottish Highlands, with the former aimed at people who want to get started or improve their skills. On the weekend course, you will learn about choosing equipment, navigation and avalanche evaluation, with plenty of time in the mountains to practise. There are instructional videos available throughout the course. The longer course also covers snow and ice climbing techniques, poor weather navigation and winter survival techniques.

Activity prices: The weekend course costs £105 per person including self-catering accommodation or £160 for full board in local hotel. The five-day course costs £250 for instruction only, £300 self-catering or £466 in a hotel.

Accommodation: On-site self-catering accommodation is available in the beautifully located and homely Calluna Lodge. Various room options. Hotel accommodation can be arranged.

Food: Not included in the price. Accommodation is self-catering. It is just a ten-minute walk to the centre of Fort William.

Equipment supplied: Technical climbing equipment is supplied. If you don't have your own plastic boots, you can hire them at £5 per day.

What to take: Personal clothing, footwear and other items. Full list sent on booking.

When to go: January to April.

Established: 1972

Safety: All instructors are MLTB qualified. The centre is approved by the Mountaineering Council of Scotland and the British Mountaineering Council.

Insurance: Mountaineering insurance is available from the centre and costs £10.70 for seven days.

Methods of payment: VISA, Mastercard, cheque, cash (3.5% surcharge on credit card payments).

Booking information: Advance booking is essential. A non-refundable 50% deposit is payable on booking. Balance paid on arrival. Cancellation within four weeks of course start date forfeits the whole course price unless replacement client is found.

Nearest airport: Glasgow.

Nearest rail station: Fort William.

AVALON ADVENTURE

The Mill House, Dulford, Cullompton, Devon EX15 2ED
Phone: +44 (0)1884 266 646
Fax: +44 (0)1884 266 646
Email: avalon-adventure@dial.pipex.com
Website: http://dialspace.dial.pipex.com/avalon.adventure/

Scottish or Alpine summits

Avalon Adventure is based in Devon where snow is rare so they operate their winter mountaineering courses in Scotland or the Alps. The Winter Mountaincraft course is designed for experienced hill walkers wishing to learn the skills for Scottish winter trips. During the course, you will climb suitable ridge routes and simple gullies and learn about winter navigation, ice axe and crampon use, snowcraft and survival techniques. An advanced course is also available for people wishing to progress on to more demanding terrain. The courses are run with a client:instructor ratio of 3:1.

Activity prices: The Winter Mountaincraft course costs £350 including B&B accommodation.

Accommodation: Included in the price.

Food: Breakfast is included.

Equipment supplied: All specialist equipment is supplied.

What to take: Personal clothing, suitable footwear.

When to go: January to February.

Established: 1992

Safety: All the instructors are fully qualified and hold first aid qualifications. The centre is licensed by the AALA and is approved by the Association of Mountaineering Instructors.

Insurance: The centre is insured though clients may wish to take out separate insurance too.

Methods of payment: VISA, Mastercard, cheques and cash.

Booking information: Advance booking is essential.

Nearest airport: Exeter. Transfers can be arranged.

Nearest rail station: Exeter. Transfers can be arranged.

CUILLIN GUIDES

Stac Lee, Glenbrittle, Isle of Skye, Inverness-shire IV47 8TA
Phone: +44 (0)1478 640 289
Fax: N/A
Email: Not available. Booking form on website.
Website: www.w-o-w.com/clients/cuillin

Skye high snow and ice

The Isle of Skye off Scotland's west coast is renowned for its dramatic wilderness scenery and the winter climbing matches the surroundings. Cuillin Guides know the area intimately and can always take you to the location with the best winter conditions. They offer three winter courses. The Mountaineering Skills course covers ice-axe self-arrest, step-cutting, movement on steep ground with and without crampons, navigation and survival techniques. There are just four clients per instructor so you will get personal attention. The Winter Mountaincraft course is designed for people with previous winter skills who want to take on more challenging routes, such as Devil's Ridge. The centre also offers a snow and ice climbing course.

Activity prices: The Mountaineering Skills course costs £200 and the Winter Mountaincraft course costs £225. The snow and ice climbing course costs £275.

Accommodation: Included in the price. Accommodation is in bothies or bunkhouses in the mountains.

Food: Not included.

Equipment supplied: Crampons and ice axes.

What to take: A full equipment list is supplied on booking.

When to go: January to March.

Established: 1972

Safety: All the guides are qualified mountain leaders.

Insurance: Clients need to arrange their own insurance.

Methods of payment: Personal cheque, cash.

Booking information: Advance booking is essential. A deposit of £20 is payable.

Nearest airport: Glasgow.

Nearest rail station: Kyle of Lochalsh.

KEVIN WALKER MOUNTAIN ACTIVITIES

74 Beacons Park, Brecon, Powys LD3 9BQ
Phone: +44 (0)1874 625111
Fax: +44 (0)1874 625111
Email: kevin@mountain-acts.freeserve.co.uk
Website: http://www.mountain-acts.freeserve.co.uk

Mountaineering in Snowdonia and the Brecon Beacons
Kevin Walker has over 20 years' experience leading courses in the Welsh Mountains and has been involved with MLTB courses for much of this time. He offers three courses that could be considered to come under the heading of mountaineering. A one-day course covering Security on Steep Ground is a must for those who want to progress safely and confidently on to increasingly steeper and more rugged terrain. In addition to hand, foot and body positions, the course covers route selection and simple rope techniques – no rock climbing is involved. As a logical extension to this one-day taster, the five-day Mountaincraft course progresses on to safety and emergency procedures, essential navigation and hazard recognition. Those wishing to go higher and steeper might want to consider the two-day Scrambling course, which takes you into the grey area between hill-walking and rock-climbing proper and includes some of the classic routes in Snowdonia National Park. Participants must be over 18 years of age and in reasonably good physical condition.

Activity prices: From £135 for a two-day course.
Accommodation: Not included in the price, although a good range of accommodation is available locally – see the brochure for recommendations.
Food: Clients to arrange their own.
Equipment supplied: All specialist equipment is provided.
What to take: Outdoor clothing and footwear suitable for the prevailing conditions (available for hire if necessary) – if in doubt, call ahead for advice.
When to go: Year round.
Established: 1979.

Safety: Kevin Walker Mountain Activities is a MLTB recognised centre, and all instructors are MLTB qualified.

Insurance: The centre carries indemnity insurance for all activities and can advise on personal accident insurance if required.

Methods of payment: Cash, cheques from British banks and sterling travellers' cheques.

Booking information: Reservations essential. A 20% deposit secures a booking, with the balance due three weeks prior to the course. Cancellation four to six weeks before the course forfeits 30% of the fee, two to four weeks before 50% and less than two weeks before 100%.

Nearest airport: Cardiff (south Wales) or Manchester (north Wales), depending on the course.

Nearest rail station: Abergavenny (south Wales) or Betws-y-Coed (north Wales).

MOUNTAIN CRAFT

Glennfinnan, Fort William PH37 4LT
Phone: +44 (0)1397 722213
Fax: +44 (0)1397 722213
Email: mail@mountaincraft.co.uk
Website: www.mountaincraft.co.uk

Winter and summer mountaineering in Scotland

Based in Fort William in the shadow of Ben Nevis, the highest mountain in the British Isles, Mountain Craft is able to offer some of the most exciting and challenging winter mountaineering and ice climbing in the world. Also within reach is Glencoe, Scotland's premier winter mountaineering arena, not to mention Torridon, the Cairngorms and the spectacular Cuillin Ridge on the Isle of Skye. Director Nigel Gregory is a MLTB instructor who has climbed and guided all over the world, and Mountain Craft specialises in courses for experienced hill walkers who want to progress to walking, mountaineering and ice climbing in the winter. More advanced courses are also available for experienced winter wanderers who want to progress on to steeper snow and ice. Private guiding and instruction can also be arranged.

Activity prices: Introductory winter mountaincraft weekends from £115. Five-day introductory course from £250.

Accommodation: Not included in the price, but can be arranged locally at a budget to suit.

Food: Not included in the price.

Equipment supplied: All technical climbing equipment is supplied.

What to take: Personal climbing clothing and boots.

When to go: January to April.

Established: 1996

Safety: All instructors are MLTB qualified.

Insurance: Insurance can be arranged directly through Mountain Craft.

Methods of payment: VISA, Mastercard and cheque.

Booking information: Advance booking and £75 deposit required.

Nearest airport: Glasgow.

Nearest rail station: Fort William.

PLAS Y BRENIN

National Mountain Centre, Capel Curig, Conwy LL24 0ET
Phone: +44 (0)1690 720 214
Fax: +44 (0)1690 720 394
Email: info@pyb.co.uk
Website: www.pyb.co.uk

Explore Scottish and Welsh Winter peaks

To feel confident above the snowline you need to be competent with your winter skills and the range of courses offered by Plas y Brenin are designed to achieve just that. In Scotland, you climb among the dramatic mountain scenery surrounding Glencoe and learn about use of crampons and ice axes, winter navigation, avalanche awareness, building snow shelters and rope techniques for overcoming cornices. Practical instruction sessions are followed by ascents of some of the classic Munros where the snow and ice conditions are always challenging due to the fickle nature of Scottish weather. In north Wales, a more flexible course structure allows students to take advantage of the even less predictable conditions in the north-facing cwms of Snowdonia. Once your confidence is cemented, you can head for the higher Alps to test out your new-found skills on one of the centre's Alpine Mountaineering courses.

Activity prices: The five-day Scottish Winter Mountaineering course costs £365; the similar Welsh course costs £295. A five-day Alpine Trek costs £270.
Accommodation: Prices for most courses include shared accommodation. The Alpine course prices do not include accommodation and food for two nights in a Valley dortoir and four nights in mountain huts.
Food: Most course prices include full board.
Equipment supplied: All specialist equipment and clothing is provided.
What to take: Personal clothing and your own equipment if you prefer to use it.
When to go: January to March for the UK and July for the Alpine Trek.
Established: 1954
Safety: All instructors hold nationally recognised qualifications and only the most capable and experienced are employed. The centre is licensed by the AALA. Great emphasis is placed on safety and the high quality equipment used is regularly checked and replaced.
Insurance: The centre carries public liability insurance for all activities and recommends that clients take out independent insurance against curtailment and cancellation of their course (available from the centre) and a personal accident policy.
Methods of payment: VISA, Mastercard, Access, personal cheque, cash.
Booking information: Reservations must be made in advance and a deposit is required.
Nearest airport: Depends on tour.
Nearest rail station: Depends on tour.

MULTI-ACTIVITY

Multi-activity courses are ideal for people who can't decide what sport they want to do or for people who get bored easily and want always to be doing something new. If you are new to the world of adventure sports then these centres offer you an introductory taster to a whole range of sports in a short space of time so you can see which ones you fancy taking up more seriously. The emphasis changes from centre to centre with some concentrating more on watersports, some on mountain sports, usually influenced by their location. The sport taster sessions can last for anything from a couple of hours to a day or so, and you can often mix and match the sports to suit your own requirements, especially if you book as a group. The sort of sports on offer include abseiling, rock climbing, windsurfing, sailing, caving and canyoning. An adventure feast indeed.

AUSTRIA

SPORTSCHULE FANKHAUSER – TIROL RAFTING
Dorfstrasse 17, A-6382 Kirchdorf, Tirol
Phone: +43 5352 62233
Fax: +43 5352 62587
Email: fanky@netwing.at
Website: www.tirolrafting.com

An adventure extravaganza in the Tirol
The Tirol region of Austria is one the most dramatic and appealing areas in Europe and the potential for adventure is almost limitless.

Sportschule Fankhauser is ideally located to take advantage of all the possibilities and they offer two multi-sport packages to suit the adrenaline junkie. Their Super Sports Day involves mountain biking, hiking, rafting and zipping down a flying fox (a cable stretched across a gorge). It all takes place in the stunning Kirchdorf area. If you really want to sate your adventure appetite then try their Adventure Week course where you do all of the above sports and canyoning, kayaking and rollerblading too. Phew!

Activity prices: The Super Sports Day costs Sch880 and the Adventure Week costs Sch3880, with the latter including accommodation.

Accommodation: Included in price for the Adventure week and for the Super Sports Day it is available at the centre, either camping or in a bunkhouse, or in a private hotel.

Food: Breakfast is included on the week course and it is available at the centre on the day course. Half-board packages are also available at the centre.

Equipment supplied: All specialist rafting equipment is supplied for all the sports.

What to take: Swimsuit, suitable footwear for hiking/biking.

When to go: Year round, daily.

Established: 1985

Safety: All the guides hold national qualifications in their specific sports. The centre is approved by the Austrian Tourist Office, the Austrian Rafting Association and the Austrian Canyoning Association.

Insurance: The centre has liability insurance but clients should arrange their own accident policy.

Methods of payment: VISA, Mastercard, Eurocard, travellers' cheques and cash.

Booking information: Advance booking is essential at least one day ahead.

No is deposit required and there are no cancellation penalties.

Nearest airport: Innsbruck, Salzburg or Munich. Transfers can be arranged.

Nearest rail station: St Johann in the Tyrol. Transfers can be arranged.

SPAIN

CASA DE LA MONTAñA

33556 Asturias
Phone: +34 8 5844189
Fax: +34 8 5844189
Email: casamont@mundivia.es
Website: http://personales.mundivia.es/casamont

Multi-activities in the Picos de Europa

The Picos de Europa was Spain's first National Park, and with views over the Atlantic Ocean from the 2,648 metre summit of Torrecerredo Peak, it remains one of the most spectacular and least visited mountain ranges in Europe. To take full advantage of this mountain sports paradise, Casa de la Montaña runs five-day multi-activity breaks with full-board accommodation, instruction and equipment included. La Casa includes a TV and lecture room, a kitchen and restaurant, an information office for those who would prefer to make their own plans, a games lawn and mountain bike rental. Canoeing, mountain biking and horse riding are all included in the itinerary, which makes the most of the landscape that surrounds the centre. It is necessary to be able to swim to take part in the canoeing, but no experience is required for either of the other activities, which are taken at a relatively leisurely pace.

Activity prices: A one-week multi-activity holiday costs around Pta59,000 per person (minimum six people), including transport, guided hiking and full board accommodation. Single days start from Pta4,000 per person, weekends from Pta8,500 and multi-day trips from Pta18,500, not including accommodation.
Accommodation: Full-board mountain refuge and centre accommodation is included in the price.
Food: All meals are included in the price.
Equipment supplied: All specialist equipment is provided.
What to take: Personal clothing, good boots, etc.
When to go: June to September.

Established: 1987

Safety: Mountain Guide Fernando Ruiz is a Professional Mountain Leader of the Asociacion Espagnola de Guias de Montaña (AEGM).

Insurance: Multi-activity insurance is available on request at an additional cost.

Methods of payment: Cash, VISA.

Booking information: A 30% deposit is required to secure a booking.

Nearest airport: Asturias & Santander (124 km). Pick-up from Santander Airport can be arranged for small groups at minimal cost.

Nearest rail station: Arriondas (22 km). Transfers can be arranged.

UNITED KINGDOM

CALL OF THE WILD
69 Dulais Road, Seven Sisters, Neath SA10 9ER
Phone: +44 (0)1639 700 388
Fax: +44 (0)1639 701 052
Email: info@callofthewild.co.uk
Website: www.callofthewild.co.uk

Mix and match adventure in Wales

The Brecon Beacons is an ideal playground for people looking for a taste of several adventure sports in a short period of time and there's great nightlife to unwind with at the end of an active day. Call of the Wild offer three levels of multi-activity courses from Untamed for the novice adventurer looking for a thrill to the intermediate Wild course and the Extreme course for more adventurous clients. Activities covered vary with each course but they include caving and pot-holing, mountain biking, climbing and abseiling, kayaking, canyoning and even scuba diving, hang gliding and paragliding. All the specialist gear is supplied and the course price is inclusive of full-board accommodation. You are just left to concentrate on having fun.

Activity prices: Prices depend on the accommodation chosen, either standard, premium or luxury. The Untamed and Wild courses cost £395/£440/£725 (or up to £1,000 depending on choice of hotel). The Extreme course costs £450/£510/£800 (to £1,200). There are no hidden extras.

Accommodation: Full-board accommodation is included, in standard places such as bunkhouses or farmhouses, premium places, such 2/3-star hotels or guesthouses, or luxury, such as 4/5-star hotels.

Food: All meals are included in the price.

Equipment supplied: All specialist equipment is provided.

What to take: Personal clothing, good walking boots.

When to go: Year round.

Established: 1998

Safety: All the centre's instructors hold national qualifications in their relevant activity and a first aid qualification. The centre is licensed by the AALA.

Insurance: Included in price.

Methods of payment: VISA, Mastercard, Switch, Delta, cheques, travellers' cheques, postal orders and cash (euros, US dollars or sterling).

Booking information: Advance booking is recommended but late bookings can often be accommodated. A 10% deposit is required on booking with the balance due 30 days before the holiday. If holiday is cancelled within 28 days of start date 100% is payable, or a credit is offered towards future dates.

Nearest airport: Cardiff.

Nearest rail station: Swansea or Neath.

ORIENTEERING

Put simply, orienteering involves navigating around a fixed course, often across remote and rugged terrain. At its most basic level it's not much more than competitive hiking, with walkers trying to find the quickest routes between checkpoints. At the most competitive level, however, it can mean complicated route planning, nightmare navigation and constant fell running for hours, or even days, on end.

Finding yourself

As well as orthodox orienteering, there's a growing trend in Europe towards multi-activity races with a navigation requirement. The Raid Gauloises, Eco-Challenge and Elf Authentique Adventure are just three of the multi-day challenges that are as long as they are gruelling, but there are shorter, more accessible races that are open to mere mortals. The Salomon Mountain Adventure is a series of two-day races throughout Europe that include mountain biking, orienteering, open canoeing and sea kayaking. No qualification is required and they are open to anyone who can put together a team of four. Other races in the UK include the Lowe Alpine Western Isles Challenge in Scotland's Inner Hebrides, the Karrimor International Mountain Marathon and the Hi-Tec Adventure Race Series. Running and map reading might not be your game, but if you like the sound of biking, hiking and kayaking in a competitive but friendly environment, then adventure racing might be just the jolly.

To prove the prescribed course has been completed, competitors have to punch unique hole-patterns in a card at each checkpoint. Often checkpoints are allocated points which contribute to an overall score – the further away the checkpoint and the harder it is to find, the more points it's worth. On a short, half-hour course the cost/benefit analysis for each checkpoint might be obvious, but in bad weather in the mountains, on a race lasting a day or more, route choice can mean the difference between winning and coming nowhere.

If all that sounds a bit daunting, orienteering needn't necessarily mean all pain and no pleasure. For many it's simply another way of enjoying the great outdoors with like-minded individuals who want to do more than just walk. Teamwork is often critical, making it a highly sociable adventure sport, and of course the fitness benefits are obvious. Runners who want something more from their training often turn to orienteering as an alternative and never look back. But be warned: it is addictive and side-effects include wearing lycra leggings and nylon base-layers with alarming frequency!

IRELAND

CELTIC ADVENTURES
Caherdaniel, Co. Kerry
Phone: +353 (0)66 9475 277
Fax: +353 (0)66 9475 277
Email: info@activity-ireland.com
Website: www.activity-ireland.com

Navigate the Irish hills
Based in the foothills of the MaeGillycuddy Reeks, near to the Derrynane National Park, Celtic Adventures is ideally located for organising orienteering runs into the surrounding countryside. Courses are tailor-made by qualified instructors to suit your own requirements and experience. Theory classes on navigation and mountain survival are also available to complement your orienteering skills. While the hills are not that high, conditions can be

challenging, though there are always wonderful views to compensate for the effort. In the evening, you can sit back in one of Caherdaniel's two pubs, listen to some Irish music and sup on a perfect pint of Guinness.

Activity prices: Trips are tailor-made to suit the clients' needs. Prices are based around I£20 per person per day from June to mid-August, I£18 otherwise. Discounts are available for students and school and scouting groups, except in December and January, depending on weather.

Accommodation: Hostel accommodation at I£8 or B&B at I£20, both per person/sharing basis. Holiday cottages and four-star campsite also available.

Food: Available at centre for approximately I£14 per day for all meals.

Equipment supplied: All specialist equipment provided.

What to take: Personal clothing and footwear.

When to go: Year round.

Established: 1988

Safety: All guides are fully qualified in their fields.

Insurance: Centre has insurance but it is recommended that clients arrange their own.

Methods of payment: VISA or personal cheque.

Booking information: Advance booking is recommended with payment requested at least 42 days in advance.

Nearest airport: Cork (2.5 hours) or Kerry (1.5 hours). Groups of clients travelling together can be collected from the airport.

Nearest rail station: Killarney (80 mins). Groups of clients travelling together can be collected from the station.

UNITED KINGDOM

PLAS Y BRENIN
National Mountain Centre, Capel Curig, Conwy LL24 0ET
Phone: +44 (0)1690 720 214
Fax: +44 (0)1690 720 394
Email: info@pyb.co.uk
Website: www.pyb.co.uk

Follow a compass needle in Snowdonia

The mountains and valleys of north Wales are full of interesting navigational challenges and the quickest and most efficient way to conquer them is to take Plas y Brenin's Introduction to Orienteering course. During an intensive weekend, you will learn about rough and fine navigation techniques, map setting, contour interpretation, pacing, using attack points and compass work. Even if you have no previous experience, you will be capable of competing in events by the end of the two days.

Activity prices: The introductory course costs £99.

Accommodation: Price includes shared accommodation.

Food: Course price includes full board.

Equipment supplied: All specialist equipment and clothing is provided.

What to take: Personal clothing and your own equipment if you prefer to use it.

When to go: March to November.

Established: 1954

Safety: All instructors hold nationally recognised qualifications and only the most capable and experienced are employed. The centre is licensed by the AALA. Great emphasis is placed on safety and the high quality equipment used is regularly checked and replaced.

Insurance: The centre carries public liability insurance for all activities and recommends that clients take out independent insurance against curtailment and cancellation of their course (available from the centre) and a personal accident policy.

Methods of payment: VISA, Mastercard, Access, personal cheque, cash.

Booking information: Reservations must be made in advance and a deposit is required.

Nearest airport: Manchester.

Nearest rail station: Llandudno. Free transfer available by prior arrangement.

PARAGLIDING

Ever since Icarus first fell from the skies beneath a blazing sun, man has been trying to find a way of flying like the birds. The Wright brothers came close at the turn of the century, but it wasn't until the invention of the hang glider in the late 1960s that pilots were able to fly with a full 360-degree view under power of wind alone. However, it was only in the late 1980s that paragliding took off as the most accessible and portable way to fly.

A paraglider basically consists of a large parachute-like canopy or wing that is attached to the pilot by a harness. To launch a paraglider, all the pilot needs is a hill and some wind in the right direction. The wing basically acts as a huge, lightweight aileron, providing lift when it has some forward speed. In the right conditions, paragliders can travel for hundreds of miles and reach heights of over 12,000 feet.

Despite the relatively recent ascent of the sport into popular parlance, paragliding is extremely well regulated in Europe, with a rigidly defined sequence of skills and courses leading to your very first solo flight. Many schools offer tandem taster sessions and one-day introductions, but for those who are bitten by the bug, this first day can usually be upgraded as part of a multi-day course. After that, mountain flying, cross-country courses and stunt sessions are just a few of the alternatives that await the certified pilot.

The secret to the success of paragliders is their simplicity. Easy to use, relatively cheap (a second-hand paraglider with all the kit can cost as little as £1,000) and weighing less than 20 kg, they can be flown from just about anywhere, by just about anyone. You don't need to be an athlete or an acrobat to master all you need to know about flying like the birds.

AUSTRIA

HIGH 5
Bahnhof 248, 6951 Lingenau
Phone: +43 5513 4140
Fax: +43 5513 4150
Email: office@outdoor.at
Website: www.outdoor.at

Fly beyond Lake Constance
High 5 is one of the leading outdoor centres in the country and their paragliding courses are suited to every level of ability. They have a number of launch sites to suit different wind conditions. There are spectacular views over the surrounding country so take your camera; just don't drop it! The instructors are all highly qualified and have many years of experience. After an exciting day flying, you have the option of spending the night sleeping in a teepee.

Activity prices: Paragliding courses cost from Sch980.
Accommodation: Available at centre, including teepees for exotic nights under canvas.
Food: Available at centre.
Equipment supplied: All specialist equipment is supplied.
What to take: Nothing special.
When to go: 1 May to 31 October.
Established: 1989
Safety: All the instructors at High 5 are nationally qualified. The centre is a member of the Austrian Outdoor Association.
Insurance: Full liability insurance cover is included in the price of the jump.
Methods of payment: Bank draft and cash.
Booking information: Advance booking is recommended.
Nearest airport: Zurich (1 hour).
Nearest rail station: Bregenz. Transfers can be arranged.

FRANCE

ALPINE FLYING CENTRE
The Flyer's Lodge, 216 rue de Bellevue, Les Houches, 74310
Phone: +33 (0)4 50 54 59 63
Fax: +33 (0)4 50 54 48 52
Email: flyerlodge@aol.com
Website: www.flyers-lodge.com

Soar over the Chamonix Valley
The stunning Alpine mountains around the Chamonix Valley offer some of the best thermal and cross-country flying in Europe, if not the world. The flying conditions change throughout the year so it is an ideal place to train. Spring is probably the best of all, though each distinct season has its advantages for various disciplines of the sport. For newly qualified pilots, there can be few more dramatic settings for flying a paraglider and the extensive cable car system and road access to launch sites means there is no carrying your gear back up hills. The centre does not cater for complete beginners. There are two five-day courses that help teach you how to get more from your flying. The Air Experience course is ideal for less-experienced pilots to learn about efficient flying techniques and accurate use of a variometer. The Mountain Thermal course covers these points but also looks more closely at weather conditions and mountain and valley conditions, so is more suited to pilots with a little experience.

Activity prices: The Air Experience and Mountain Thermal courses both cost FFr2,000. Daily fly guiding service costs FFr160 per day.
Accommodation: The centre is based at the lovely Flyer's Lodge. B&B accommodation costs Fr195 and half board Fr310.
Food: Included in accommodation costs (see above). Excellent three-course evening meals are cooked every night except one.
Equipment supplied: None.
What to take: You need to take all your own flying equipment and personal flying clothing. Check with centre for full list.

When to go: Year round.

Established: 1994

Safety: All instructors hold BHPA or FFVL flying qualifications and are highly experienced.

Insurance: Clients must arrange their own medical, travel/cancellation and flying insurance.

Methods of payment: VISA, Mastercard, travellers' cheques, cash.

Booking information: Advance booking is essential. A deposit of FFr500 per person is required and full payment for accommodation is due six weeks prior to arrival. Less than 30 days' notice of cancellation means you still pay the full holiday cost. Course and guiding payments are made at end of your stay.

Nearest airport: Geneva.

Nearest rail station: Les Houches.

SWITZERLAND

ALPIN RAFT
Postfach 78, 3800 Matten
Phone: +41 33 823 4100
Fax: +41 33 823 4101
Email: mail@alpinraft.ch
Website: www.alpinraft.ch

Paragliding in the Swiss Alps

The Jungfrau region of Switzerland offers some of the best paragliding in Europe. No previous experience is required for tandem flights as all pilots are fully qualified and will provide all necessary instructions before take-off. Passengers are strapped to a harness in front of the pilot, ensuring an uninterrupted view of the spectacular Alpine scenery, and guaranteeing some great opportunities for aerial photography. No specialist equipment is required and transport is included for most flights. The starting height, which determines the length of time spent in the air, varies from 500 metres to 2,000 metres.

Activity prices: From SFr120 to SFr230, depending on the location and height of the launch point.

Accommodation: Backpacker accommodation available at the centre.

Food: None provided.

Equipment supplied: All paragliding equipment.

What to take: Hiking clothes and a good pair of walking shoes.

When to go: April to October.

Established: 1988

Safety: All instructors are certified passenger pilots.

Insurance: Clients must arrange their own insurance.

Methods of payment: All common methods of payment accepted.

Booking information: Book by phone or email. Full payment is charged for cancellation on the day of trip.

Nearest airport: Bern.

Nearest rail station: Interlaken.

UNITED KINGDOM

ACORN ACTIVITIES
PO Box 120, Hereford HR4 8YB
Phone: +44 (0)1432 830083
Fax: +44 (0)1432 830110
Email: sales@acornactivities.co.uk
Website: www.acornactivities.co.uk

Paragliding throughout the UK
Acorn Activities runs paragliding courses in a number of locations, so there's a chance it'll be nearer than you think. Given a gentle slope and a slight breeze, the paraglider's wing is easily inflated. From the first day your feet will be off the ground. By the end of the four-day course you will gain your Elementary Pilot's Certificate, enabling you to fly solo for long distances while under supervision. As with hang gliding, weather is a crucial consideration: accommodation can be booked through Acorn on the understanding that the dates might have to be rearranged, although this is at the discretion of the accommodation supplier. Acorn Activities will accept no responsibility for cancelled accommodation costs should they arise.

Activity prices: £140 for a two-day course, £280 for a four-day course.

Accommodation: Not included in the price, although accommodation can be arranged at a budget to suit.

Food: Not included.

Equipment supplied: All specialised equipment is provided.

What to take: Warm, windproof clothes and sturdy shoes or boots.

When to go: Year round, weather permitting.

Established: 1990

Safety: All instructors are BHPA qualified.

Insurance: Insurance is required, although this can be arranged through Acorn Activities.

Methods of payment: VISA, Mastercard, cheque and cash.

Booking information: Late bookings are welcomed. A non-refundable deposit of £10 per day is required. Cancellation charges apply on a sliding scale from 80% for over 43 days before departure to 100% for up to 14 days.

Nearest airport: Depends on location.

Nearest rail station: Depends on the itinerary.

ADVENTURE SPORTS

Carnkie Farmhouse, Carnkie, Redruth, Cornwall TR16 6RZ
Phone: +44 (0)1209 218 962
Fax: +44 (0)1209 314 118
Email: holidays@adventure-sports.co.uk
Website: www.adventure-sports.co.uk

Soaring over Cornish cliffs

Adventure Sports is based in Cornwall in south-west England and has access to some of the most spectacular coastline and hill areas in the country, ideal for learning to paraglide. Their courses are all aimed at the adult market and are very good social affairs too, with groups and singles welcome. There is no need for previous experience as the highly qualified course instructors cover everything from the principles of flying to the basic techniques needed for getting airborne. Adventure Sports do not have a fixed location for paragliding as it is weather dependent. Instead, they use their excellent local knowledge to decide where to run each course for the best flying conditions. The centre caters for many adventure sports so you can mix and match to suit your desires.

Activity prices: A three-day camping stay with two days of activities costs from £76 (low season) to £100 (high season) and prices go up to £329 for a seven night/seven activity days course.

Accommodation: Included in price. You have a choice of camping, self-catering chalets or a converted self-catering farmhouse. There are many social options nearby or on the site.

Food: Not included.

Equipment supplied: All specialised equipment is provided.

What to take: Personal clothing and suitable footwear.

When to go: Summer months only.

Established: 1982

Safety: All instructors are BHPA qualified and very experienced.

Insurance: Insurance is required. Policies are offered by the centre.

Methods of payment: VISA, cheque and cash.

Booking information: Advance booking is required. A £50 deposit is payable.

Nearest airport: Newquay.

Nearest rail station: Redruth. Transfers can be arranged.

DERBYSHIRE FLYING CENTRE

Cliffside, Church Street, Tideswell, Derbyshire SK17 8PE
Phone: +44 (0)1298 872 313
Fax: +44 (0)1298 872 313
Email: hg-pg@d-f-c.freeserve.co.uk
Website: www.d-f-c.freeserve.co.uk

Experience Peak paragliding

The Peak District National Park is one of the most attractive places to fly in the UK. The Derbyshire Flying Centre has access to over 20 training hills so whatever the wind direction there is always a place to fly from. The beginners' course lasts for two days and involves hands-on flying from day one. Expert instructors will take you through the basic principles of flying a paraglider and show you the techniques for controlling your movement. If you are hooked then you can progress to become an

Elementary Pilot on a five-day course (three days after the taster course) before becoming a Club Pilot following a further five-day course. Once you are off the ground you won't want to come back down.

Activity prices: The Taster course costs £85 with two-day BHPA membership costing a further £10. The Elementary Pilot Course costs £195 if booked in one block, with BHPA membership for three months costing £35. The Club Pilot course also costs £195 with an upgrade to full BHPA membership costing £44.

Accommodation: Not included in the price, but centre can help to organise it if necessary.

Food: Not included. Lunch is normally taken at a local pub (alcohol not permitted) or café.

Equipment supplied: All flying equipment is provided.

What to take: Sensible, suitable clothing (warm layers is best) and strong comfortable supportive footwear.

When to go: Year round subject to weather.

Established: 1989

Safety: All instructors are BHPA qualified.

Insurance: BHPA membership (compulsory) includes third party insurance. Personal insurance is up to the client. Policies are offered at centre.

Methods of payment: Cheque and cash.

Booking information: Two weeks' advance booking is preferred. Courses or days that are cancelled due to weather are credited to the client.

Nearest airport: Manchester.

Nearest rail station: Hope. Transfers can be arranged.

HIGH ADVENTURE

Sandpipers, Coastguard Lane, Freshwater Bay, Isle of Wight PO40 9QX
Phone: +44 (0)1983 752 322
Fax: +44 (0)1983 755 063
Email: phil@high-adventure.demon.co.uk
Website: www.high-adventure.co.uk

A Wight flight experience
The Isle of Wight is a great flying location as it generally has better weather conditions throughout the year than the rest of the UK,

and there are plenty of launch sites so wind direction is never a problem either. High Adventure was the first hang gliding school in the UK to start teaching paragliding too. They have eight BHPA qualified instructors who can teach courses to suit from beginner level right up to the more experienced paragliders looking to hone their skills. The aim of the short taster courses is to get you flying as soon as it is safe and practicable. After an introduction to the principles of the sport you are then taken to the training slopes where demonstrations of technique should allow you to start practising ground handling yourself. After a couple of hours you are taking off on short hops before, hopefully, you get to fly from the top of the slope.

Activity prices: A one-day taster course during the week costs £55 including BHPA membership. At weekends, the taster day costs £69. A two-day introductory course costs £100 (weekday) or £130 (weekend), both plus £10 for BHPA membership. The three to four-day Student Pilot course costs £225 (plus £35 BHPA fee); the four to five-day Club Pilot course costs £295 (plus £35 BHPA fee).

Accommodation: Not included in the price. Choice of hotels nearby.

Food: Not included. Available on site.

Equipment supplied: All flying equipment is provided.

What to take: Sensible, suitable clothing (warm layers is best) and strong, comfortable, supportive footwear.

When to go: March to October.

Established: 1981

Safety: All the centre's instructors are qualified with the BHPA. The centre is a member of the Isle of Wight Tourist Board and the BHPA.

Insurance: Third party insurance, via BHPA, is included in the price. Personal insurance should be arranged by client.

Methods of payment: VISA, Mastercard, cheque and cash.

Booking information: Advance booking is necessary and a deposit required. The deposit is non-refundable if cancellation is not for good reason.

Nearest airport: Southampton.

Nearest rail station: Lymington. Daily transfers from 10.15 a.m. ferry from Lymington.

SKY SYSTEMS LTD

66 Woodbourne Avenue, Brighton, East Sussex BN1 8EJ
Phone: +44 (0)1273 556695
Fax: +44 (0)1273 566330
Email: skyinfo@skysystems.co.uk
Website: www.skysystems.co.uk

Paragliding in the South Downs
Rising up from the white cliffs of Dover and stretching almost 100 km
from Winchester in the west to Eastbourne in the east, the South
Downs boast some of the best paragliding country in England.
Situated less than an hour from London and a stone's throw from the
bright lights of Brighton, Sky Systems is one of the United Kingdom's
largest paragliding centres, offering a variety of courses for beginners
and experts alike. A taster flight in a tandem paraglider with a
qualified instructor costs just £39, but the best way to progress to
your first solo flight is to take the Elementary Pilot course. BHPA
approved, the course takes most people around five days to
complete, and finishes with a solo flight from 600–700 feet. Pre-
booking is required, but training days do not have to be taken
consecutively.

Activity prices: From £99 per day. Elementary Pilot course from £330.

Accommodation: Clients must arrange their own.

Food: Snacks available.

Equipment supplied: All specialist equipment is supplied.

What to take: Personal clothing.

When to go: Year round, weather permitting.

Established: 1985

Safety: All instructors are BHPA qualified.

Insurance: Insurance is mandatory and can be arranged at the centre on the
day of attendance.

Methods of payment: All common payment methods accepted.

Booking information: Advance booking is essential.

Nearest airport: London Gatwick.

Nearest rail station: Brighton.

SUSSEX HANG GLIDING AND PARAGLIDING

Dairy Farm House, Wick Street, Firle, East Sussex BN8 6NB

Phone: +44 (0)1273 858 170

Fax: +44 (0)1273 858 177

Email: sussexhgpg@mistral.co.uk

Website: www.airbase.co.uk/sussexhgpg/

Soar over the South Downs

Some of the best flying conditions in the UK exist on the South Downs on England's south coast and this centre has access to some of the best launch sites in the area to take advantage of all wind conditions. Their introductory courses operate throughout the year and within a weekend you will be making your first flights from the top of the training hill. You can then choose to join the Student Pilot course that lasts for four days leading to a certificate. You learn the theory of flying and how to handle equipment and be able to take off, turn and land safely. Once you complete the following Club Pilot course you can buy and own your own paraglider.

Activity prices: A one-day introductory course costs £65, a two-day weekend introductory course costs £105. The Student Pilot course costs £285. A dual flight costs £40.

Accommodation: Not included in course price. The centre can help you organise accommodation in Brighton.

Food: Not included. Take some snacks and sandwiches with you.

Equipment supplied: All specialist flying equipment is provided.

What to take: Warm, windproof clothing with separate waterproof and strong supportive boots.

When to go: Year round subject to weather.

Established: 1995

Safety: All the instructors used are BHPA qualified and the centre is a member of the same organisation.

Insurance: BHPA membership (compulsory) includes third party insurance. You will need to join on arrival. Other insurance is client's responsibility.

Methods of payment: Cheque and cash.

Booking information: Advance booking is advised.

Nearest airport: London Gatwick.

Nearest rail station: Preston Park or Brighton.

WILTSHIRE HANG GLIDING AND PARAGLIDING CENTRE

Old Yatesbury Airfield, Yatesbury, Calne, Wiltshire SN11 8FA

Phone: +44 (0)1672 861 555

Fax: +44 (0)1672 861 555

Email: hamish.a@virgin.net

Website: http://business.virgin.net/hamish.a

Marlborough air time

Located near Avebury, this centre launches from various sites on hills at the edge of the beautiful Vale of Pewsey and the Marlborough Downs. They run courses to take you from novice to Club Pilot level and beyond. During the one-day taster course, you will learn about ground inflation of the canopy and how to control it, with your first hops coming around lunchtime. In the afternoon, you move further up the hill as you continue to improve. The two-day course builds your skill still further with the goal of your completing simple flying tasks from a height of about 100 feet. The four-day Elementary Pilot course takes those skills to a competent level ready for the Club Pilot course.

Activity prices: The one-day taster course costs from £69, the two-day course from £119; the Elementary Pilot Certificate course lasts four days and costs from £220.

Accommodation: Not included in course price. The centre can help you organise accommodation in the local area.

Food: Not included.

Equipment supplied: All specialist flying equipment is provided.

What to take: Warm clothing with separate windproof and waterproof top and supportive footwear.

When to go: Year round subject to weather.

Established: 1980

Safety: All the instructors used are BHPA qualified and the centre is a member of the same organisation and the Association of Free Flight Professionals.

Insurance: BHPA membership (compulsory) includes third party insurance.
You will need to join on arrival. Other insurance is client's responsibility.

Methods of payment: Cheque and cash.

Booking information: Advance booking is advised.

Nearest airport: Bristol.

Nearest rail station: Chippenham.

RAFTING

Few adventure sports are as accessible or as exciting as white water rafting. No experience is needed and anyone who's happy in water can ride some of the biggest rapids in Europe in complete safety.

Rafts tend to hold six to eight people including the instructor, who guides the raft down the rapids avoiding any obvious obstacles. Typically each rafter will be given a paddle, a helmet, a buoyancy aid and a wetsuit, and will negotiate the rapids with instructions from the guide. On especially big white water, clients may simply hang on to the safety rope around the edge of the raft and move their weight around to punch through big waves or 'holes'. Whatever people might tell you otherwise, a buoyancy aid and a white water helmet are essential on any river, regardless of grade. Check to make sure these items are provided. If they're not, go elsewhere – there are usually a few companies offering the same or similar trips.

Rafting trips in Europe are generally half-day or one-day, but some companies do offer multi-day trips, particularly on longer rivers like the Çoruh in Turkey. Because rafts are so big and buoyant, provisions and equipment can be stowed on the raft and carried downriver, making it the ideal wilderness experience for those without the time or the inclination to learn to canoe.

White water grades

International Grading of white water uses the following approximate guidelines:

Grade I – Some small waves, but basically little more than a bob.
Grade II – Slightly bigger waves and a few obstacles, but nothing that cannot be anticipated well in advance.

Grade III – Heavier white water with numerous obstacles, through which an obvious line can be negotiated.

Grade IV – Usually much more powerful and continuous – a safe line may only be apparent after inspection from the bank.

Grade V – As for IV, but often bigger and more technically demanding; even after inspection, the safest line is not obvious. This is the highest grade that can be commercially rafted.

Grade VI – The limit of possibility, and runnable only at particular water levels – awareness, anticipation and reactive skills must be completely reliable.

Although running a grade V in a loaded raft is accessible to people without any experience of white water, negotiating the same rapid in a kayak is a different thing altogether. While kayaks might be more manoeuvrable, their relative size, shape and buoyancy make them much less forgiving, and much more intimidating – without a guide to take responsibility, any mistakes you make are yours alone. By the same token, the rewards for a successful run are all the sweeter!

AUSTRIA

ADVENTURE TOURS – SPORTSAGENTUR STROBL
A-8940 Liezen, Hauptplatz 3
Phone: +43 3612 25343
Fax: +43 3612 253439
Email: strobl@ennstal.at
Website: www.rafting.at

A dash of Austrian Salza
Hartwig Strobl's Adventure Tours has been running rafting trips since 1988 on two of Austria's most beautiful rivers, the Enns and the Salza. With rapids graded between II and IV, the rivers are ideal for beginners and more experienced paddlers. The very experienced guides will give you a complete rundown on all the necessary paddling skills and safety measures you will need to make your rafting trip successful. They run a

particularly popular weekend package where you get two nights' accommodation, a barbecue and two rafting trips, one on each river.

Activity prices: A single rafting trip costs DM75. The weekend package tour, with two rafting trips, two nights' hotel accommodation and a barbecue, costs DM305.

Accommodation: Not included in single rafting tour price. Various levels of accommodation are available locally. See above for inclusive weekend package.

Food: Not included in price. Available locally.

Equipment supplied: All specialist rafting equipment is supplied.

What to take: Swimsuit and towel.

When to go: 15 April to 15 October.

Established: 1988

Safety: All the rafting guides are nationally qualified and most have over ten years of experience. The centre is a member of Tourismusverband Grimming-Gesäuse.

Insurance: The centre is fully covered.

Methods of payment: Travellers' cheques and cash.

Booking information: Advance booking is recommended.

Nearest airport: Salzburg (180 km).

Nearest rail station: Selzthal (35 km). Transfers can be arranged.

HIGH 5
Bahnhof 248, 6951 Lingenau
Phone: +43 5513 4140
Fax: +43 5513 4150
Email: office@outdoor.at
Website: www.outdoor.at

A Constance source of white water
High 5 is one of the leading providers of adventure sports in Austria from its base near Lingenau on the shores of the impressive Lake Constance. There are several rivers in the area that offer rafting opportunities but High 5 concentrates on the best of them, the Bregenzer Ach. The skill levels needed to paddle the river successfully vary with the put-in point, but it has rapids to test almost all levels of ability. The qualified instructors will give you a comprehensive

introduction to the paddling, safety and rescue techniques necessary
for making your journey as exciting and safe as possible.

Activity prices: The rafting trips cost from Sch80 per day. There are three-day
options too.

Accommodation: Available at centre, including teepees for exotic nights
under canvas.

Food: Available at centre.

Equipment supplied: All specialist equipment is supplied.

What to take: Swimsuit and towel.

When to go: 1 May to 31 October.

Established: 1989

Safety: All the rafting guides at High 5 are nationally qualified. The centre is a
member of the Austrian Outdoor Association.

Insurance: Full liability insurance cover is included in the price.

Methods of payment: Bank draft and cash.

Booking information: Advance booking is recommended.

Nearest airport: Zurich (1 hour).

Nearest rail station: Bregenz. Transfers can be arranged.

SPORTSCHULE FANKHAUSER – TIROL RAFTING
Dorfstrasse 17, A-6382 Kirchdorf, Tirol
Phone: +43 5352 62233
Fax: +43 5352 62587
Email: fanky@netwing.at
Website: www.tirolrafting.com

A Tirol rafting extravaganza
The rafting in the Tirol region of Austria is some of the best in Europe and
Sportschule Fankhauser are ideally placed to take advantage of the most
exciting rivers. They offer a variety of rafting trips in the Haiming area,
ranging from easier routes, such as the Entenloch Gorge, through the
awesome Imster Canyon run that is known as Europe's Grand Canyon, to
the extreme white water of the Ötztaler. The experienced guides will fully
brief you on paddling skills and safety and rescue techniques before you
enter the water – and then you come face to face with the rapids.

Activity prices: The Imster trip costs Sch490 per person and the Ötztaler run costs Sch780. You can do both for Sch1,180.

Accommodation: Available at centre, either camping or in a bunkhouse.

Food: Breakfast and half-board packages are available at the centre.

Equipment supplied: All specialist rafting equipment is supplied, including wetsuits, neoprene shoes, helmets and buoyancy aids.

What to take: Swimsuit.

When to go: Year round, daily.

Established: 1985

Safety: All the rafting guides hold national qualifications. The centre is approved by the Austrian Tourist Office and the Austrian Rafting Association.

Insurance: The centre has liability insurance but clients should arrange their own accident policy.

Methods of payment: VISA, Mastercard, Eurocard, travellers' cheques and cash.

Booking information: Advance booking is essential at least one day ahead. No deposit is required and there are no cancellation penalties.

Nearest airport: Innsbruck. Transfers can be arranged.

Nearest rail station: Ütztalf-Bahnhof. Transfers can be arranged.

FRANCE

SNOW SAFARI LIMITED

Chalet Savoy, 1351 route des Chavants, 74310 Les Houches
Phone: +33 (0)4 50 54 56 63;
UK bookings & information number 01279 600 885
Fax: +33 (0)4 50 54 57 19
Email: Chalsavoy@aol.com
Website: www.chaletsavoy.com

Rafting the rivers around Mont Blanc
The rivers of the French Alps, and the Chamonix region in particular, offer some of the most continuous and exciting white water in Europe. The Chalet Savoy offers a two-hour introduction to rafting, which involves basic instruction on a 5 km descent of the Chamonix Valley. Also available is a day-trip to the dramatic Dranse River, which

Surf's up! Once you can stand up, surfing becomes very addictive.

Leaping around rocks can add a bit of extra spice to a hike.

Whilst trekking, some bridges may only just seem better options than crossing rivers.

A swooping downhill ride on single track can wipe away
in an instant the pain of many uphills.

Surf kayaking provides a rapid, all-action return to the beach.

Crossing tumultuous water is part and parcel of a days coasteering.

Whilst caving, try not to get caught between a rock and a hard place.

Half the fun of winter mountaineering is getting up into the mountains in the first place.

There's not much to beat the buzz of a challenging downhill run.

The amber nectar is a fitting reward for a perfect landing.

The hard part of the climb over, take a minute to sit back and admire the view.

includes a visit to the spectacular Horseshoe Falls. Last but not least is the Dora Baltea River in Italy, which is known in rafting circles as the 'Colorado of the Alps'. Prices include all transport, equipment and instruction while on the river.

Activity prices: From FFr220 for a one-hour introduction, FFr530 for a half-day and FFr650 for a full day.

Accommodation: Available at the Chalet Savoy. Summer prices start from FFr140 for B&B accommodation or FFr2,050 for seven days and seven nights.

Food: Half-board included in the accommodation price.

Equipment supplied: All equipment supplied.

What to take: Swimsuit, towel and warm change of clothes.

When to go: May to September.

Established: 1987

Safety: All guides and leaders are fully qualified for the relevant activity.

Insurance: Clients must arrange their own insurance.

Methods of payment: VISA, Mastercard.

Booking information: Contact Snow Safari for booking form and full terms and conditions.

Nearest airport: Geneva.

Nearest rail station: Les Houches.

ITALY

CENTRO CANOA RAFTING DIMARO
Val Di Sole, Via Gole 105 – 38025 Dimaro, Trentino
Phone: +39 (0)463 974 332/973 278
Fax: +39 (0)463 973 200
Email: rafting@tin.it
Website: www.raftingcenter.it

Rafting in the Valley of the Sun
The swift waters of the River Noce flow through one the most stunning parts of northern Italy, the Val Di Sole. There are four levels of one-day rafting trips to suit all abilities on offer at the Dimaro Canoeing and Rafting Centre. The shortest course for

beginners covers 4 km while the longest course, over 25 km, provides a sterner test of endurance, lasting four and a half hours. For those wishing to sharpen their rafting skills still further, a five-day course turns novices into competent paddlers with a series of theory lessons and lots of time on the water. After a hard day paddling, you can relax in the campsite swimming pool, play tennis or simply build up your energy levels for the next day by eating pizza in the restaurant.

Activity prices: One-day rafting trips cost: 4 km L40,000; 10 km L68,000; 15 km L85,000; 25 km L120,000. The five-day basic rafting course including camping and equipment costs L350,000, or L370,000 for advanced level.
Accommodation: Four-star camping is available at the centre and is free for clients booking weekend or one-week courses. Local hotel accommodation can also be arranged by the centre.
Food: Special prices are available for clients at the campsite restaurant.
Equipment supplied: All specialist equipment is supplied.
What to take: Swimsuit, trainers, t-shirt.
When to go: May to September.
Established: 1984
Safety: All rafting guides are qualified teachers with AIRAF.
Insurance: Cover is included in the course price.
Methods of payment: VISA, travellers' cheques, cash.
Booking information: A minimum of two weeks' advance booking is recommended. A deposit of 20% is required.
Nearest airport: Verona Villafranca. Clients can be picked up from the airport on request.
Nearest rail station: Trento – Trento Mal({?}

SLOVENIA

TOP EXTREME
TOP d.o.o., Vojkova 9, 5000 Nova Gorica
Phone: +38 (0)66 522 006
Fax: +38 (0)66 522 006

Email: info@top.si
Website: www.top.si

Down a world championship river

Slovenia's Soča river is one of the most beautiful rivers in Europe and was host to the 1991 World Kayaking Championships, so you know it can serve up a challenging and exciting rafting ride too. On Top Extreme's two-hour course, based at the company's Alpine centre near Bovec, you will get to experience it up close and personal. After a briefing session on paddling techniques and safety, you enter the fast-flowing waters. There are three courses to choose from. The standard run of 9.5 km starts from Boka Waterfall, the soft course is 8 km long from the confluence of the Koritnica and Soča rivers and the full-on long course joins the two together. During the first 5 km you get used to paddling together, and then you take on the river's thrilling rapids. En route, you pull into the bank for a picnic in a pine forest.

Activity prices: The standard course costs DM55, the soft option DM48 and the long course DM75. Group and student discounts available.

Accommodation: Not included. Available locally.

Food: Picnic included during day. Other food is available locally.

Equipment supplied: Wetsuits, shoes, helmet, lifejacket and waterproof jacket.

What to take: swimsuit, t-shirt and towel.

When to go: April to November.

Established: 1993

Safety: The centre's rafting staff are all qualified instructors.

Insurance: Accident insurance is included in the price. The company also has liability insurance.

Methods of payment: Eurocard, Mastercard and cash.

Booking information: Advance booking is essential.

Nearest airport: Ljubljana (100 km).

Nearest rail station: Most na Soci (30 km).

SWITZERLAND

ALPIN RAFT
Postfach 78, 3800 Matten
Phone: +41 33 823 4100
Fax: +41 33 823 4101
Email: mail@alpinraft.ch
Website: www.alpinraft.ch

A Swiss white water rush
Nowhere else in Europe is the water as exciting and continuous as the Alps, and Switzerland is no exception. Alpin Raft offers a half-day of rafting on the Lutschine, a fast, action-packed river featuring continuous grade III–IV rapids. Alpine meltwater can be cold, even in the middle of summer, so wetsuits are provided, but off the water expect to be blissfully sunbaked. Lunch is always a highlight and the scenery is the stuff that chocolate boxes are made of – snow-capped mountain peaks, plunging valleys and sweeping Alpine meadows.

Activity prices: SFr88 for a half day.
Accommodation: Backpacker accommodation available at the centre.
Food: Lunch included.
Equipment supplied: Wetsuit, booties, helmet and buoyancy aid.
What to take: Swimsuit and towel.
When to go: May to October.
Established: 1988
Safety: Instructors must have a white water rafting certificate and are trained in river rescue and first aid.
Insurance: Clients must provide their own insurance.
Methods of payment: All common methods of payment accepted.
Booking information: Book by phone or email. Full payment is charged for cancellation on the day of trip.
Nearest airport: Bern.
Nearest rail station: Interlaken.

UNITED KINGDOM

ACORN ACTIVITIES
PO Box 120, Hereford HR4 8YB
Phone: +44 (0)1432 830083
Fax: +44 (0)1432 830110
Email: sales@acornactivities.co.uk
Website: www.acornactivities.co.uk

Rafting throughout England, Scotland and Wales
With the British weather as it is, white water rafting is generally best in the winter months, but Acorn Activities guarantee a white water experience whatever the weather and whatever the season. They operate from a number of locations in the UK, so if you're prepared to brave the winter wonderland of Scotland or Wales, you might be in for some of the biggest white water in the UK. If you'd prefer to drift and splash through warmer waves, the summer months might be your best bet for a fuller flavour. Wetsuits, buoyancy aids and helmets are provided year round, and time spent on the river totals about two hours. The second half of the day includes a choice of alternative, dry-land activities (see below), presumably to warm up!

Activity prices: £45 for two hours of rafting, followed by your choice of canoeing, abseiling, archery, clay-pigeon shooting and obstacle course.
Accommodation: Not included in the price, but can be arranged nearby at a budget to suit.
Food: Not included.
Equipment supplied: Wetsuits, buoyancy aids and helmets are provided.
What to take: Towel, warm clothes to change into, etc.
When to go: Year round, but water levels are best from November to March.
Established: 1990
Safety: All guides are fully qualified.
Insurance: Insurance is required, although this can be arranged through Acorn Activities.
Methods of payment: VISA, Mastercard, cheque and cash.

Booking information: Late bookings are welcomed. A non-refundable deposit of £10 per day is required. Cancellation charges apply on a sliding scale from 80% for over 43 days before departure to 100% for up to 14 days.

Nearest airport: Cardiff or Birmingham International.

Nearest rail station: Depends on the itinerary.

BLACK MOUNTAIN ACTIVITIES

PO Box 5, Hay on Wye, Hereford HR3 5YB
Phone: +44 (0)1497 847 897
Fax: +44 (0)1497 847 897
Email: enquiries@blackmountain.co.uk
Website: www.blackmountain.co.uk

Take on south Wales' white water

If you have never experienced white water then rafting is the ideal way to get started. When the rains come, the rivers of south Wales rise significantly and offer plenty of adrenaline-pumping action for paddlers. Your experienced river guide will keep you on the right line but it's up to you and the rest of the team to provide the power. You will complete a lesson in safety techniques and self-rescue in case you end up swimming in the rapids. If rafting is not possible due to water levels, you get to choose between gorge walking and Canadian canoeing.

Activity prices: Rafting trips cost £30.

Accommodation: Not included in the price. There is a range of accommodation available locally and the centre will advise you.

Food: Not included. Packed lunches can be arranged.

Equipment supplied: All specialist equipment is supplied.

What to take: Personal clothing, swimsuit, suitable footwear.

When to go: Year round.

Established: 1992

Safety: All the centre's staff are fully qualified in their respective sports, hold first aid qualifications and are highly professional. All equipment used meets national safety standards. The centre is licensed by the AALA and the Welsh Tourist Board.

Insurance: The centre is insured, though clients may wish to take out separate insurance too.

Methods of payment: Personal cheque and cash.

Booking information: Advance booking is recommended, though late bookings may be possible.

Nearest airport: Depends on tour. Cardiff and Bristol are nearest to the centre.

Nearest rail station: Depends on the itinerary. Hereford and Abergavenny are nearest to the centre.

CROFT-NA-CABER

Kenmore, Loch Tay, Perthshire
Phone: +44 (0)1887 830 236
Fax: +44 (0)1887 830 649
Email: info@croftnacaber.co.uk
Website: www.croftnacaber.co.uk

Riding a white Tay

The River Tay is one of Scotland's most exciting and most popular rivers for rafting. Croft-na-Caber's half-day trips take in three different sections, including Grandtully, a challenging ride that has been used in the British white water kayaking championships. There are gentler runs more suited to beginners, such as the one around Cat's Hole. The whole tour takes around three hours. It is a wonderfully scenic river, too – if you ever get the chance to take a breather from the action and look around.

Activity prices: The rafting runs cost £28 per person, depending on which section you tackle.

Accommodation: Self-catering log cabins or hotel accommodation is available at the centre.

Food: Hotel restaurant and bar at centre.

Equipment supplied: All specialist equipment is supplied.

What to take: Personal clothing, swimsuit, suitable footwear.

When to go: Year round.

Established: 1974

Safety: All the centre's staff are fully qualified in their respective sports, hold first aid qualifications and are highly professional. All equipment used meets national safety standards. The centre is licensed by the AALA.

Insurance: The centre is insured up to £6 million for liability, but clients may wish to take out separate insurance for accidents/cancellation.

Methods of payment: VISA, Mastercard, cheques and cash.

Booking information: Advance booking is essential. Payment of 20% deposit is required. Tour must be confirmed or cancelled at least seven days in advance.

Nearest airport: Edinburgh. Transfers can be arranged.

Nearest rail station: Perth, Pitlochry. Transfers can be arranged.

ROCK CLIMBING

Unlike the rush of bungee jumping and the in-your-face fun of white water rafting, climbing is meticulously slow and serene. Most climbs, whether they're 20 or 200 feet high, have a critical or 'crux' move that can take minutes to complete – legs start to shake, arms get tired and fingers start to sweat. Just when you think you're going to have to give up and abseil back down, you go for it one last time, pull yourself up and grab the next hold with a deep breath of satisfaction . . . and relief. The rewards of that patient search for a solution is what brings climbers back to the wall again and again.

Initially, the complications of climbing seem to outweigh any likelihood of enjoyment. To the untrained eye all the knots, ropes and gear can be as daunting as the climb itself. By far the best way to learn is to take an introductory course that will introduce you to the basics of technique, safety and ropework. Within just a few hours you will be able to tie a few basic knots and climb with a partner using a rope, and after a couple of days you'll be setting up your own climbs. Once you've mastered the basics, it's only a matter of time and practice before it becomes second nature and you're able to climb without supervision.

If you can't get to the mountains (or it's simply too wet and cold to climb), it's worth popping along to your local climbing wall, where evening classes and crash courses for beginners are almost always on offer. Because all the holds are man-made, climbing walls give an added sense of confidence in a safe and controlled environment. It's also a good idea to find someone to climb with – more than anything, climbing is a social sport that by its very nature engenders trust and friendships that can last a lifetime.

How hard is hard severe? Rock climbing grades

Rock climbing grades in Britain have developed since climbing began and the standard system is now a slightly complex but very flexible method for grading how hard climbs are. Different grading systems are used in Europe, the United States and Australia, just to keep you guessing! In Britain, the adjectival grades give an overall picture of the route. These grades in ascending order of difficulty are: Moderate, Difficult, Very Difficult, Severe, Hard Severe, Very Severe, Hard Very Severe and Extremely Severe (this latter category then has E number ratings too, up to E9 at the moment – a route that looks like polished glass to most people!). so Hard Severe is a route slightly above the middle difficulty and it is a grade that beginner climbers can aspire to reasonably quickly, given proper tuition. These gradings are then matched with a Technical Grade. This gives an indication of the hardest move on a pitch, where 4a is little more than a scramble and 8c is at the cutting edge of climbing. The higher the number and letter the more technical the move. The two grades are combined in guidebooks like this: Hard Very Severe (HVS) 4c.

AUSTRIA

SPORTSCHULE FANKHAUSER – TIROL RAFTING
Dorfstrasse 17, A-6382 Kirchdorf, Tirol
Phone: +43 5352 62233
Fax: +43 5352 62587
Email: fanky@netwing.at
Website: www.tirolrafting.com

A Tirol rock fest
The Tirol region in Austria has great potential for people looking to get to grips with a rock challenge. Sportschule Fankhauser has a wide range of course options to suit climbers of all abilities from complete beginners to experienced rock freaks looking to test their skills to the limit. The majority of their half-day trips take place in the Haiming region and are led by fully qualified instructors.

Activity prices: The half-day rock climbing courses cost Sch490 per person.

Accommodation: Available at centre, either camping or in a bunkhouse.

Food: Breakfast and half-board packages are available at the centre.

Equipment supplied: All specialist climbing equipment, except footwear, is supplied.

What to take: Personal clothing and suitable footwear, preferably climbing shoes.

When to go: Year round, daily, depending on the weather.

Established: 1985

Safety: All the climbing guides hold national qualifications. The centre is approved by the Austrian Tourist Office.

Insurance: The centre has liability insurance but clients should arrange their own accident policy.

Methods of payment: VISA, Mastercard, Eurocard, travellers' cheques and cash.

Booking information: Advance booking is essential at least one day ahead. There is no deposit required and no cancellation penalties.

Nearest airport: Innsbruck. Transfers can be arranged.

Nearest rail station: Ütztal-Bahnhof. Transfers can be arranged.

BULGARIA

BULGARIAN MOUNTAINS ADVENTURE

Kancho Shipkov, Kv. Dianabad bl 18 vh.A, 1172 Sofia
Phone: +359 2 620 688
Fax: N/A
Email: kancho@bglink.net
Website: http://pss.bglink.net/mysite/explorebg.html

A Bulgarian rock treat

Been around the European climbing scene and seen it all? Looking for somewhere different, somewhere that adds an extra edge to the adventure? Then why not head for the spectacular mountains of Bulgaria, one of Europe's least explored adventure destinations. Bulgarian Mountains Adventure is a company based around members of the national mountain rescue service. They offer personal and tailor-made guiding services and can provide trips to suit climbers of varying standards. The most popular faces and routes in the country are in north-western Rila in the Maljovitsa region. However, there are plenty of other options, including the Pirin Mountains and the Balkan Mountains. Wherever you choose, you are unlikely to bump into the usual crowd of climbers from your local crag.

Activity prices: The trips are all tailor-made to suit your requirements and cost around US$50 per day, or less, depending on what you do and where you go. The centre will advise you on the possibilities. The price also includes local transportation.

Accommodation: Food and lodging during the activity are included in the price and organised by the centre. Hotels and meals at the start and end of your trip are not included but the centre can help you arrange them.

Food: Food is included during the activity, but not at the start and end of your trip.

Equipment supplied: All specialist equipment is supplied, though you can take your own if you have it.

What to take: Personal clothing and climbing shoes.

When to go: Year round, though winter is only for the crazy!

Established: 1997

Safety: At least one of the guides in every group is a qualified rescuer from the Bulgarian Mountain Rescue Service. They have plentiful experience and excellent local knowledge.

Insurance: Clients can arrange their own policy or the centre can arrange it on the spot.

Methods of payment: Bank transfer and cash.

Booking information: Advance booking is essential and a 30% deposit is payable. Cancellation penalties may apply.

Nearest airport: Sofia. Transfers can be arranged.

Nearest rail station: Sofia Central. Transfers can be arranged.

FRANCE

INTERNATIONAL SCHOOL OF MOUNTAINEERING, SWITZERLAND

Hafod Tan y Graig, Nant Gwynant, Gwynedd LL55 4NW , UK
Phone: +44 (0)1766 890441
Fax: +44 (0)1766 890599
Email: ism@dial.pipex.com
Website: http//:ds.dial.pipex.com/ism

Classic Alpine rock

ISM's rock-climbing course is for people who enjoy climbing on cliffs and crags but would like to progress on to climbs on a much bigger scale in a high mountain setting. The week begins on the great limestone cliffs of the Swiss Prealpes, which offer routes up to 20 pitches long, at altitudes up to 3,000 metres, before moving on to one of the prime granite areas, such as central Switzerland or the Mont Blanc region. The course encompasses a wide range of climbing styles, from bolt protection to long Alpine ridges. Climbers must be able to tackle second Alpine grade V (British Very Severe), but ISM can offer training in the UK for anyone wishing to reach the required standard.

Activity prices: Six-day Alpine course prices range from £365 to £995. UK courses range from £45 to £130 per day depending on group size.
Accommodation: All Alpine courses include hotel accommodation. In the UK guesthouse or hotel accommodation can be arranged.
Food: All Alpine courses include full board. In the UK food can be arranged.
Equipment supplied: All specialist equipment is provided.
What to take: Personal clothing and footwear.
When to go: August and September in the Alps, year round in the UK.
Established: 1960
Safety: All guides hold the International Carnet, the highest qualification available in mountaineering.
Insurance: Relevant insurance required for all Alpine courses.
Methods of payment: All common payment methods accepted.

Booking information: Contact ISM for booking form and full terms and conditions.

Nearest airport: Manchester for UK-based courses. Various for Alps-based courses.

Nearest rail station: Bangor for UK-based courses. Various for Alps-based courses.

MOUNTAIN ACTIVITY EXPERIENCE

93 avenue Michel Croz, 74400 Chamonix
Phone: +33 4 50 55 80 80
Fax: +33 4 53 48 50
Email: M.A.X@wanadoo.fr
Website: montblanconeline.fr/max/max.htm

Scaling Chamonix's rock routes
Numerous crags and crevices stake out the Chamonix Valley, the Aiguilles Rouges and the Cluses Valley, and there are routes to suit all abilities, from the first-timer to the very best in the world. Half-day, full-day and five-day introductory courses are available, with groups progressing very much at their own pace. After only a few days, newcomers to the sport usually improve dramatically, allowing them to venture higher into the heart of the Mont Blanc range, via the Aiguille du Midi cable car or the Montenvers train. And, as the company's promotional material promises, 'In such surroundings, magic operates.' For more experienced climbers, high altitude climbing is offered in smaller groups of one or two. Prices do not include rental of helmet, harness and rock shoes, but do include all group equipment. Five-day prices include all transportation and cable-car passes, and picnic and half-board for the high altitude course.

Activity prices: Private tuition costs FFr1,350 per day, FFr750 per half-day. Group rates (four to six people) are FFr340 per person for a full day and FFr190 for a half-day. Introductory or improver's five-day courses cost from FFr3,000 per person (six to eight people) to FFr5,400 per person (two people). High altitude five-day courses cost FFr3,500 per person for two people and FFr6,500 for private guiding.

Accommodation: Not included in the price.

Food: Picnic and half-board are included only on the high altitude course.

Equipment supplied: Technical group equipment such as ropes and climbing hardware.

What to take: Helmets, harnesses and rock shoes are not included, but can be rented at the centre.

When to go: Summer only.

Established: 1997

Safety: All instructors are nationally qualified high mountain guides.

Insurance: Clients must provide their own insurance.

Methods of payment: Cheques and cash.

Booking information: A deposit is required to secure a booking. Cancellation within a month of the course forfeits the deposit.

Nearest airport: Geneva.

Nearest rail station: Chamonix.

ODYSSEE MONTAGNE
101 Les Marmottières, 74310 Les Houches
Phone: +33 (0)4 50 54 36 01
Fax: +33 (0)4 50 54 35 74
Email: odyssee@odyssee-montagne.fr
Website: http://odyssee-monatgne.fr

Rock climbing on Mont Blanc granite
Mont Blanc, the Dolomites, Verdon, Les Drus, the Matterhorn – all offer classic rock routes, and all are found in the Alps. The Mont Blanc region boasts hundreds of exceptional granite routes for climbers of all abilities, from one or two pitches to 3,000-foot walls. Further south, meanwhile, the Ecrins Range features some spiritual climbs away from the crowds. Finally, the limestone of southern France, and in particular the Verdon Gorge, provides the perfect escape for those seeking a bit of sun and sand. Odyssée Montagne offers foundation courses for novice climbers and indoor climbers, in

addition to more technical courses for those who climb up to French grade 6a and above. Courses vary from four days/three nights to six days/five nights, although guiding and instruction can be tailored to individual requirements depending on weather conditions and technical ability.

Activity prices: From FFr2,260 for four days and three nights to FFr3,950 for six days and five nights.

Accommodation: Included.

Food: All food is included in the price.

Equipment supplied: All technical equipment is included.

What to take: Personal equipment including harness and rock shoes.

When to go: Year round.

Established: 1993

Safety: All mountain guides are members of the Ecole National de Ski et d'Alpinisme.

Insurance: Comprehensive insurance can be provided at an additional 5% of the full price.

Methods of payment: Travellers' cheque, VISA, Mastercard, Swift bank transfer, etc.

Booking information: A deposit of 30% is required at the time of booking.

Bookings will be accepted no later than 15 days before departure.

Nearest airport: Geneva. Airport collection available on request.

Nearest rail station: Saint Gervais.

SNOW SAFARI LIMITED
Chalet Savoy, 1351 Route des Chavants, 74310 Les Houches
Phone: +33 (0)4 50 54 56 63;
UK bookings & information number 01279 600 885
Fax: +33 (0)4 50 54 57 19
Email: Chalsavoy@aol.com
Website: www.chaletsavoy.com

Rock climbing in the Chamonix Valley
In addition to some of the world's finest rock-climbing, Les Houches also features an excellent climbing wall to learn on and

an indoor wall just a few minutes'walk from the chalet. A three-hour introductory course is available for complete beginners, and the price of FFr240 includes all specialist equipment and a video of your endeavours. More experienced climbers can choose from some of the finest routes in the Chamonix Valley. The price of FFr350 for a half-day or FFr500 for a full day includes all equipment (except climbing shoes) and the services of a local climbing instructor.

Activity prices: From FFr240 for a three-hour taster session to FFr350 for a half-day and FFr500 for a full day.
Accommodation: Available at the Chalet Savoy. Summer prices start from FFr140 per person per night for B&B or FFr2,050 per person for seven days and seven nights.
Food: Half-board included in the accommodation price.
Equipment supplied: All specialised climbing equipment. Climbing shoes can be rented locally.
What to take: Normal hiking clothes.
When to go: May to September.
Established: 1987
Safety: All guides and leaders are fully qualified for the relevant activity.
Insurance: Clients must arrange their own insurance.
Methods of payment: VISA, Mastercard.
Booking information: Contact Snow Safari for booking form and full terms and conditions.
Nearest airport: Geneva.
Nearest rail station: Les Houches.

IRELAND

CELTIC ADVENTURES
Caherdaniel, Co. Kerry
Phone: +353 (0)66 9475 277
Fax: +353 (0)66 9475 277
Email: info@activity-ireland.com
Website: www.activity-ireland.com

Guinness climbers

Learning to climb is exciting anywhere in the world, but taking a course in the magnificent, unspoilt south-west of Ireland has an added touch of magic. Celtic Adventures offer only introductory rock climbing courses so you won't feel overawed by surrounding classes of experienced rock rats. There are several climbing location options available, including sea cliffs and mountain routes, and the course will be tailor-made to suit your abilities and desire for progression. The instructors are fully trained and will ensure that your safety is paramount. After scaling the heights you can kick back and relax with a pint of Guinness in a cosy village pub or explore nearby historic sites.

Activity prices: Trips are tailor-made to suit the clients' needs. Prices are based around I£20 per person per day from June to mid-August, I£18 otherwise. Discounts available for students and school and scouting groups.

Accommodation: Hostel accommodation at I£8 or B&B at I£20 both per person/sharing basis. Holiday cottages and four-star campsite also available.

Food: Available at centre for approximately I£14 per day for all meals.

Equipment supplied: All specialist equipment provided.

What to take: Personal clothing and footwear.

When to go: Year round except December and January, depending on weather.

Established: 1988

Safety: All guides are fully qualified in their fields.

Insurance: Centre has insurance but it is recommended that clients arrange their own.

Methods of payment: VISA or personal cheque.

Booking information: Advance booking is recommended with payment requested at least 42 days in advance.

Nearest airport: Cork (2.5 hours) or Kerry (1.5 hours). Groups of clients travelling together can be collected from the airport.

Nearest rail station: Killarney (80 mins). Groups of clients travelling together can be collected from the station.

CANYON ADVENTURES
Via Mateotti 57/b, 38069 Torbole sul Garda (TN)
Phone: +39 (0)464 505 072
Fax: +39 (0)464 505 647
Email: flipper@anthesi.com
Website: www.garda.com/flipper

On your Garda cliffs
Lake Garda is a stunningly beautiful part of Italy and the world-famous Arco climbing walls are on its northern shore. Canyon Adventures offer courses with nationally qualified guides to suit all levels of ability, from beginners to advanced rock lovers. For those climbers looking for a bigger experience, the centre runs trips to the inspiring and awesome walls and pinnacles of the Dolomites (used to film the opening scenes of Stallone's *Cliffhanger*).

Activity prices: One-day climbing courses cost from L70,000 to L120,000. Prices for longer trips to the Dolomites are available on request.

Accommodation: Not included in course price. Clients normally arrange their own but the centre can help.

Food: Full-day tours include lunch, otherwise clients arrange their own. There are many options in the Garda area.

Equipment supplied: All specialist equipment is provided.

What to take: Personal clothing.

When to go: Daily from April to the end of October.

Established: 1992

Safety: All rock climbing guides are nationally qualified. The centre is also a member of the Associazione Italiana Guide Alpine.

Insurance: The centre has full liability insurance. Clients are advised to take out their own accident insurance.

Methods of payment: Postal order or travellers' cheques.

Booking information: Advance booking is essential. Full payment is due at

time of booking. Cancellations must be notified in writing at least one week
before activity date.

Nearest airport: Verona.

Nearest rail station: Rovereto.

SWITZERLAND

ADVENTURE'S BEST

PO Box 9, Via Basilea 28, CH-6903 Lugano
Phone: +41 91 966 11 14
Fax: +41 91 966 12 13
Email: info@asbest.ch
Website: www.asbest.ch

Climbing in southern Switzerland

Ticino is the southern-most state, or *canton*, of Switzerland, and its
lakes, rivers and mountains make the region an adventure sports
paradise. The climbing is particularly impressive, with remote peaks
towering as high as 3,400 metres. All climbing activities are instructed
by a nationally qualified Alpine guide. Accommodation is not
included in the price but is available at the centre.

Activity prices: Contact the centre for the latest prices.

Accommodation: Not included in the price, but is available at the centre.
Shared dorms cost an additional SFr20 per person, a double room SFr40 per
person, a double room with en suite bath/shower SFr50 per person and a single
room with en suite bath/shower SFr60 per person.

Food: Not included in the price, but is available at the centre. Buffet breakfast
costs SFr15 per person.

Equipment supplied: All specialist equipment is provided.

What to take: Personal clothing.

When to go: Year round, weather permitting.

Established: 1994

Safety: All instructors hold recognised qualifications from the relevant
national or international governing body.

Insurance: Clients are responsible for arranging their own insurance.

Methods of payment: VISA, Mastercard, Amex, travellers' cheques and cash.

Booking information: No deposit required.

Nearest airport: Lugano-Agno (5 km).

Nearest rail station: Lugano (200 metres).

ALPIN CENTER ZERMATT

Mountain Guides' Association

3920 Zermatt

Switzerland

Phone: +41 (0)27 966 2460

Fax: +41 (0)27 966 2469

Email: alpincenter@zermatt.ch

Website: www.zermatt.ch/alpincenter

Scale Switzerland's best rock faces

Whether you are only starting out on your rock career or you fancy challenging your well-honed techniques on some outstanding rock, then the Alpin Center Zermatt offers it all. Beginners can choose from one-day, three-day or one-week courses that cover basic climbing skills, belaying methods and development of movement techniques. More experienced rock jocks can take on the south-facing rock at Riffelhorn, where you are surrounded by 4,000 foot high Alpine peaks, or on the glacier-polished rock at Dossen. There are also a couple of artificial walls nearby for those rainy days. Courses with highly experienced guides can be tailor-made to suit your requirements.

Activity prices: One-day course costs SFr120; three-day course costs SFr720 (including half-board); one-week course costs SFr830. Advanced climbing courses cost SFr180 per day with a maximum group size of two per instructor.

Accommodation: A wide range of accommodation is available in the Zermatt area. The centre can assist with arranging it. Half-board accommodation is included on some of the courses.

Food: Food is included on some of the courses. There are plenty of eating options in Zermatt.

Equipment supplied: Specialist equipment is available.

What to take: Specialist equipment that you own. Check with centre for recommended list. Personal mountain clothing and suitable footwear.

When to go: June to October.

Established: 1982

Safety: All the Alpin Center guides are fully licensed, qualified and highly experienced.

Insurance: Clients must arrange their own personal accident insurance and it is recommended that you also take out Rescue Insurance with Air Zermatt for SFr20 per week or SFr30 per year. Forms available from the Alpin Center.

Methods of payment: VISA, cash or bank transfer.

Booking information: Advance booking is essential.

Nearest airport: Zurich.

Nearest rail station: Zermatt.

FOUR SEASONS GUIDES

Chalet L'Aurore, 1936 Verbier
Phone: +41 27 771 7683
Fax: +41 27 771 1603
Email: hans@verbier.ch
Website: www.swissguides.com

Climb your Alpine heart out

The big advantage of booking through a private guide is that you can do exactly what you want to do without compromising to the demands of big groups and set itineraries. The UIAGM-qualified guides are also among the most experienced people available for leading you into the mountains. So if you fancy climbing some of Switzerland's classic rock faces, such as those in the Trient area, whether it be in summer or winter (weather permitting), for a day, a week or even a month, then Four Seasons Guides can oblige. If you want guidance on where to go then the guides will advise once they know your experience levels.

Activity prices: Guiding fees are SFr400 per day for one to two clients. For this, the guide will also arrange local travel and hotel bookings and the itinerary (clients pay directly to the hotel, bus company, etc.).

Accommodation: Not included in the price. There is a large range of accommodation options in the area and the guide will help you to arrange it.

Food: Not included in the price, but there are plenty of eating options in the area too. While in the mountains, clients pay for their own food and that of the guide.

Equipment supplied: Specialist equipment can be hired in Verbier.

What to take: All specialist mountain clothing.

When to go: Year round.

Established: 1990

Safety: All guides hold UIAGM qualifications.

Insurance: Clients are recommended to buy helicopter rescue insurance which costs SFr30 for one year.

Methods of payment: VISA, Mastercard, Amex, travellers' cheques and cash.

Booking information: Payment in full is required one week in advance. Full refunds are available for acceptable cancellation.

Nearest airport: Geneva. Transfers can be arranged.

Nearest rail station: Le Chable. Transfers can be arranged.

YO YO ROCK CLIMBING SCHOOL

Kletterschule Yo Yo, Sihlquai 244, CH-8005 Zurich
Phone: +41 1 273 1861
Fax: +41 1 273 1803
Email: yoyo@kletterschule.ch
Website: www.kletterschule.ch

Get high on Swiss rock

Yo Yo Rock Climbing School is a dynamic centre that offers climbing courses to suit everyone around the major Swiss crags and further afield in France, Italy and Spain. The basic courses are split into three parts that all last a weekend, where you learn the basics of ropework, climbing techniques and safety. The locations used in Switzerland include Berner Oberland and Ticino. Highly qualified and very experienced instructors who know the mountain environment intimately supervise all the courses. Many of the guides speak English. Group sizes are limited to a maximum of eight.

Activity prices: Courses cost from SFr320 for weekends including accom-modation, guide, breakfast and dinner. Week-long courses cost from SFr840 to SFr1,360 depending on location and difficulty.

Accommodation: Included in the price.

Food: Some is included in the price.

Equipment supplied: Some specialist equipment is provided.

What to take: Some personal climbing gear (a full list is sent on booking), and personal clothing.

When to go: Year round, weather permitting.

Established: 1996

Safety: All instructors hold recognised qualifications from the relevant national or international governing body. Second guides can be trainee guides. All the guides are members of the Swiss Mountain Guide Federation.

Insurance: Clients are responsible for arranging their own insurance.

Methods of payment: International bank draft, travellers' cheques and cash.

Booking information: Advance booking is recommended. A sliding scale of cancellation penalties is used. Cancellation insurance is available from the centre.

Nearest airport: Zurich.

Nearest rail station: Depends on course location.

UNITED KINGDOM

ACORN ACTIVITIES
PO Box 120, Hereford HR4 8YB
Phone: +44 (0)1432 830083
Fax: +44 (0)1432 830110
Email: sales@acornactivities.co.uk
Website: www.acornactivities.co.uk

Rock climbing in Snowdonia, Scotland and the Lake District
Acorn Activities runs rock climbing courses throughout the UK for those who really want to get to grips with the rock. Half-day, full-day, two-day and five-day options are all on offer. Using a variety of rock faces, fully qualified guides will teach you everything from the basics of technique and belaying through to leading and seconding. On the

five-day course in particular, there will be ample opportunity to follow some classic harder routes as your skills progress to multi-pitch climbs. All specialist equipment is provided and accommodation is included on weekend breaks and holidays, but not on single days or courses.

Activity prices: £25 for a half-day, £40 for a full day, £120 for a two-day course, £300 for a five-day course. Two-day breaks cost £175, six-day breaks £475.

Accommodation: B&B accommodation is included on the two and five-day breaks.

Food: Dinner costs an additional £14 per night on the two and five-day breaks, otherwise not included.

Equipment supplied: All specialist equipment is provided.

What to take: Warm, windproof and dry clothes, depending on conditions.

When to go: Year round.

Established: 1990

Safety: All instructors are BMC qualified.

Insurance: Insurance is required, although this can be arranged through Acorn Activities.

Methods of payment: VISA, Mastercard, cheque and cash.

Booking information: Late bookings are welcomed. A non-refundable deposit of £10 per day is required. Cancellation charges apply on a sliding scale from 80% for over 43 days before departure to 100% for up to 14 days.

Nearest airport: Depends on course location.

Nearest rail station: Depends on the itinerary.

ADVENTURE SPORTS
Carnkie Farmhouse, Carnkie, Redruth, Cornwall TR16 6RZ
Phone: +44 (0)1209 218 962
Fax: +44 (0)1209 314 118
Email: holidays@adventure-sports.co.uk
Website: www.adventure-sports.co.uk
Cornish cliff climbers
Cornwall is among the most beautiful coastal regions in the UK and the sea cliffs here are ideal for learning to rock climb. There is a huge selection of routes to choose from to suit every level of ability so you

could justify spending a whole week learning to climb there. Adventure Sports use only highly qualified instructors who will take you through the fundamental principles of rock climbing, including ropework and how to move on rock. More advanced climbers can be advised on how to improve their skills, including safety and lead climbing. The location for climbing is chosen on a daily basis to take advantage of the best weather conditions. The centre offers a range of sports so you can mix climbing with other adventures during your stay.

Activity prices: A three-day camping stay with two days of activities costs from £76 (low season) to £100 (high season) and prices go up to £329 for a seven night/seven activity days course.

Accommodation: Included in price. You have a choice of camping, self-catering chalets or a converted self-catering farmhouse. There are many social options nearby or on the site.

Food: Not included.

Equipment supplied: All specialised equipment is provided.

What to take: Personal clothing and suitable footwear.

When to go: Summer months only.

Established: 1982

Safety: All the centre's climbing instructors hold nationally recognised qualifications and are very experienced. The centre is a member of the West Country Tourist Board.

Insurance: Insurance is required. Policies are offered by the centre.

Methods of payment: VISA, cheque and cash.

Booking information: Advance booking is required. A £50 deposit is payable.

Nearest airport: Newquay.

Nearest rail station: Redruth. Transfers can be arranged.

ALAN KIMBER

Calluna, Heathercroft, Fort William PH33 6RE
Phone: +44 (0)1397 700 451
Fax: +44 (0)1397 700 489
Email: mountain@guide.u-net.com
Website: www.guide.u-net.com

Rocky highs in the Scottish Highlands

Alan Kimber has climbed in many of the world's greatest mountain ranges and is one of the most experienced mountain guides in the UK. There are several rock climbing courses offered to suit every level of ability from beginner to advanced. The five-day Introductory Easy Rock course teaches the basics of safe and efficient movement on rock faces, choosing equipment and using it properly, tying the correct knots, abseiling, belaying and rope management. And it is all taught on location at the stunning crags of Glen Coe, Glen Nevis and Ben Nevis. With a 1:3 instructor:client ratio you can be sure that your progress will be closely monitored. Once you are content climbing grade VS then you can join the Skye Rock course, where you get to climb some of the UK's classic routes on the Isle of Skye.

Activity prices: The starter course costs £235 for instruction only, £290 self-catering or £330 in a hotel. The five-day Skye Rock course costs £320 for instruction only, £380 in a hostel or £410 in a hotel.

Accommodation: On-site self-catering accommodation is available in the beautifully located and homely Calluna Lodge. Various room options. Hotel accommodation can be arranged. The Skye Rock self-catering accommodation is at an independent hostel.

Food: Not included in the price. Accommodation is self-catering. It is just a ten-minute walk to the centre of Fort William.

Equipment supplied: Technical climbing equipment is supplied. If you don't have your own rock climbing shoes, you can hire them at £4 per day.

What to take: Personal clothing, footwear and other items. Full list sent on booking.

When to go: May to September.

Established: 1972

Safety: All instructors are MLTB qualified. The centre is approved by the Mountaineering Council of Scotland and the BMC.

Insurance: Mountaineering insurance is available from the centre and costs £10.70 for seven days.

Methods of payment: VISA, Mastercard, cheque, cash (3.5% surcharge on credit card payments).

Booking information: Advance booking is essential. A non-refundable 50%

deposit is payable on booking. Balance paid on arrival. Cancellation within four weeks of course start-date forfeits the whole course price unless replacement client is found.

Nearest airport: Glasgow.

Nearest rail station: Fort William.

AVALON ADVENTURE

The Mill House, Dulford, Cullompton, Devon EX15 2ED
Phone: +44 (0)1884 266 646
Fax: +44 (0)1884 266 646
Email: avalon-adventure@dial.pipex.com
Website: http://dialspace.dial.pipex.com/avalon.adventure/

Rock around Europe

Although Avalon Adventure are based in Devon where there is some excellent sea cliff climbing, they operate their climbing courses throughout the UK and parts of Europe. Their five-day Introduction to Rock Climbing course is a great way to become confident on rock in a short space of time. The syllabus covers ropework, belaying, protection placement, arranging belay stances, anchors, route-finding, emergency procedures and equipment selection. The Intermediate course takes you on to lead climbing on multi-pitch routes. They also offer bouldering courses in Fontainebleau, the French mecca, classic rock courses around the UK and trips to the Costa Blanca in Spain.

Activity prices: The Introduction course costs £180 and the Intermediate course from £150 to £250 depending on location.

Accommodation: Not included in the price. The centre will help you arrange accommodation to suit your budget.

Food: Not included.

Equipment supplied: All specialist equipment is supplied.

What to take: Personal clothing, suitable footwear.

When to go: April to August.

Established: 1992

Safety: All the instructors are fully qualified and hold first aid qualifications.

The centre is licensed by the AALA and is approved by the Association of Mountaineering Instructors.

Insurance: The centre is insured, though clients may wish to take out separate insurance too.

Methods of payment: VISA, Mastercard, cheques and cash.

Booking information: Advance booking is essential.

Nearest airport: Exeter. Transfers can be arranged.

Nearest rail station: Exeter. Transfers can be arranged.

BLACK MOUNTAIN ACTIVITIES
PO Box 5, Hay on Wye, Hereford HR3 5YB
Phone: +44 (0)1497 847 897
Fax: +44 (0)1497 847 897
Email: enquiries@blackmountain.co.uk
Website: www.blackmountain.co.uk

Scaling south Welsh rock
Rock climbing has never been so popular and Black Mountain have courses to suit beginners and improvers, with real emphasis on teaching techniques in a way that makes it easy to progress to harder routes. The Real Rock Taster Days are designed for novices and teach you basic rope techniques and how to move on rock. On full-day courses, you also get the chance to try abseiling. Improvers' courses involve more challenging climbs, learning belay techniques and equipment selection.

Activity prices: A Taster course costs £30 for a full day and £20 for a half-day. Improvers' courses last a full day and cost £35.

Accommodation: Not included in the price. There is a range of accommodation available locally and the centre will advise you.

Food: Not included. Packed lunches can be arranged.

Equipment supplied: All specialist equipment is supplied.

What to take: Personal clothing, suitable footwear.

When to go: Year round.

Established: 1992

Safety: All the centre's staff are fully qualified in their respective sports, hold first aid qualifications and are highly professional. All equipment used meets national safety standards. The centre is licensed by the AALA and the Welsh Tourist Board.

Insurance: The centre is insured, though clients may wish to take out separate insurance too.

Methods of payment: Personal cheque and cash.

Booking information: Advance booking is recommended, though late bookings may be possible.

Nearest airport: Depends on tour. Cardiff and Bristol are nearest to the centre.

Nearest rail station: Depends on the itinerary. Hereford and Abergavenny are nearest to the centre.

HIGH TREK SNOWDONIA

Tal y Waen, Deiniolen, Caernarfon, Gwynedd LL55 3NA
Phone: +44 (0)1286 871 232
Fax: +44 (0)1286 870 576
Email: high.trek@virgin.net
Website: www.hightrek.co.uk

A personal climb in Wales

High Trek Snowdonia specialise in very personalised rock climbing courses with a client:instructor ratio of just 2:1 so you are guaranteed to improve your skills. There is virtually no time spent in classrooms as the learning is done out on the crags that have made Snowdonia one of the most famous spots in European climbing. Starting on single pitch routes, you will learn the basics of tying on, using a belay plate and the climbing calls used to tell your partner what you are doing. You will then be shown how to use protection equipment and the secrets of moving well on rock. You will also learn how to abseil. In addition, there is an improvers' course where you can learn to lead or simply make the swap from gym climbing to real rock.

Activity prices: Both the beginners' and the improvers' course cost £265 for three days and three nights all-inclusive.

Accommodation: Included in the price. You stay at the homely Tal y Waen farmhouse in bunk-bed accommodation.

Food: Included in price. You get full board including wine with dinner and a packed lunch.

Equipment supplied: All specialist equipment is supplied, except climbing shoes.

What to take: Personal clothing, suitable footwear or climbing shoes.

When to go: April to October.

Established: 1985

Safety: All the centre's climbing instructors hold the Mountain Instructor Award and a first aid qualification. The centre is approved by the Association of Mountaineering Instructors and the Wales Tourist Board.

Methods of payment: VISA, Matercard, Switch, cheques, cash.

Booking information: Advance booking is recommended though late bookings may be possible. A £75 deposit is payable and full payment is due four weeks in advance. Sliding scale for cancellation.

Nearest airport: Manchester.

Nearest rail station: Bangor.

INTERNATIONAL SCHOOL OF MOUNTAINEERING, SWITZERLAND

Hafod Tan y Graig, Nant Gwynant, Gwynedd LL55 4NW, UK
Phone: +44 (0)1766 890441
Fax: +44 (0)1766 890599
Email: ism@dial.pipex.com
Website: http//:ds.dial.pipex.com/ism

Rock climb the classic crags of north Wales
ISM uses the wonderful climbing crags of Snowdonia to train people for their overseas trips to the Alps. However, you don't have to be Alps-bound to join their courses. They offer tuition with highly qualified instructors on a personal basis and will be able to supply you with all the skills necessary to tackle single and multi-pitch rock routes. They will teach you about belaying, rope management, protection selection, route finding, movement and anything else you need to know.

Activity prices: From £45 to £130 per day depending on group size.

Accommodation: In the UK guesthouse or hotel accommodation can be arranged.

Food: In the UK food can be arranged.

Equipment supplied: All specialist equipment.

What to take: Personal clothing and footwear.

When to go: Year round.

Established: 1960

Safety: All guides hold the International Carnet, the highest qualification available in mountaineering.

Insurance: Relevant insurance required for all Alpine courses.

Methods of payment: All common payment methods accepted.

Booking information: Contact ISM for booking form and full terms and conditions.

Nearest airport: Manchester.

Nearest rail station: Bangor.

KEVIN WALKER MOUNTAIN ACTIVITIES

74 Beacons Park, Brecon, Powys LD3 9BQ
Phone: +44 (0)1874 625111
Fax: +44 (0)1874 625111
Email: kevin@mountain-acts.freeserve.co.uk
Website: http://www.mountain-acts.freeserve.co.uk

Climbing in north and south Wales

Wales boasts stunning mountain scenery, the most extensive cave system in the UK and more sheep than people! Kevin Walker Mountain Activities has been offering courses and short breaks in the Welsh Mountains for over 20 years, with the emphasis always on small group size and personal tuition. Most courses are led by Kevin, who has published a number of books on mountaineering and climbing and has been involved with MLTB courses for many years. Two and five-day introductory courses are offered on the superlative mountain crags of Snowdonia. No previous climbing experience is necessary, but all participants must be over 18 years of age, and should be reasonably fit and healthy. Two-day courses include instruction on basic technique and ropework with an emphasis on safety, while five-day courses take in the larger crags. Ensuring there are no more than two clients per instructor maximises attention, individual instruction and enjoyment.

Activity prices: From £155 for a two-day course.

Accommodation: Not included in the price, although a good range of accommodation is available locally – see the brochure for recommendations.

Food: Clients to arrange their own.

Equipment supplied: All specialist equipment is provided.

What to take: Outdoor clothing and footwear suitable for the prevailing conditions (available for hire if necessary) – if in doubt, call ahead for advice.

When to go: April to October.

Established: 1979

Safety: Kevin Walker Mountain Activities is a MLTB recognised centre, and all instructors are MLTB qualified.

Insurance: The centre carries indemnity insurance for all activities and can advise on personal accident insurance if required.

Methods of payment: Cash, cheques from British banks and sterling travellers' cheques.

Booking information: Reservations essential. A 20% deposit secures a booking, with the balance due three weeks prior to the course. Cancellation four to six weeks before the course forfeits 30% of the fee, two to four weeks before 50%, and less than two weeks before 100%.

Nearest airport: Cardiff (south Wales) or Manchester (north Wales), depending on the course.

Nearest rail station: Abergavenny (south Wales) or Betws-y-Coed (north Wales).

PEAK ACTIVITIES

Rock Lea Activity Training Centre, Station Road, Hathersage, Hope Valley, Derbyshire S32 1DD
Phone: +44 (0)1433 650 345
Fax: +44 (0)1433 650 342
Email: admin@iain.co.uk
Website: www.iain.co.uk

Getting to grips with Derbyshire grit

Hathersage is right in the middle of a little piece of rock climbing heaven. Just look out the door of the centre and you can see the famous, 5 km long gritstone crags of Stanage – one of the best places to climb in the UK – Millstone Edge and Bole Hill Quarry. If you want a change from those then Burbage Edge and Frogatt Edge are just five minutes' drive away. There are numerous and varied routes suitable for absolute beginners as well as grades to test the best. It's not all rock, though, and the weekends are great social occasions too. The course content includes basic safety, knot-tying, ropework, belaying techniques, moving on rock, setting up top rope systems and safe methods for leading climbs. Once through the beginners course, you can take on the Follow Up Climbing Weekend, where the instructors work closely with you to polish your rock skills.

Activity prices: Beginners' Rock Climbing Weekends cost £120 per person for two full days of tuition. A Follow Up Climbing Weekend costs £149. Climbing is also included on the multi-activity weekend at £149 per person. Personal one-to-one tuition can also be arranged.

Accommodation: Not included in the tour price. There is a large range of options within easy reach of the centre, ranging from hostels and B&B to farmhouses and hotels.

Food: Not included in tour price, but there are plenty of local eateries to suit all budgets.

Equipment supplied: All specialist equipment and bad weather gear if necessary.

What to take: Personal clothing and suitable footwear. Full list supplied on booking.

When to go: Year round, depending on weather.

Established: 1979

Safety: All the climbing instructors used by Peak Activities are qualified with SPSA, MIA and MIC{?} and have first aid qualifications too. Staff carry radios and first aid kits. The company is licensed by the AALA and is a member of the Heart of England Tourist Board. Supplied specialist equipment is of a high standard and regularly maintained and replaced.

Insurance: All Peak Activity tours are fully insured for public and third party liability. Optional additional insurance can be taken out to guard against cancellation, illness, loss of property, etc.

Methods of payment: VISA, Mastercard, Eurocard, personal cheques.

Booking information: A 50% deposit is requested with all bookings.

Nearest airport: Leeds (45 mins), Manchester (45 mins), Birmingham (90 mins) or Sheffield (12 mins). Transfers can be arranged.

Nearest rail station: Hathersage. Transfers can be arranged.

PLAS Y BRENIN

National Mountain Centre, Capel Curig, Conwy LL24 0ET
Phone: +44 (0)1690 720 214
Fax: +44 (0)1690 720 394
Email: info@pyb.co.uk
Website: www.pyb.co.uk

Scaling Snowdonia's rock routes

Plas y Brenin is one of the foremost outdoor centres in the UK and has been operating since 1954. It is based right in the heart of Snowdonia, which has a plethora of classic rock climbing locations, including sea cliffs at Gogarth and the mountain crag of Clogwyn D'ur Arddu. The centre operates a whole range of climbing courses that can take you from complete novice to competent lead climber and beyond. The beginners' course, which has a low student/ instructor ratio of 4:1, covers basic ropework, equipment selection, bouldering, top-roping and single and multi-pitch route techniques. The Introduction to Lead Climbing course takes you through understanding guidebooks, route selection and choosing protection on the climb. There's even a course for indoor gym climbers to help them convert to real rock. And the whole time you are surrounded by some of the most dramatic mountain and coastal scenery in the UK.

Activity prices: There is a multitude of courses on offer. An Introduction to Climbing weekend course costs £150, while an Introduction to Lead Climbing course costs £170. A weekend transition course to convert from indoor climbing to the real thing costs £150.

Accommodation: Prices for most courses based at Plas y Brenin include shared accommodation at the centre. Many rooms are twin-bedded with en suite facilities. A self-catering cottage and a bunkhouse are also available at the centre.

Food: Most course prices include full board.

Equipment supplied: All specialist equipment and clothing is provided.

What to take: Personal clothing and your own equipment if you prefer to use it.

When to go: March to October.

Established: 1954

Safety: All instructors hold nationally recognised qualifications and only the most capable and experienced are employed. The centre is licensed by the AALA. Great emphasis is placed on safety and the high quality equipment used is regularly checked and replaced.

Insurance: The centre carries public liability insurance for all activities and recommends that clients take out independent insurance against curtailment and cancellation of their course (available from the centre) and a personal accident policy.

Methods of payment: VISA, Mastercard, Access, personal cheque, cash.

Booking information: Reservations must be made in advance and a deposit is required.

Nearest airport: Manchester.

Nearest rail station: Llandudno Junction. Free transfer is available by prior arrangement.

ROCK AND ICE

Birch Tree House, Shirley, nr Ashbourne, Derbyshire DE6 3AS
Phone: +44 (0)1335 360 490
Fax: N/A
Email: rock.ice@bigfoot.com
Website: www.rockandice.demon.co.uk

Take on the crags of the Derbyshire Dales
Rock and Ice are based in the heart of the Derbyshire Dales, home to some of the UK's best climbing crags. They offer a selection of courses run by qualified instructors to suit a variety of climbing abilities. Their two-day introductory course covers moving on rock,

equipment, ropework and knots, and basic safety skills. It is not necessary to have any previous experience though this course can be tailored to suit people who have a little experience and wish to gain more confidence. The groups are small and friendly. The intermediate course takes you on to steeper rock and introduces you to multi-pitch climbing and double rope techniques, while the advanced course helps you progress up the route grades and includes traverses and overhangs. Pump up those muscles!

Activity prices: Prices are based around £80 to £100 per day for one to one tuition and £50 per person on a one instructor to two clients basis.

Accommodation: Not included in the tour price. The centre will help you to arrange accommodation in the local area.

Food: Not included in price but there are local eateries to suit all budgets.

Equipment supplied: All specialist equipment.

What to take: Personal clothing and suitable footwear. Suggested list supplied on booking.

When to go: Year round, depending on weather.

Established: 1987

Safety: The instructors employed by Rock and Ice are all qualified by the national governing bodies.

Insurance: The centre recommends outdoor pursuits travel insurance that starts at £12.50 for up to four days.

Methods of payment: Cheques and cash.

Booking information: A 50% deposit is requested with all bookings. Balance is due 28 days before course. Cancellation penalties are applied.

Nearest airport: Manchester.

Nearest rail station: Derby. Transfers can be arranged.

THE ROCK CENTRE

Chudleigh, Devon TQ13 OEE
Phone: +44 (0)1626 852717
Fax: +44 (0)1626 852717
Email: trc@globalnet.co.uk
Website: www.rockcentre.co.uk

Climbing on Devon limestone

Devon features some fantastic limestone climbing at all grades, as well as the infamous granite tors of Dartmoor National Park, and the Rock Centre is ideally situated to take advantage of these opportunities. The centre itself is set in 10 acres of rural countryside, with mossy dells and its own limestone cliffs, creating an ideal learning resource within a few minutes' walk of the onsite accommodation. Chudleigh rock offers both north and south-facing limestone climbs for all standards, while the options in the surrounding area include world-class coastal climbing. Particularly popular is sea-traversing on Torbay's apparently inaccessible cliffs and coves. Traversing involves scrambling sideways just above the high tide mark – fixed ropes and excellent holds make it ideal for beginners. For those with some experience who want to work towards a recognised climbing qualification, the Rock Centre runs Single Pitch Award training and assessment courses throughout the year. This basic climbing qualification is run under the auspices of the BMC and the MLTB and covers such skills as choice of venue, rope management, correct use of equipment, group management, emergency procedures and crag etiquette.

Activity prices: £10 per half-day, £20 per full day for groups of four or more. For individuals or groups smaller then four, an instructor costs £40 per half-day and £80 per full-day. SPA courses cost £50 per head for training and £60 per head for assessment.

Accommodation: Not included in the price, although a good range of accommodation is available locally. Camping at the Rock Centre costs £1 per person, bunkhouse accommodation £2 per person. B&B accommodation can be arranged at a price to suit.

Food: Clients to arrange their own.

Equipment supplied: All specialist equipment is provided.

What to take: Personal clothing and footwear suitable for the prevailing conditions – if in doubt, call ahead for advice.

When to go: Year round.

Established: 1978

Safety: All staff hold national governing body qualifications and the centre is licensed by the AALA.

Insurance: The centre carries indemnity insurance for all activities and can advise on personal accident insurance if required.

Methods of payment: Cash or cheque.

Booking information: Reservations must be made in advance, although a deposit is not normally required.

Nearest airport: Exeter or Plymouth.

Nearest rail station: Exeter or Newton Abbot. Clients can be picked up by prior arrangement.

TWR-Y-FELIN NO LIMITS

The TYF Group, 1 High Street, St Davids, Pembrokeshire SA62 6QS
Phone: +44 (0)1437 721 611
Fax: +44 (0)1437 721 692
Email: info@tyf.com
Website: www.tyf.com

Climb the cliffs of Pembrokeshire

Based in Britain's smallest city, the TYF No Limits centre has access to the north Pembrokeshire climbing area with its challenging sea cliff routes. The centre also has its own climbing wall where you can practise your technique to your heart's content.

Their Introduction to Climbing course starts you off on easier sandstone slab routes on the peninsula's south coast. These are classic routes that are open to all levels. You will learn about ropework, equipment, belay techniques, and basic climbing and abseiling skills. The Improvers' course includes more advanced techniques, protection placement, rescue procedures and equipment and route selection. For those looking to lead climbs, a course is offered to teach the rope and safety techniques needed.

Activity prices: The Introduction to Climbing course costs £240 for three days with full board or £132 for camping. Both the Improvers' and Lead courses follow the same pricing plan.

Accommodation: Included in price. You can either camp or have B&B, half board or full board accommodation in the Twr-y-Felin Hotel, a beautiful converted 18th-century windmill.

Food: Included in hotel-based course prices (see above).

Equipment supplied: All specialist equipment is provided.

What to take: Personal clothing and suitable footwear

When to go: April to October.

Established: 1986

Safety: All the climbing instructors hold national qualifications. The centre is approved by the AALA and is a member of the Welsh Tourist Board.

Insurance: The centre has liability insurance but recommends that clients take out independent insurance against curtailment and cancellation of their course (available from the centre) and a personal accident policy.

Methods of payment: VISA, Mastercard, Switch, cheques and cash.

Booking information: Advance booking is required.

Nearest airport: Cardiff.

Nearest rail station: Haverfordwest. Transfers can be arranged.

UIST OUTDOOR CENTRE

Cearn Dusgaidh, Lochmaddy, Isle of North Uist, Outer Hebrides, HS6 5AE
Phone: +44 (0)1876 500480
Fax: +44 (0)1876 500480
Email: alyson@keiller.u-net.com
Website: www.uistoutdoorcentre.co.uk

Rock climbing the cliffs and sea stacks of the Outer Hebrides
Nowhere in Britain is more remote or inaccessible than the arch-ipelago of the Outer Hebrides, but the rewards of such isolation speak for themselves. The North Atlantic forms a spectacular and often foreboding backdrop to the sea cliffs, sea stacks and crags that provide the perfect rock-climbing environment. Half-day, full-day and multi-day courses are offered and all specialist climbing equipment is provided. All activities are of course weather dependent, but with walking, wildlife watching and sea kayaking also on offer, it's unlikely you'll be stuck for something to do.

Activity prices: From £35 per day for adults, £18 per day for under-12s.

Accommodation: Bunkhouse accommodation costs an additional £9 per night with bedding and £7 per night without bedding.

Food: Full board can be arranged but there are plenty of facilities for self-catering.

Equipment supplied: All specialist equipment is supplied.

What to take: Personal clothing.

When to go: Activities are available year round, but suitable climbing conditions are most likely from May to September.

Established: 1991

Safety: All instructors hold nationally recognised qualifications.

Insurance: The centre is insured for all licensed activities.

Methods of payment: Only cash and cheque accepted.

Booking information: Book by phone, post or email. A 10% deposit is required to secure a booking.

Nearest airport: Benbecula.

Nearest rail station: N/A. The nearest ferry terminal is in Lochmaddy. All clients can be picked up from the ferry or airport at no extra cost.

SAILING

Sailing is perhaps one of the oldest adventure sports in this book, and it's still one of the most popular. The reasons, perhaps, lie in its inherent flexibility: the basic skills and decisions used to sail a one-man topper around a sheltered bay are no different from those used by skippers leading a 12-man crew on a round-the-world yacht race. And of course, the thrill is the same: wind rushing past the sail, spray pluming up from the prow and the indescribable feeling of flying along under the power of the wind alone.

Perhaps because of its heritage and history, sailing is extremely well regulated all over Europe, with a well-established progression of qualifications for those who want to enjoy the freedom of sailing on their own. For those less certain of their sea legs, most sailing centres offer two or three-hour introductory sessions that should be more than enough to give you a taste for the salt-water life. And at its simplest level, there's very little demand for physical or financial fitness, as introductory courses tend to be cheap and cheerful.

After mastering the basics of rigging the boat, setting the sail and tacking into the wind, you'll progress on to bigger and faster boats, until eventually, after years of practice and a lifetime of learning, you too might be skippering your own yacht round the world. In fact, if that sounds like your cup of rum, there are even companies that allow you to train aboard a round-the-world yacht without any experience whatsoever. But be warned: a month-long leg in the Indian Ocean is as much about drive and determination as the health of your bank balance.

TURKEY

BITEZ YACHTING
Neyzen Tevfik Caddesi 142, 48400 Bodrum
Phone: +90 252 316 2139/2454
Fax: +90 252 316 3101
Email: ecomail@turk.net
Website: http://www.holidaybank.co.uk/bitezyachting

Sailing the Turkish coast and the Greek islands
Participation is the essence of Bitez Yachting's one and two-week trips in the idyllic waters of the Turkish coast and the Greek islands. On board the traditional Aegean-type wooden yachts *Yeke* or *Diwa*, participants assist with setting the sails and other chores on board, as well as tending the helm, although no previous experience is required as all training will be given. A typical day involves a few hours' sailing, time spent idling in quiet bays and swimming in turquoise-blue waters, and visits ashore to some of the villages and harbours along the coast. The sailing programmes can also be combined with a few days' trekking or scuba-diving.

Activity prices: From US$335 for one week to US$545 for two weeks in the low season, and US$380 to US$625 in the high season.
Accommodation: On-board accommodation is included in the price.
Food: Food on board operates on a kitty system that is not included in the price.
Equipment supplied: All specialist equipment is provided.
What to take: Personal clothing and footwear suitable for the prevailing conditions – if in doubt, call ahead for advice.
When to go: May to October.
Established: 1986
Safety: All the English/Dutch-speaking guides are highly experienced.
Insurance: Clients are responsible for arranging their own insurance.
Methods of payment: Cash and/or bank transfer.

Booking information: A 25% deposit is required to confirm a booking, with the balance paid on arrival. There is a 5% charge for a cancellation within two weeks of the departure date.

Nearest airport: Dalaman and Bodrum. Tranfers to and from the airport are included in the price.

Nearest rail station: N/A.

UNITED KINGDOM

ACORN ACTIVITIES
PO Box 120, Hereford HR4 8YB
Phone: +44 (0)1432 830083
Fax: +44 (0)1432 830110
Email: sales@acornactivities.co.uk
Website: www.acornactivities.co.uk

Sailing throughout the UK
Acorn Activities boasts a number of locations throughout the UK for sailing, all of which are ideally suited for beginners. Two-day and five-day courses are available for those who want to make their own accommodation arrangements, but there are also two, three and five-day breaks for those who would prefer the whole package. Sailors on the two-day and three-day courses will be instructed to RYA Level 1, while sailors on the five-day holiday will be instructed to RYA Level 2. Wetsuits are provided for all sailing courses, and Wayfarer dinghies and Toppers are used for all instruction. Accommodation is arranged at one of a number of family-run hotels within easy driving distance of the sailing centres, and all bedrooms have private en suite facilities.

Activity prices: £165 for a two-day course, £250 for a three-day course and £440 for a five-day course.

Accommodation: Family-run hotel accommodation included in the price.

Food: Breakfast is included, but dinner costs an extra £14 per person per night.

Equipment supplied: All specialist equipment is provided, including wetsuits.

What to take: Warm clothes and shoes that can get wet.

When to go: April to October.

Established: 1990

Safety: All instructors are RYA qualified.

Insurance: Insurance is required, although this can be arranged through Acorn Activities.

Methods of payment: VISA, Mastercard, cheque and cash.

Booking information: Late bookings are welcomed. A non-refundable deposit of £10 per day is required. Cancellation charges apply on a sliding scale from 80% for over 43 days before departure to 100% for up to 14 days.

Nearest airport: Cardiff or Birmingham International.

Nearest rail station: Depends on the itinerary.

ADVENTURE SPORTS

Carnkie Farmhouse, Carnkie, Redruth, Cornwall TR16 6RZ
Phone: +44 (0)1209 218 962
Fax: +44 (0)1209 314 118
Email: holidays@adventure-sports.co.uk
Website: www.adventure-sports.co.uk

Sailing under a Cornish sky

Cornwall is one of the UK's most beautiful coastal regions with towering cliffs, caves and sandy beaches. Add to this the reliable winds and you have a great location for learning to sail. To maximise sailing time and to ensure the best conditions on any given day, Adventure Sports use a variety of locations around the area. The centre's instructors are RYA qualified and can get complete novices handling a sailboat with confidence during a short course. There are many other activities on offer at the centre, so you can mix sailing with other sports during your stay. The courses are very socially orientated and aimed at the adult market, so you will have a fun time out of the water too.

Activity prices: A three-day camping stay with two days of activities costs from £76 (low season) to £100 (high season) and prices go up to £329 for a seven night/seven activity days course.

Accommodation: Included in price. You have a choice of camping, self-catering chalets or a converted self-catering farmhouse. There are many social options nearby or on the site.

Food: Not included.

Equipment supplied: All specialised equipment is provided.

What to take: Swimsuit, suitable footwear.

When to go: Summer months only.

Established: 1982

Safety: All the centre's sailing instructors hold RYA qualifications and are very experienced.

Insurance: Insurance is required. Policies are offered by the centre.

Methods of payment: VISA, cheque and cash.

Booking information: Advance booking is required. A £50 deposit is payable.

Nearest airport: Newquay.

Nearest rail station: Redruth. Transfers can be arranged.

CALSHOT ACTIVITIES CENTRE
Calshot Spit, Fawley, Southampton SO45 1BR
Phone: +44 (0)23 8089 2077
Fax: +44 (0)23 8089 1267
Email: acocal@hants.gov.uk
Website: www.hants.gov.uk/calshot

Learn where the instructors learn

Calshot Activities Centre is located right at the water's edge on the Solent, a perfect sheltered place for learning to sail. The centre has been operating for over 30 years and is used to train the RYA instructors, so you know the standards are high. They have a large fleet of dinghies to choose from, such as Optimists for beginners and Toppers for race training, and a team of experienced instructors to guide you through each course. The courses emphasise the practical side of sailing within a safe learning environment. Courses are tailored to meet your requirements but can be residential or non-residential.

Activity prices: There are so many course options and package prices that you should call the centre with your specific requirements.

Accommodation: Included in price. There is room for 150 people at the centre with various room options.

Food: Included. Three cooked meals per day plus drinks with residential courses. Meals on other courses can be booked to suit.

Equipment supplied: All equipment is provided.

What to take: Swimsuit, suitable footwear.

When to go: April to October.

Established: 1969

Safety: All the centre's sailing instructors are RYA qualified. The centre is licensed by the AALA and is a member of the RYA.

Insurance: Insurance is required. Policies are offered by the centre that cover you from the day of booking for cancellation through sickness or injury.

Methods of payment: VISA, Mastercard, cheque and cash.

Booking information: Advance booking is required. Full payment is needed on booking for all courses of up to four days' duration. A non-refundable £25 deposit is needed for longer courses with balance paid eight weeks before arrival.

Nearest airport: Southampton or Bournemouth.

Nearest rail station: Southampton Central or Beaulieu Road, Brockenhurst.

CROFT-NA-CABER

Kenmore, Loch Tay, Perthshire
Phone: +44 (0)1887 830 236
Fax: +44 (0)1887 830 649
Email: info@croftnacaber.co.uk
Website: www.croftnacaber.co.uk

Windy days on Loch Tay
Set among beautiful forested hills, Loch Tay is a lovely place to sail. Croft-na-Caber are approved by the RYA and run a full range of RYA certificate courses. You can choose from half-day or one-day taster courses or take on the RYA 1-star and 2-star courses over a full day. Higher-level courses take up to five days to complete. The sailing is mainly done in dinghies though the centre has a choice of boat styles, including a catamaran.

Activity prices: Sailing courses range from £40 for half a day to £69 for a full day. Longer courses are available.

Accommodation: Self-catering log cabins and hotel accommodation are available at centre.

Food: Hotel restaurant and bar at centre.

Equipment supplied: All specialist equipment is supplied.

What to take: Personal clothing, swimsuit, suitable footwear.

When to go: Year round.

Established: 1974

Safety: All the centre's staff are fully qualified in their respective sports, hold first aid qualifications and are highly professional. All equipment used meets national safety standards. The centre is licensed by the AALA and is recognised by the RYA.

Insurance: The centre is insured up to £6 million for liability but clients may wish to take out separate insurance for accidents/cancellation.

Methods of payment: VISA, Mastercard, cheque and cash.

Booking information: Advance booking is essential. Payment of 20% deposit is required. Tour must be confirmed or cancelled at least seven days in advance.

Nearest airport: Edinburgh. Transfers can be arranged.

Nearest rail station: Perth, Pitlochry. Transfers can be arranged.

HOVE LAGOON WATERSPORTS

Hove Lagoon, Kingsway, Hove BN3 4LX
Phone: +44 (0)1273 424842
Fax: +44 (0)1273 421919
Email: windsurf@hovelagoon.co.uk
Website: www.hovelagoon.co.uk

Sailing the English Channel

The Channel boasts a long and distinguished sailing history, and the sheltered waters of Hove Lagoon provide the ideal environment to get to grips with the mainsail and master the mizzen. The best way to learn to sail is to take the RYA Level 1 course, which takes you step by step through the basics of rigging, launching and sailing in sheltered waters. Successful completion of the course enables budding sailors to hire dinghies in the lagoon. After that, the ocean's the limit as RYA courses 2 and 3 take you beyond the harbour walls and out to sea. A combination of courses can be taken at a discount, and there is also a catamaran sailing course for beginners. All courses are flexible and can include weekends, weekdays or evenings.

Activity prices: From £20 for two hours to £120 for a full weekend, including all instruction and specialist equipment. Private tuition, nationally recognised certification and group discounts also available.
Accommodation: Local B&B and hotel accommodation can be arranged from £15 per night, but is not included in the price.
Food: Catering facilities and a licensed bar are available, but are not included in the price.
Equipment supplied: All specialist equipment is supplied.
What to take: Personal clothing, swimsuit, towel and a pair of shoes that can get wet.
When to go: March to November.
Established: 1994
Safety: All instructors have qualifications recognised by the national governing body for the appropriate activity (e.g. RYA, BCU, etc).
Insurance: The centre is insured for all licensed activities.
Methods of payment: All common methods of payment are accepted.
Booking information: Advance booking required by phone, post or email. A 50% deposit is required to secure a booking.
Nearest airport: London Gatwick.
Nearest rail station: Hove.
Getting there: Pick-up can be arranged for groups.

WINDSPORT INTERNATIONAL
Mylor Yacht Harbour, Falmouth, Cornwall TR11 5UF
Phone: +44 (0)1326 376 191/363
Fax: +44 (0)1326 376 192
Email: windsport.international@btinternet.com
Website: www.windsport-int.com

Sail a Cornish estuary

The Carrick Roads estuary is a picturesque area that offers all the excitement of ocean sailing but in protected waters. Courses are available in a range of boat styles, including catamarans, Lasers and RS boats, to suit all levels of ability and experience, from complete novice to race coaching. Personal tuition can be arranged to focus on your needs or you can join a group. You can also combine sailing with other activities on offer, such as land yachting or windsurfing. Windsport International also have a centre at Rutland.

Activity prices: Tuition varies from £184 for a five-day junior course to £30 per hour for intensive personal coaching. Boat hire is also available.

Accommodation: Clients to arrange own. There are plenty of options in Falmouth.

Food: Clients to arrange own.

Equipment supplied: All safety equipment and clothing provided.

What to take: Suitable footwear for watersports.

When to go: Year round.

Established: 1985

Safety: All instructors are RYA qualified and the centre is licensed by the AALA and recognised by the RYA.

Insurance: Insurance is required and a scheme is offered by the centre

Methods of payment: VISA, Mastercard, Switch, Delta, cheque with bank card and bankers' drafts.

Booking information: Advance booking is preferred, though tuition and boat hire are available on the day. A 25% deposit is required and cancellation policy may be applied.

Nearest airport: Newquay. Connections to London airports.

Nearest rail station: Truro.

SCUBA DIVING

Superlatives seem to go hand in hand with many adventurous activities, and often for good reason, but it's probably fair to say that the world's oceans remain the largest and least developed wilderness on earth. There's something other-worldly about being suspended beneath the surface of the water in complete darkness, with your torch pressed against your chest and only the phosphorescence of the waves above to light the life that surrounds you. Despite the bubbles of your own breathing, it's as still and quiet as anywhere you've ever been.

Unlike many surface sports, scuba-diving is blissfully calm and unhurried. The basic equipment encompasses a face-mask and flippers, a buoyancy compensator and weight belt (to control ascent and descent below the surface), an air-tank and regulator (to regulate the flow of air from the tank), and, in Europe at least, a wetsuit. Essential safety equipment also includes an underwater watch, a depth gauge and a pressure gauge, all of which are critical for measuring how much time you have left in the water.

The only safe way to learn to scuba dive is to enrol in a nationally or internationally accredited course. Here, not only will you learn the basics of breathing and swimming underwater, you will also be taught about how equipment works, the way the body behaves underwater, and a few essential safety procedures.

If you can't learn somewhere warm and wonderful, the local swimming pool might be a welcome alternative, and many clubs offer weekend and evening classes. It's also worth noting that while you don't have to be an athlete to take part, scuba diving is dependent on certain medical requirements – if you're in any doubt contact your doctor.

Monster of the deep

Of all the dive-sites in Europe, Scotland's Corryvreckan is arguably one of the most demanding and intimidating. Tortuous tidal currents and a 200 metre (600 foot) pinnacle reaching to just 30 metres (100 feet) below the surface conspire to produce the third largest whirlpool in the world. Only an option in slack water at low tide, the site can be dived to the top of the pinnacle, but the safety margin is measured in minutes, and the skill of the boat pilot is every bit as important as the experience and judgement of the dive-team. Porpoise Dive Charters in Oban offer trips to the site for highly experienced divers only.

GREECE

NAUTILUS DIVING CORFU
Episkopiana 49084, Corfu
Phone: +30 661 76684 extn. 344 (May to October) or
+30 661 75393 (winter)
Fax: N/A
Email: lindsay@otenet.gr
Website: http://website.lineone.net/~lindsay.hollingdale/

A Greek underwater treat
Nautilus Diving is based on the popular and beautiful Greek island of Corfu and they run a full range of diving courses and recreational dives to suit all levels of ability, including beginners. Their scuba courses are approved by the British Sub Aqua Club (BSAC) and CMAS. The leisure dives for qualified divers are run off the west coast of the island and those for beginners or the less experienced off the east coast. The centre has two boats, a 13.6 metre hard boat and a 5.5 metre Rigid Inflatable Boat (usually referred to as a RIB) that is used on the west coast trips.

Activity prices: Taster dives cost Dr10,000. The BSAC Ocean Diver course costs Dr150,000, while the CMAS 1-star course costs Dr95,000. Leisure diving costs Dr11,000 if you hire all the gear, Dr9,500 for just a bottle and weights. A six-dive package with all gear costs Dr60,000 and with only bottle and weights Dr52,000.

Accommodation: Not included in price. The centre is situated in the grounds of the Messonghi Beach Hotel, Moraitika. There are plenty of other hotels in the nearby villages. Pick-ups can be arranged from other resorts.

Food: Not included in price.

Equipment supplied: All the diving equipment is available for hire.

What to take: Own dive gear if you have it, swimsuit.

When to go: May to October.

Established: 1984

Safety: All the scuba instructors are fully qualified. The centre is a member of BSAC and CMAS.

Insurance: The centre has third party insurance. Clients should arrange their own travel and accident policy.

Methods of payment: VISA and cash.

Booking information: Advance booking with deposit is preferred.

Nearest airport: Corfu. Transfers can be arranged.

Nearest rail station: N/A.

IRELAND

SKELLIGA AQUATICS
Caherdaniel, Co. Kerry
Phone: +353 (0)66 9475 277
Fax: +353 (0)66 9475 277
Email: skelliga@iol.ie
Website: www.activity-ireland.com

Emerald Isle diving
Skelliga Aquatics is part of the Celtic Adventures Activity Centre (see section on Hiking) located between the mountains and sea in gorgeous south-west Ireland. The warm waters of the Gulf Stream that flow past the coast ensure that the marine life is both plentiful and uniquely exotic for this part of the world. Dolphins, killer whales, porpoise and turtles all ply the route while seals, large fish and lobsters

are often encountered underwater. The centre's purpose-built, fully-equipped dive boat will take you in comfort to the area's dive spots, including the famous Skelliga Rock. For those who just want to taste diving the short 'Try-a-Dive' course shows you the basics and gets you in the water, while the more committed can undergo the full PADI (Professional Association of Diving Instructors) open water qualification over four and a half days. If you want to learn more about the intricate web of sea animals, then try the marine biology course.

Activity prices: Try-a-Dive costs I£30 while the PADI open water qualification course over four and a half days costs I£295.
Accommodation: Hostel accommodation at I£8 or B&B at I£20 both per person/sharing basis. Holiday cottages and four-star campsite also available.
Food: Available at centre for approximately I£14 per day for all meals.
Equipment supplied: All specialist scuba diving equipment provided.
What to take: Personal clothing and footwear.
When to go: Year round except December and January, depending on weather.
Established: 1988
Safety: All diving personnel are fully PADI-qualified. Skelliga Aquatics is a member of the Irish Association of Adventure Sports and is promoted by the Irish Tourist Board, Bord Failte.
Insurance: Centre has insurance but it is recommended that clients arrange their own.
Methods of payment: VISA or personal cheque.
Booking information: Advance booking is recommended with payment requested at least 42 days in advance.
Nearest airport: Cork (2.5 hours) or Kerry (1.5 hours). Groups of clients travelling together can be collected from the airport.
Nearest rail station: Killarney (80 mins). Groups of clients travelling together can be collected from the station.

MALTA

FRANKIE'S GOZO DIVING CENTRE
Mgarr Road, Xewkija, Gozo
Phone: +356 551 315

Fax: +356 560356
Email: frankie@digigate.net
Website: www.digigate.net/frankie

Dive Malta's crystal waters

Gozo is one of the few remaining Mediterranean islands that remains relatively untouched by tourism. The lack of visitors means that the diving is some of the best on offer in the region and Frankie's Gozo Diving Centre is a fun place to explore from. There are drop-offs, caves, tunnels and wrecks and a profusion of marine life to keep even experienced divers enthralled. The dive centre has a special deep diving pool and great shore diving nearby that are ideal for beginners to get used to the equipment before heading for the open sea. Several hard dive boats are available to take experienced divers out to the more distant dive sites. It is a PADI centre so novices can become qualified after a short course while the centre can train up to Assistant Instructor level.

Activity prices: Prices are very competitive on the island so contact the centre for the latest offers.

Accommodation: Frankie has several properties available for rent on the island, including converted farmhouses.

Food: Properties are self-catering but there are restaurants nearby.

Equipment supplied: All specialist scuba diving equipment provided.

What to take: Swimsuit.

When to go: Year round.

Established: 1987

Safety: All diving staff and instructors are PADI-qualified and the centre is a member of the Gozo Tourism Association.

Insurance: The centre has its own insurance but clients are advised to take out their own travel insurance to cover them for scuba diving too.

Methods of payment: VISA, Mastercard, Eurocheques, cash.

Booking information: Advance booking is recommended, though late bookings are accepted.

Nearest airport: Malta International. Transfers can be arranged.

Nearest rail station: N/A.

SPAIN

SAFARI DIVING LANZAROTE

Playa de la Barilla 4, 35510 Puerto Del Carmen, Lanzarote,
Canary Islands
Phone: +34 (0)928511992
Fax: +34 (0)928510496
Email: info@safaridiving.com
Website: www.safaridiving.com

Volcanic diving

The island of Lanzarote, with its bizarre, lunar-like lava landscape, is unique among the Canary Islands. As a side-effect of the volcanic activity, numerous lava-based reefs have sprung up all around the island, making it a fascinating place to scuba dive. Safari Diving is a five-star PADI centre and they run a comprehensive range of courses for divers of all abilities. The Discover Scuba half-day course allows complete novices to get a taste of underwater life while the two to three-day Open Water course, which involves theory and practice sessions, leads to an internationally recognised qualification that allows you to dive anywhere in the world. For those wishing to go further, the centre runs all the courses to take you to Assistant Instructor level. They also offer speciality courses, such as Underwater Photographer and Night Diver. There are a number of shipwrecks in the area and the reefs are home to plenty of big fish, including tuna, barracuda, moray eels and rays. Whales and dolphins are occasionally seen too. All with year-round warm water temperatures. Bliss!

Activity prices: Course prices start from Pta30,000. Contact the centre for full list. Dive packages for qualified divers start from Pta30,265 for six dives with all hired gear to Pta58,000 for 12 dives. If you have your own gear the prices go down. Group discounts available.
Accommodation: Not included in the course price. Apartments and other accommodation are available close to the centre.

Food: Not included in course price. There are many restaurants close to the centre.

Equipment supplied: All specialist scuba diving equipment is included in course prices.

What to take: Take your own scuba gear to get a price reduction on dive packages.

When to go: Year round.

Established: 1986

Safety: All diving instructors and assistants are PADI-qualified. Owner Rene Van Leeuwen is recognised as a leader in diver training. The centre is a member of the Lanzarote Tourist Board.

Insurance: Centre has full insurance.

Methods of payment: VISA, Mastercard, travellers' cheques, cash.

Booking information: Advance booking is required for the courses with a non-refundable deposit.

Nearest airport: Arrecife Lanzarote. Transfers arranged free of charge.

Nearest rail station: N/A.

SWITZERLAND

ADVENTURE'S BEST
PO Box 9, Via Basilea 28, CH-6903 Lugano
Phone: +41 91 966 11 14
Fax: +41 91 966 12 13
Email: info@asbest.ch
Website: www.asbest.ch

Scuba diving in the rivers of southern Switzerland
Tucked away in the southernmost reaches of the Swiss Alps, the state of Ticino is an area of approximately 3,500 sq km characterised by lakes, rivers and mountains. Adventure's Best has been offering scuba diving in the world famous River Verzasca since 1994, and all dives are led by instructor Learco Benaglia, who holds an internationally recognised PADI instructor's qualification.

Activity prices: Contact the centre for the latest prices.

Accommodation: Not included in the price, but is available at the centre. Shared dorms cost SFr20 per person, a double room SFr40 per person, a double room with en suite bath/shower SFr50 per person and a single room with en suite bath/shower SFr60 per person.

Food: Not included in the price, but is available at the centre. Buffet breakfast costs SFr15 per person.

Equipment supplied: All specialist equipment is provided.

What to take: Personal clothing.

When to go: May to October.

Established: 1994

Safety: All instructors hold recognised qualifications from the relevant national or international governing body.

Insurance: Clients are responsible for arranging their own insurance.

Methods of payment: VISA, Mastercard, Amex, travellers' cheques and cash.

Booking information: No deposit required.

Nearest airport: Lugano-Agno (5 km).

Nearest rail station: Lugano (200 metres).

TURKEY

BITEZ YACHTING
Neyzen Tevfik Caddesi 142, 48400 Bodrum
Phone: +90 252 316 2139/2454
Fax: +90 252 316 3101
Email: ecomail@turk.net
Website: http://www.holidaybank.co.uk/bitezyachting

Diving the Turkish coast
The Bitez Yachting dive programme is organised through the European Diving Centre in Fethiye, the only British-owned and run diving business in Turkey. As a beginner you'll join the five-day PADI Open Water course, which then qualifies you to dive at any dive centre worldwide. The course is divided into theory and practical lessons, starting with basic skills and progressing to a maximum depth of 18 metres. Experienced divers are also welcome and can

be buddied up with divers of similar experience if required. Accommodation is at a pension a few minutes' walk from the dive centre, and breakfast and lunch are provided. The remaining two days of the seven-day programme are spent trekking in the unspoilt region of Kocagol.

Activity prices: Introductory courses cost from US$775 for one week (five days' diving and two days' trekking) in the low season to US$850 in the high season. Experienced divers' prices range from US$565 in the low season to US$625 in the high season.

Accommodation: Nearby pension accommodation is included in the price.

Food: Breakfast and lunch are included in the price.

Equipment supplied: All specialist equipment is provided.

What to take: Personal clothing and footwear suitable for the prevailing conditions – if in doubt, call ahead for advice.

When to go: May to October.

Established: 1986

Safety: All the English/Dutch-speaking guides are highly experienced.

Insurance: Clients are responsible for arranging their own insurance.

Methods of payment: Cash and/or bank transfer.

Booking information: A 25% deposit is required to confirm a booking, with the balance paid on arrival. There is a 5% charge for a cancellation within two weeks of the departure date.

Nearest airport: Dalaman and Bodrum. Tranfers to and from the airport are included in the price.

Nearest rail station: N/A.

UNITED KINGDOM

ACORN ACTIVITIES
PO Box 120, Hereford HR4 8YB
Phone: +44 (0)1432 830083
Fax: +44 (0)1432 830110
Email: sales@acornactivities.co.uk
Website: www.acornactivities.co.uk

Learning to scuba dive

Acorn Activities have a number of locations across the United Kingdom where specialist diving courses are run under the auspices of both PADI and BSAC. All courses are taught by fully qualified instructors, and the five-day course has been specifically arranged by Acorn so that students gain a qualification from both associations, enabling any successful participant to dive anywhere in the world. The five-day course includes pool work, lectures and five open-water dives in the sea or inland lakes, depending on the location. Participants must be able to swim 200 metres, and a medical statement must be signed – this will be sent on confirmation of booking.

Activity prices: £540 for a five-day course.

Accommodation: Six nights B&B included in the price.

Food: Dinner costs an additional £13 per night.

Equipment supplied: All specialist equipment is provided.

What to take: Masks, fins and snorkels. These can be purchased at individual dive centres at competitive prices if you're unsure what to buy.

When to go: May to September.

Established: 1990

Safety: All instructors are BSAC or PADI qualified.

Insurance: Insurance is required, although this can be arranged through Acorn Activities.

Methods of payment: VISA, Mastercard, cheque and cash.

Booking information: Late bookings are welcomed. A non-refundable deposit of £10 per day is required. Cancellation charges apply on a sliding scale from 80% for over 43 days before departure to 100% for up to 14 days.

Nearest airport: Cardiff or Birmingham International.

Nearest rail station: Depends on the itinerary.

UIST OUTDOOR CENTRE

Cearn Dusgaidh, Lochmaddy, Isle of North Uist, Outer Hebrides HS6 5AE

Phone: +44 (0)1876 500480

Fax: +44 (0)1876 500480

Email: alyson@keiller.u-net.com
Website: www.uistoutdoorcentre.co.uk

Scuba diving the islands of the Outer Hebrides
Underwater activities in the North Atlantic are not for the cold-blooded, but those willing to brave the water are likely to have the islands' unique underwater world to themselves. Courses cater for all abilities and dive-sites vary from sheltered sea lochs to ocean drop-offs – really experienced divers can even charter the centre's RIB powerboat to explore the possibilities for themselves. Lochmaddy is designated a Marine Area of Conservation, and divers can expect to share the water with mako shark, seals, porpoises and dolphins as well as the usual array of sunfish, soft corals and anemones. Bunkhouse accommodation is available at the centre, and alternative accommodation can be arranged according to requirements.

Activity prices: From £35 per day for adults, £18 per day for under-12s. RIB dive boat hire costs £145 per day.

Accommodation: Bunkhouse accommodation costs an additional £9 per night with bedding and £7 per night without bedding.

Food: Full board can be arranged but there are plenty of facilities for self-catering.

Equipment supplied: Personal diving gear is not provided.

What to take: Personal diving equipment and clothing.

When to go: Year round.

Established: 1991

Safety: All instructors hold nationally recognised qualifications for the relevant activity.

Insurance: The centre is insured for all licensed activities.

Methods of payment: Only cash and cheque accepted.

Booking information: Book by phone, post or email. A 10% deposit secures a booking.

Nearest airport: Benbecula.

Nearest rail station: N/A. The nearest ferry terminal is in Lochmaddy. All clients can be picked up from the ferry or airport at no extra cost.

SEA KAYAKING

Unlike the short, rounded kayaks favoured by white water rock-hoppers, sea kayaks are long and thin, making them much more suitable for paddling over longer distances without the benefit of a current. Additional storage space for equipment makes sea kayaks ideal for longer trips in remote areas. A rudder is often used to take the strain out of turning with the paddle. With tents, sleeping bags and provisions safely stowed away in specially designed waterproof bulkheads, sea paddlers can go for days without seeing another soul. In fact, at the time of writing, two mad paddlers from north Wales have just set off to paddle from the UK to Australia!

While it may lack the glamour of the raging river, the sea can be every bit as exciting and challenging as the biggest white water rapids, with treacherous tidal races, unpredictable currents and crashing surf. For most people, however, sea kayaking offers an opportunity for peace and tranquillity. Compact, quiet and environmentally friendly, sea kayaks offer the perfect platform to view the wildlife and scenery of the world's most spectacular coastlines. You can even get wooden-framed kayaks that collapse down into a backpack for easy travelling. So there's no excuse. Next time you need to cross the English Channel, forget the ferry and take your kayak (er . . . just watch out for the big ships because they certainly won't be looking out for you!).

ITALY

CANYON ADVENTURES
Via Mateotti 57/b, 38069 Torbole sul Garda (TN)

Phone: +39 (0)464 505 072
Fax: +39 (0)464 505 647
Email: flipper@anthesi.com
Website: www.garda.com/flipper

A kayak tour of Lake Garda

With its impressive mountain surroundings, the famous Lake Garda is one of the most beautiful parts of Italy and it is the country's biggest lake. Canyon Adventures offer a range of sea kayak tours, starting from half-day trips and going up to full week-long expeditions. On the multi-day tours, you sleep in tents at the various campsites around the lake. You carry all the tents, cooking gear and sleeping bags in the kayak but no previous experience is required as Lake Garda is generally quite calm.

Activity prices: Half-day kayak trips cost L60,000 and full-day trips L90,000. Prices for longer trips are available on request.

Accommodation: Not included in course price. Clients normally arrange their own but the centre can help.

Food: Full-day tours include lunch, otherwise the client arranges their own. There are many options in the Garda area.

Equipment supplied: All specialist equipment is provided.

What to take: Personal clothing for changing into, sandals, towel, sunglasses.

When to go: Daily from April to end of October.

Established: 1992

Safety: All sea kayaking guides are nationally qualified.

Insurance: The centre has full liability insurance. Clients are advised to take out their own accident insurance.

Methods of payment: Postal order or travellers' cheques.

Booking information: Advance booking is essential. Full payment is due at time of booking. Cancellations must be notified in writing at least one week before activity date.

Nearest airport: Verona.

Nearest rail station: Rovereto.

SWITZERLAND

ALPIN RAFT
Postfach 78, 3800 Matten
Phone: +41 33 823 4100
Fax: +41 33 823 4101
Email: mail@alpinraft.ch
Website: www.alpinraft.ch

Sea kayaking in the Swiss Alps
The gin-clear waters of Lake Thun provide the perfect setting for sea kayaking, and there's no better way to get away from the crowds. Paddling in specially designed boats, kayakers glide past peaceful bays, secluded beaches and cascading waterfalls. Alpin Raft supplies all the necessary specialist equipment.

Activity prices: From SFr30.
Accommodation: Backpacker accommodation available at the centre.
Food: Not included.
Equipment supplied: All specialist equipment provided.
What to take: Old trainers and a dry change of clothes.
When to go: April to October.
Established: 1988
Safety: All the guides hold national kayaking qualifications.
Insurance: Clients must arrange their own insurance.
Methods of payment: All common methods of payment accepted.
Booking information: Book by phone or email. Full payment is charged for cancellation on the day of trip.
Nearest airport: Bern.
Nearest rail station: Interlaken.

UNITED KINGDOM

ACORN ACTIVITIES
PO Box 120, Hereford, HR4 8YB

Phone: +44 (0)1432 830083
Fax: +44 (0)1432 830110
Email: sales@acornactivities.co.uk
Website: www.acornactivities.co.uk

Sea kayaking throughout the UK
Acorn Activities is one of the biggest providers of outdoor pursuits in the UK, and they use a variety of centres to teach sea kayaking in safe and sheltered waters. Novices can take half or full-day taster courses with a BCU-qualified instructor to take them through the basics of the BCU 1-star award, including paddling in a straight line (never as easy as it sounds!), paddling backwards and turning. These sessions can be tailor-made to suit the ability of the group, so if you're working towards a BCU star-test qualification there's no better way to get added tuition and practice. Wetsuits and all additional equipment are provided. Accommodation is not included, but can be arranged nearby at a budget to suit.

Activity prices: £25 per half-day, £40 per day.

Accommodation: Not included in the price, but can be arranged locally.

Food: Not included.

Equipment supplied: All specialist equipment, including wetsuits if required.

What to take: Warm clothing and footwear that can get wet.

When to go: Year round.

Established: 1990

Safety: All instructors are BCU qualified.

Insurance: Insurance is required, although this can be arranged through Acorn Activities.

Methods of payment: VISA, Mastercard, cheque and cash.

Booking information: Late bookings are welcomed. A non-refundable deposit of £10 per day is required. Cancellation charges apply on a sliding scale from 80% for over 43 days before departure to 100% for up to 14 days.

Nearest airport: Cardiff or Birmingham International.

Nearest rail station: Depends on the itinerary.

CALSHOT ACTIVITIES CENTRE
Calshot Spit, Fawley, Southampton SO45 1BR
Phone: +44 (0)23 8089 2077
Fax: +44 (0)23 8089 1267
Email: acocal@hants.gov.uk
Website: www.hants.gov.uk/calshot

A top paddle on the Solent
Calshot is recognised as being one of the UK's premier sea kayaking
centres and is approved by the BCU. They offer a range of courses to
suit all ability levels. Beginners take to the water in the more protected
parts of the Solent before moving out on to open water. With the aid
of their highly qualified and experienced guides, you will learn about
paddle strokes, weather prediction, tides and safety procedures.
Once a year, the centre runs a major sea kayak expedition for more
skilled paddlers; recent trips have gone to the south-west of Ireland,
the Scilly Isles and the Outer Hebrides.

Activity prices: There are so many course options and package prices that you
should call the centre with your specific requirements.
Accommodation: Included in price. There is space for 150 people at the
centre with various room options.
Food: Included. Three cooked meals per day plus drinks with residential
courses. Meals on other courses can be booked to suit.
Equipment supplied: All equipment is provided.
What to take: Swimsuit, suitable footwear.
When to go: April to October.
Established: 1969
Safety: All the centre's kayaking staff are BCU qualified. The centre is
licensed by the AALA and is a member of the BCU.
Insurance: Insurance is required. Policies are offered by the centre which cover
you from the day of booking for cancellation through sickness or injury.
Methods of payment: VISA, Mastercard, cheque and cash.
Booking information: Advance booking is required. Full payment is needed on
booking for all courses of up to four days' duration. A non-refundable £25 deposit
is needed for longer courses with balance paid eight weeks before arrival.

Nearest airport: Southampton or Bournemouth.

Nearest rail station: Southampton Central or Beaulieu Road, Brockenhurst.

PLAS Y BRENIN

National Mountain Centre, Capel Curig, Conwy LL24 0ET

Phone: +44 (0)1690 720 214

Fax: +44 (0)1690 720 394

Email: info@pyb.co.uk

Website: www.pyb.co.uk

Paddle Britain's high seas

The complex tidal patterns and the stunning scenery around the coast of north Wales provide an ideal classroom for learning to sea kayak. Plas y Brenin's Introduction to Sea Kayaking weekend course is based around the coast of Anglesey and the Llyen Peninsula. It teaches you about paddling techniques in salt water, how coastal water behaves, planning a sea kayaking journey, weather forecasting and sea safety. To further enhance your skills, there is also a five-day course available. Once you are comfortable in the sea, you can choose to head north for the centre's Sea Kayaking Expedition to Scotland, which involves six days of wilderness paddling and camping along the ruggedly beautiful west coast. Daily paddle distance is 10–12 miles.

Activity prices: The introductory course costs £99 while the five-day course costs £295. The Scottish expedition costs £335.

Accommodation: Prices include shared accommodation.

Food: Course prices include full board.

Equipment supplied: All specialist equipment and clothing is provided.

What to take: Personal clothing and your own equipment if you prefer to use it.

When to go: July to September for the Welsh courses and June to September for the Scottish trip.

Established: 1954

Safety: All instructors hold nationally recognised qualifications and only the most capable and experienced are employed. The centre is licensed by the AALA. Great emphasis is placed on safety and the high quality equipment used is regularly checked and replaced.

Insurance: The centre carries public liability insurance for all activities and recommends that clients take out independent insurance against curtailment and cancellation of their course (available from the centre) and a personal accident policy.

Methods of payment: VISA, Mastercard, Access, personal cheque, cash.

Booking information: Reservations must be made in advance and a deposit is required.

Nearest airport: Manchester (for Welsh courses).

Nearest rail station: Llandudno (for Welsh courses). Free transfer available by prior arrangement.

PRESELI VENTURE

Parcynole Fach, Mathry, Haverfordwest, Pembrokeshire SA62 5HN
Phone: +44 (0)1348 837 709
Fax: +44 (0)1348 837 656
Email: sophie@preseliventure.com
Website: www.preseliventure.com

Sea and surf in west Wales

The dramatic coastline of the Pembrokeshire National Park, with its ragged coves, isolated beaches and high cliffs, and an abundance of wildlife, make for a great sea kayaking experience. Preseli Ventures offers courses ranging from half a day to five days to suit all levels of ability from complete novice to advanced paddlers. If you want to break up the adventure, the sea kayaking can be combined with coasteering and mountain biking. The BCU-qualified instructors not only ensure your safety but will also help you improve your paddling skills and awareness of sea conditions and trip planning. When you are all paddled out, the delicious home-cooked food available at the centre is sure to re-energise you.

Activity prices: £30 for a half-day and £159 for an all-inclusive weekend course. You can also combine sea kayaking with coasteering and mountain biking.

Accommodation: Included in the weekend course price. The Preseli Venture Lodge sleeps up to 30 people.

Food: Great home-cooked food is available at the centre and is included in the weekend course price.

Equipment supplied: All specialist kayaking equipment. Full wetsuit, buoyancy jacket, and helmet.

What to take: Swimsuit, training shoes, towel.

When to go: Year round, daily.

Established: 1987

Safety: All the guides have relevant BCU national coaching qualifications, specific on-site training and lifesaving and first aid qualifications. Preseli Venture is a member of the BCU and the WCA and is part of the Welsh Tourist Board Accreditation Scheme.

Insurance: Clients can arrange their own insurance, but it is available via Preseli Venture.

Methods of payment: VISA, Mastercard, Amex, travellers' cheques and cash.

Booking information: Advance booking is recommended. A non-refundable 50% deposit is required with booking.

Nearest airport: Cardiff.

Nearest rail station: Haverfordwest. Transfer from this station or from Fishguard ferry port or Fishguard station can be arranged.

TWR-Y-FELIN NO LIMITS

The TYF Group, 1 High Street, St Davids, Pembrokeshire SA62 6QS

Phone: +44 (0)1437 721 611

Fax: +44 (0)1437 721 692

Email: info@tyf.com

Website: www.tyf.com

Paddle Pembrokeshire's dramatic coastline

Based in Britain's smallest city, the TYF No Limits centre has access to some of the UK's best coastal kayaking. Their Introduction to Sea Kayaking course is aimed at people who already know the basics of paddling and want to learn specific techniques for open water in order to explore the coves, remote islands and headlands. Theory work comprises prediction of tides and weather, chart work, rescues and forward paddling. By the end of the three-day course you should be at

BCU 3-star level. For those wanting to see more of the coast, a Celtic Sea Kayak trip will take you to the best parts of the Pembrokeshire Coast National Park at a leisurely pace.

Activity prices: The Introduction to Sea Kayaking course costs from £89 if you camp up to £160 full board. The Celtic trip costs £160 for two days' full board or £240 for three days. Camping options available too.

Accommodation: Included in price. You can either camp or have B&B, half board or full board accommodation in the Twr-y-Felin Hotel, a beautiful converted 18th-century windmill.

Food: Included in hotel-based course prices (see above).

Equipment supplied: All specialist equipment and clothing is provided.

What to take: Personal clothing and your own equipment if you prefer to use it.

When to go: April to September for Introduction courses and June to November for the Celtic trip.

Established: 1986

Safety: All instructors hold BCU qualifications and are very experienced.

Insurance: The centre has liability insurance but recommends that clients take out independent insurance against curtailment and cancellation of their course (available from the centre) and a personal accident policy.

Methods of payment: VISA, Mastercard, Switch, cheques and cash.

Booking information: Advance booking is required.

Nearest airport: Cardiff.

Nearest rail station: Haverfordwest. Transfers can be arranged.

UIST OUTDOOR CENTRE

Cearn Dusgaidh, Lochmaddy, Isle of North Uist, Outer Hebrides HS6 5AE
Phone: +44 (0)1876 500480
Fax: +44 (0)1876 500480
Email: alyson@keiller.u-net.com
Website: www.uistoutdoorcentre.co.uk

Sea kayaking the islands of the Outer Hebrides
North Uist has been described as the jewel in the Hebridean crown, offering adventure seekers some of the most remote and spectacular

wilderness in the British Isles. The region is characterised by towering sea cliffs and exposed sea stacks, sheltered inland lochs enclosed by rolling moorland, and endless beaches of pure white sand. Sea kayaking is arguably the best way to explore these areas and to experience the unique wildlife of the region, which includes dolphins, porpoises, seals, basking sharks and killer whales. Week-long courses are available for paddlers of all abilities, and guided tours – including multi-day expeditions – can be arranged.

Activity prices: £35 per day for adults, £18 per day for under-12s. Six-day courses for introductory to advanced paddlers cost from £375 per person including all instruction and equipment, full board and an overnight expedition to a remote area. Training and assessment weekends for BCU qualifications are also available. Call ahead for specific dates of all courses.

Accommodation: Bunkhouse accommodation costs an additional £9 per night with bedding, and £7 per night without bedding.

Food: Full board can be arranged but there are plenty of facilities for self-catering.

Equipment supplied: All specialist equipment is supplied.

What to take: Personal clothing.

When to go: April to September.

Established: 1991

Safety: All instructors hold nationally recognised qualifications.

Insurance: The centre is insured for all licensed activities.

Methods of payment: Only cash and cheque accepted.

Booking information: Book by phone, post or email. A 10% deposit is required to secure a booking.

Nearest airport: Benbecula.

Nearest rail station: N/A. The nearest ferry terminal is in Lochmaaddy. All clients can be picked up from the ferry or airport at no extra cost.

SKI TOURING

If you spend the summer months exploring the mountains with your backpack and wish to continue when winter descends, then why not give ski touring a try? Reaching parts that other skiers just can't reach, you will be privy to some wonderful scenic delights and the blissful silence that remote mountain areas offer. When you reach a summit, you can just clip your heels back into your skis and enjoy the awesome experience of skiing fresh powder in a mountain bowl with not another soul in sight. If you really want to go further, then carry some mountaineering gear and you can ascend even the most challenging peaks and ski back off them.

The secret to skiing uphill is 'skins'. These synthetic-haired strips stick to the bottom of your skis, allowing them to slide forward, when the hair lies flat, but not backwards, when the hair rises and grips. Special ski bindings allow you to unclip the heel of your boot to move uphill more easily and then clip back in to act like a downhill ski binding. You can easily carry a full-size backpack too, so it's a great way to get out into remote areas on more than a day trip. Of course, you should always employ a qualified guide if you are new to an area as you will be entering potential avalanche zones; and anyway, the guides will be able to show you the best and most isolated spots. Once you have tried it, skiing on-piste will be like going to the supermarket for a quiet break.

FRANCE

INTERNATIONAL SCHOOL OF MOUNTAINEERING, SWITZERLAND
Hafod Tan y Graig, Nant Gwynant, Gwynedd LL55 4NW, UK

Phone: +44 (0)1766 890441
Fax: +44 (0)1766 890599
Email: ism@dial.pipex.com
Website: http//:ds.dial.pipex.com/ism

On skins in the French Alps

Renowned for steep downhill descents and monstrous moguls, the
French Alps also provide almost limitless opportunities for cross-
country skiing. ISM offers a week-long introduction to ski touring
which promises to convert downhill skiers into avid tourers. The
comprehensive course is ideally suited to people who plan to ski tour
on their own or those who simply want to try cross-country skiing for
the first time. The six-day course covers all aspects of multi-day ski-
touring from traversing techniques to avalanche avoidance, and
includes ascents of a number of passes in the Leysin area. The course
culminates in a three-day tour of Les Hautes Alpes, staying in
mountain huts and making ascents of suitable summits. Confidence
on red runs and the ability to make controlled parallel turns are
prerequisites for the course.

Activity prices: £695 for six-day course.

Accommodation: All Alpine courses include hotel accommodation.

Food: Alpine courses include full board.

Equipment supplied: All specialist equipment.

What to take: Personal ski clothing and footwear.

When to go: November to April.

Established: 1960

Safety: All guides hold the International Carnet, the highest qualification
available in mountaineering.

Insurance: Relevant insurance required for all Alpine courses.

Methods of payment: All common payment methods accepted.

Booking information: Contact ISM for booking form and full terms and
conditions.

Nearest airport: Geneva.

Nearest rail station: Leysin.

MOUNTAIN ACTIVITY EXPERIENCE
93 avenue Michel Croz, 74400 Chamonix
Phone: +33 4 50 55 80 80
Fax: +33 4 53 48 50
Email: M.A.X@wanadoo.fr
Website: montblanconeline.fr/max/max.htm

Ski touring in the Chamonix Valley
If you're an intermediate or expert skier and you fancy getting away
from the on-piste crowd to do some 'mountaineering', then high
altitude ski touring might be the answer. Within a few hours' hike of
the major resorts, the Mont Blanc range presents numerous back-
country routes. One-day, weekend and week-long tours are all
possible. Guides are happy to adapt the itinerary to suit the group, but
lunch on a mountain pass and unrivalled views of Mont Blanc are
guaranteed . . . weather permitting. Mountain Activity Experience
even promises you'll hear the snow quality change as you ski down
the untouched north face. Touring skis, bindings, boots, skins and an
avalanche transceiver are not provided, but can be rented for an
additional fee.

Activity prices: From FFr350 per person per day (minimum four people). Three-
day weekends FFr1,990 per person (minimum four people), five-day Mont
Blanc Tour FFr2,600 per person (minimum four people).
Accommodation: Not included in the price.
Food: Not included.
Equipment supplied: None provided.
What to take: Touring skis, boots and bindings are not included, but can be
rented at the centre.
When to go: Winter only.
Established: 1997
Safety: All instructors are nationally qualified high mountain guides.
Insurance: Clients must provide their own insurance.
Methods of payment: Cheques and cash.
Booking information: A deposit is required to secure a booking. Cancellation
within a month of the course forfeits the deposit.

Nearest airport: Geneva.

Nearest rail station: Chamonix.

ODYSSEE MONTAGNE

101 Les Marmottieres

74310 Les Houches

Phone: +33 (0)4 50 54 36 01

Fax: +33 (0)4 50 54 35 74

Email: odyssee@odyssee-montagne.fr

Website: http://odyssee-monatgne.fr

Explore remote parts of the Mont Blanc Massif

The traditional way to tour the Alps in winter, and still the best. Odyssée Montagne offers Alpine tours for telemark skiers of all levels who want to explore the authentic high-mountain wilderness away from the crowds. To get to the summits often requires a basic level of fitness or natural endurance, and clients should expect some steady climbs lasting up to two or three hours, but the rewards speak for themselves. The routes chosen include some of the best in the Alps and can be tailored to suit the ability of the group. A two-day summit route might be suitable for experienced cross-country skiers, but a six-day tour allows more time for acclimatisation and more chance of a successful summit attempt.

Activity prices: From FFr2,400 for two days and one night, FFr3,800 for six days and five nights.

Accommodation: Included.

Food: All food is included in the price.

Equipment supplied: All the specialist ski equipment is available from the centre.

What to take: Personal clothing for skiing.

When to go: March to May.

Established: 1993

Safety: All mountain guides are members of the Ecole National de Ski et d'Alpinisme.

Insurance: Comprehensive insurance can be provided at an additional cost of 5% of the full price.

Methods of payment: Travellers' cheques, VISA, Mastercard, Swift bank transfer, etc.

Booking information: A deposit of 30% is required at the time of booking.

Bookings will be accepted no later than 15 days before departure.

Nearest airport: Geneva.

Nearest rail station: Saint Gervais.

SWITZERLAND

ADVENTURE'S BEST

PO Box 9, Via Basilea 28, CH-6903 Lugano
Phone: +41 91 966 11 14
Fax: +41 91 966 12 13
Email: info@asbest.ch
Website: www.asbest.ch

Ski touring in southern Switzerland

Measuring 90 km by 40 km, the region of Ticino is a mountain wilderness tucked away in the southernmost corner of Switzerland. Untroubled by the tourist masses, it's ideally suited to ski-touring, with 3,000 metre peaks and snow from December to May. All ski tours are led by a nationally certified alpine guide and can be tailor-made to suit your ability and requirements. Accommodation is not included in the price, but the centre offers a variety of options, from shared dorms to single rooms with en suite showers.

Activity prices: Contact the centre for the latest prices.

Accommodation: Not included in tour price but is available at the centre. Shared dorms cost an additional SFr20 per person, a double room SFr40 per person, a double room with en suite bath/shower SFr50 per person and a single room with en suite bath/shower SFr60 per person.

Food: Not included in the price, but is available at the centre. Buffet breakfast costs SFr15 per person.

Equipment supplied: All specialist equipment is provided.

What to take: Personal clothing.

When to go: December to May.

Established: 1994

Safety: All instructors hold recognised qualifications from the relevant national or international governing body.

Insurance: Clients are responsible for arranging their own insurance.

Methods of payment: VISA, Mastercard, Amex, travellers' cheques and cash.

Booking information: No deposit required.

Nearest airport: Lugano-Agno (5 km).

Nearest rail station: Lugano (200 metres).

FOUR SEASONS GUIDES
Chalet L'Aurore, 1936 Verbier
Phone: +41 27 771 7683
Fax: +41 27 771 1603
Email: hans@verbier.ch
Website: www.swissguides.com

Explore the Alpine wilderness

Verbier is situated close to a whole host of 3,000 and 4,000 metre high mountains, many of which offer superb ski touring and ski mountaineering opportunities. A favourite area for combining skiing and climbing is in the Pinennine Alps on the mountains between Mont Blanc and the Matterhorn. Hiring a personal guide will allow you to take full advantage of the possibilities with the added confidence of being with one of the most experienced mountain people available. For tourers, trips can be arranged to last anything from one day to one week, taking advantage of the well-developed lift system to make the trip easier. 'Skinning' times can be altered to suit your ability.

Activity prices: Guiding fees are SFr400 per day for one to two clients. For this, the guide will also arrange local travel and hotel bookings and the itinerary (clients pay directly to the hotel, bus company, etc.). Helicopter fees are extra.

Accommodation: Not included in the price. There is a large range of accommodation options in the area and the guide will help you to arrange it.

Food: Not included in the price, but there are plenty of eating options in the area too. While in the mountains, the client pays for his own food and that of the guide.

Equipment supplied: Specialist equipment can be hired in Verbier.

What to take: All specialist mountain clothing.

When to go: January to June.

Established: 1990

Safety: All guides hold UIAGM qualifications.

Insurance: Clients are recommended to buy helicopter rescue insurance which costs SFr30 for one year.

Methods of payment: VISA, Mastercard, Amex, travellers' cheques and cash.

Booking information: Payment in full is required one week in advance. Full refunds are available for acceptable cancellation.

Nearest airport: Geneva. Transfers can be arranged.

Nearest rail station: Le Chable. Transfers can be arranged.

UNITED KINGDOM

PLAS Y BRENIN

National Mountain Centre, Capel Curig, Conwy LL24 0ET
Phone: +44 (0)1690 720 214
Fax: +44 (0)1690 720 394
Email: info@pyb.co.uk
Website: www.pyb.co.uk

Ski from Wales to the Alps

Plas y Brenin offers ski mountaineering preparation courses in Scotland for people who are looking to head off on tours to the Alps. Their courses are very comprehensive, covering ski mountaineering techniques and safety and rescue skills. The instructors at the centre are very highly qualified and have plenty of experience. They also run tours to the Alps.

Activity prices: The Ski Mountaineering Preparation Weekend costs £99. The Alpine Ski Touring course and the Alpine Ski Mountaineering course cost £425 each.

Accommodation: Prices include shared accommodation, except nights spent in mountain huts.

Food: Course prices include full board, except for the nights spent in mountain huts.

Equipment supplied: All specialist equipment and clothing is provided.

What to take: Personal clothing and your own equipment if you prefer to use it.

When to go: January for the preparation course, April for the Alpine courses.

Established: 1954

Safety: All instructors hold nationally recognised qualifications and only the most capable and experienced are employed. The centre is licensed by the AALA. Great emphasis is placed on safety and the high quality equipment used is regularly checked and replaced.

Insurance: The centre carries public liability insurance for all activities and recommends that clients take out independent insurance against curtailment and cancellation of their course (available from the centre) and a personal accident policy.

Methods of payment: VISA, Mastercard, Access, personal cheque, cash.

Booking information: Reservations must be made in advance and a deposit is required.

Nearest airport: Depends on course.

Nearest rail station: Depends on course.

SKIING

The ski industry is booming like never before. The advent of more user-friendly and lower-priced equipment and cheaper ski holiday packages has promoted skiing to the rank of the second holiday that families have to have. Whether you spend a weekend skiing downhill at your favourite resort, clip on your free-heel skis for a spot of cross-country action or get airlifted by helicopter to pristine mountain bowls where deep fresh powder awaits, you are sure to enjoy this addictive sport. The potential for on-piste skiing is vast in Europe, with the whole Alpine region offering extensive lift systems and ski infrastructure. There is no way we could do this justice in a multi-sport book and we haven't tried. Instead, we have selected a few centres to give you a taste of the variety on offer.

Heli-skiing started over in Canada, but soon caught on in Europe. However, concerns about the safety aspects (the choppers can set off avalanches) led to heli-skiing being banned in several European countries. Switzerland and Italy still allow it, though. Just flying into the mountains is exciting enough, but when you land and stand with only your guide and companions above untouched powder, the thrill factor is as high as it gets with skiing. It is not for beginners, though, as the isolation and challenging descents require great skill and experience. And it isn't cheap either.

On the edge of extreme

When you get into the high mountain environment found in the heart of the Alps, you may see some skiers, slightly crazed or highly spiritual, skiing the most ridiculously steep and dangerous off-piste routes. Almost always, there is no escape route and so once they commit, it really is a case of fly or die (or at least badly injure yourself). One skier in particular, Glen Plake, has caught the public's imagination with his wild punk hairstyles and his breathtaking new test runs. If you ever get the chance to visit Argentière at the head of the Chamonix Valley, then take the lift up to the top station, called Grand Montets. Just out of the station is a fenced-off gully where merely standing near the edge gives you nauseous vertigo. The narrow gully is bordered by daunting black rock and it is fenced off for a reason: one slip and you would be off down to the Mer de Glace glacier far below. If you ever get there and stand looking at the frightening void, just remember, Glen Plake skied down that gully!

Cross-country skiing is a very different way of enjoying the snow. It is more akin to hiking and is an excellent way to get fit. The world's top cross-country skiers are some of the fittest athletes around. Many European ski centres have pisted cross-country runs on offer.

BULGARIA

BULGARIAN MOUNTAINS ADVENTURE
Kancho Shipkov, Kv. Dianabad bl 18 vh.A, 1172 Sofia
Phone: +359 2 620 688
Fax: N/A
Email: kancho@bglink.net
Website: http://pss.bglink.net/mysite/explorebg.html

Off the beaten Bulgarian piste
Bulgaria has a well-established ski industry even though it is not as busy as the centres around the Alps. However, the real advantage of this is that there are just loads of relatively unexplored off-piste and cross-country skiing opportunities for the more experienced skier. Bulgarian Mountains Adventure is a company based around members of the national mountain rescue service and they offer a

personal, tailor-made guiding service that can take you into any of the country's ranges.

Activity prices: The trips are all tailor-made to suit your requirements and cost around US$50 per day, or less, depending on what you do and where you go. The centre will advise you on the possibilities. The price also includes local transportation.

Accommodation: Food and lodging during the activity are included in the price and organised by the centre. Hotels and meals at the start and end of your trip are not included but the centre can help you arrange these.

Food: Food is included during the activity, but not at the start and end of your trip.

Equipment supplied: Ski equipment is available but take your own if you have it.

What to take: Personal ski and mountain clothing.

When to go: December to March, though the season varies greatly depending on snow conditions.

Established: 1997

Safety: At least one of the guides in every group is a qualified rescuer from the Bulgarian Mountain Rescue Service. They have plentiful experience and excellent local knowledge.

Insurance: Clients can arrange their own policy or the centre can arrange it on the spot.

Methods of payment: Bank transfer and cash.

Booking information: Advance booking is essential and a 30% deposit is payable. Cancellation penalties may apply.

Nearest airport: Sofia. Transfers can be arranged.

Nearest rail station: Sofia Central. Transfers can be arranged.

FRANCE

MOUNTAIN ACTIVITY EXPERIENCE
93 avenue Michel Croz, 74400 Chamonix
Phone: +33 4 50 55 80 80
Fax: +33 4 53 48 50

Email: M.A.X@wanadoo.fr
Website: montblanconeline.fr/max/max.htm

Downhill skiing in the Chamonix Valley
Mountain Activity Experience offers so many skiing courses that
you'd be hard pushed to find one that doesn't suit your ability,
budget or timing. Level 1 three and five-day courses take you
through the basics, from turning on your first green runs after
three days, to a 12 km traverse down to Vallercine (a quiet village
on the Swiss border) after five days. Levels 2 and 3 take you
through progressively steeper slopes and introduce you to the
possibilities of off-piste skiing on straightforward classics. By the
end of Level 2/3 you'll be ready to take on the 22 km Vallée
Blanche – point downhill and just follow the guide! Level 4/5 is the
next logical step with off-piste potential on glaciers and high-
mountain runs, followed by your first forays into deep powder,
steep slopes and big moguls.

Activity prices: From FFr800 per person for a three-day course and FFr1,300
for a five-day course (five to eight people in both cases).
Accommodation: Not included in the price.
Food: Not included.
Equipment supplied: None provided.
What to take: Skis, boots poles and personal skiing clothing are not provided,
but can be rented at the centre.
When to go: Winter only.
Established: 1997
Safety: All instructors are nationally qualified ski instructors.
Insurance: Clients must provide their own insurance.
Methods of payment: Cheques and cash.
Booking information: A deposit is required to secure a booking. Cancellation
within a month of the course forfeits the deposit.
Nearest airport: Geneva.
Nearest rail station: Chamonix.

MOUNTAIN ACTIVITY EXPERIENCE
93 avenue Michel Croz, 74400 Chamonix
Phone: +33 4 50 55 80 80
Fax: +33 4 53 48 50
Email: M.A.X@wanadoo.fr
Website: montblanconeline.fr/max/max.htm

Heli-skiing the Mont Blanc Massif
Powder skiing is arguably the ultimate goal for any recreational skier, but without the need for lifts, passes and other people, it's easy to see why aficionados describe heli-skiing as unbeatable. Airlifted to one of 22 different summits around Mont Blanc, you'll be given a preview of the route on the way up, followed by an extreme close-up on the way back down! And just when you thought it couldn't get any better, pasta in a cosy pension awaits those who've been ploughing through the white stuff all day.

Activity prices: FFr1,500 per person.

Accommodation: Not included in the price.

Food: A home-made pasta meal at a cosy pension is included in the price.

Equipment supplied: None provided.

What to take: Skis, boots and poles are not included, but can be rented at the centre.

When to go: Winter only.

Established: 1997

Safety: All instructors are nationally qualified high mountain guides and ski instructors.

Insurance: Clients must provide their own insurance.

Methods of payment: Cheques and cash.

Booking information: A deposit is required to secure a booking. Cancellation within a month of the course forfeits the deposit.

Nearest airport: Geneva.

Nearest rail station: Chamonix.

MOUNTAIN ACTIVITY EXPERIENCE
93 avenue Michel Croz, 74400 Chamonix
Phone: +33 4 50 55 80 80
Fax: +33 4 53 48 50
Email: M.A.X@wanadoo.fr
Website: montblanconeline.fr/max/max.htm

Off-piste skiing in the Mont Blanc Massif
The ski areas of Chamonix can be so vast that it's sometimes difficult
to know where to start, even for the experienced skier. Mountain
Activity Experience specialises in taking intermediate and expert skiers
off the beaten piste and introducing them to the powder possibilities of
the area. 'Blacker than Black' offers skiers the chance to steepen their
fall-line, while the 24 km Vallée Blanche run will leave you, quite
literally, breathless. You don't have to be an expert skier, but some
fitness and finesse might help. And if that's not enough to powder
your toes, for just FFr310 per person (minimum 10 people) you can
share a meal at the famous Requin Mountaineering Hut and ski the
Vallée Blanche by moonlight (not surprisingly, drinks aren't included).

Activity prices: From FFr800 per person (five to eight people) to FFr2,200 per
person (two to three people) for a three-day course, and from FFr1,300 per
person to FFr3,700 per person for a five-day course.
Accommodation: Not included in the price.
Food: Not included.
Equipment supplied: None provided
What to take: Skis, boots, poles and other personal skiing equipment are not
included, but can be rented.
When to go: Winter only.
Established: 1997
Safety: All instructors are nationally qualified ski instructors.
Insurance: Clients must provide their own insurance.
Methods of payment: Cheques and cash.
Booking information: A deposit is required to secure a booking. Cancellation
within a month of the course forfeits the deposit.
Nearest airport: Geneva. Nearest rail station: Chamonix.

SNOW SAFARI LIMITED

Chalet Savoy, 1351 route des Chavants, 74310 Les Houches
Phone: +33 (0)4 50 54 56 63; UK bookings & information number
01279 600 885
Fax: +33 (0)4 50 54 57 19
Email: Chalsavoy@aol.com
Website: www.chaletsavoy.com

Pistes of Champions
Chamonix–Les Houches is the regular venue for Chamonix's world
cup races and boasts some of the best downhill skiing in the world.
The Savoy is situated at the foot of Mont Blanc, and the ski slopes
are only five minutes' walk from the chalet – in normal conditions it's
possible to ski right back to the front door. Chalet Savoy's unique
Safari pass accesses 17 ski areas within an hour's drive of Les
Houches. Europe's longest ski-run, the Vallée Blanche, can be
reached by the world's highest cable car, the Aiguille du Midi, while
the more adventurous can heli-ski in Italy or Switzerland. Instruction
and equipment rental are also available for skiing and snowboarding.

Activity prices: 17 area ski costs FFr240 per day for adults, or FFr1,100 for six
days, including trips to four different ski areas and a money back guarantee
for days not skied. Concessions available for children, OAP's and
unemployed.
Accommodation: Available at the Chalet Savoy. Prices from FFr2,750 per
person for seven days and seven nights, which includes free use of the sauna
and daily transport to the slopes.
Food: Half-board included in the accommodation price.
Equipment supplied: Equipment rental is available.
What to take: Personal skiing equipment, sunglasses, sunscreen, etc.
When to go: December to April.
Established: 1987
Safety: All guides and leaders are fully qualified for the relevant activity.
Insurance: Clients must arrange their own insurance.
Methods of payment: VISA, Mastercard.

Booking information: Contact Snow Safari for booking form and full terms and conditions.

Nearest airport: Geneva.

Nearest rail station: Les Houches.

SWITZERLAND

FOUR SEASONS GUIDES
Chalet L'Aurore
1936 Verbier
Switzerland
Phone: +41 27 771 7683
Fax: +41 27 771 1603
Email: hans@verbier.ch
Website: www.swissguides.com

Ski like a Swiss bird
Verbier is surrounded by beautiful Alpine peaks and some of them can be accessed by helicopter for a virgin powder ski-run of a lifetime. One of the best places to try this exciting sport is on the Plateau of Trient Glacier. There are numerous options for powder or spring snow from January to June. This is not for beginners. You should be used to skiing on changeable snow conditions and be in good physical shape because you will be out in the wilds for a while. No chair lifts round here! This centre also offers some superb off-piste skiing opportunities.

Activity prices: Guiding fees are SFr400 per day for one to two clients. For this, the guide will also arrange local travel and hotel bookings and the itinerary (clients pay directly to the hotel, bus company, etc.). Helicopter fees are extra.
Accommodation: Not included in the price. There is a large range of accommodation options in the area and the guide will help you to arrange it.
Food: Not included in the price, but there are plenty of eating options in the area too. While in the mountains, clients pay for their own food and that of the guide.

Equipment supplied: Specialist equipment can be hired in Verbier.

What to take: All specialist mountain clothing.

When to go: January to June.

Established: 1990

Safety: All guides hold UIAGM qualifications.

Insurance: Clients are recommended to buy helicopter rescue insurance which costs SFr30 for one year.

Methods of payment: VISA, Mastercard, Amex, travellers' cheques and cash.

Booking information: Payment in full is required one week in advance. Full refunds are available for acceptable cancellation.

Nearest airport: Geneva. Transfers can be arranged.

Nearest rail station: Le Chable. Transfers can be arranged.

SKYDIVING

'One thousand, two thousand, three thousand, check canopy!' These words, or something very similar, will be ringing in your ears long after you do your first parachute jump.

Parachuting can be divided into two distinct disciplines: static line jumping and free falling. Static line jumps tend to be from around 2,000 feet with a parachute that opens automatically a few seconds after exit. Free falling requires you to open your own parachute and is generally from much, much higher.

After a day's training on the ground learning the basics of exiting the aircraft, the free fall position and landing, your first few parachute jumps will almost certainly be static line jumps. Five or six good static line jumps (where the exit and body position are stable all the way) are required before you can free fall. After that, the sky really is the limit.

For those who don't have the time or the patience to go through the rigours of practice jumps, a tandem parachute jump offers all of the excitement with none of the responsibility. After a basic briefing you're attached to the torso of an instructor, who then does everything for you – including jumping put of the plane! They're more expensive than static line jumps, but they do mean you can jump from 10,000 feet first time out. The only requirements are that you are over 16, healthy and not overweight. Some centres require a doctor's certificate and a declaration of fitness before you jump.

SPAIN

CENTRO DE PARACAIDISMO COSTA BRAVA
Aerodromo de Empuriabrava, Apartado 194, 17487 Empuriabrava
Phone: +34 972 45 01 11

Fax: +34 972 45 07 49
Email: cpcb@gna.es
Website: http://skyrats.com

Skydiving in northern Spain
The Centro de Paracaidismo is one of the biggest dive-sites in Europe, with an enormous programme of death-defying leaps for every level of skydiver. Located on the Mediterranean coast just north of Barcelona, the centre boasts year-round sun and features a bar/restaurant, hot showers and bunkhouse accommodation, swimming pool and tennis courts. Tandem dives, introductory free fall courses and accelerated free fall programmes are all available, and the more you dive, the cheaper it becomes. A tandem flight with a qualified instructor assumes no previous experience and requires only a 15-minute briefing and a 20-minute flight, before a whole minute of free fall from 12,000 feet. The Introductory Free Fall course involves a tandem jump followed by an assisted free fall jump, with two instructors giving direct help throughout. If that's not enough, the next step is the Accelerated Free Fall Course, which continues with assisted jumps until you're ready to go solo (usually seven levels). And if you need to unwind, windsurfing, scuba diving, jet skiing and microlighting are all available in the immediate area, not to mention miles of sandy beaches . . .

Activity prices: The tandem flight with an instructor costs Pta23,000, an introductory free fall course costs Pta67,000, and the accelerated free fall course costs Pta215,000. For qualified divers, jumps cost Pta3,200 or Pta75,000 for a block of 25. Group prices are also available.
Accommodation: Not included in the price, but can be arranged nearby at a budget to suit.
Food: Not included in the price, but various options are available as part of the accommodation arrangements. Food is also available at the centre.
Equipment supplied: All specialist equipment is supplied for introductory courses. Equipment can also be hired by qualified divers.
What to take: Personal clothes and a good pair of shoes or canvas boots.
When to go: Year round.

Established: 1985

Safety: All instructors are Spanish Aerosports Federation qualified and have between 5,000 and 9,000 jumps' experience.

Insurance: Insurance is recommended for all courses, but is included in the price of the tandem jump.

Methods of payment: Cash, VISA, Mastercard, Maestro, Amex, travellers' cheques, etc.

Booking information: A deposit may be required to secure a booking.

Nearest airport: Barcelona or Girona.

Nearest rail station: Figueres.

REAL AERO CLUB DE SANTANDER

C/Castilla, 19 – Pta 23-A, 39009 Santander
Phone: +34 (0)639 666 242/(0)607 288 002
Fax: +34 (0)942 272 742
Email: rmontaraz@mundivia.es *or* rblanco@mundivia.es
Website: http://personales.mundivia.es/rmontaraz/

Fly those Spanish skies

If you are afraid of heights look elsewhere for an adrenaline fix. Without any previous jumping experience, you are strapped to an instructor, flown to 13,500 feet and launched from the plane for a whole minute and 5,000 feet of mind-blowing 200 kph free fall. With the highly qualified instructor controlling the whole flight and landing, you can just soak up the bird's-eye view of northern Spain. Preparation and the jump take up almost a whole day. For those who fear nothing, the intensive Accelerated Free Fall course should take you from novice to independent skydiver within eight jumps. There is no time for nerves as, after ground training, you go immediately into independent skydiving with two highly trained instructors by your side to assist you throughout each jump. Mid-air instructions are given via radio and there is hands-on help when needed, so it's a very safe way to scare yourself senseless.

Activity prices: Tandem jumps cost Pta23,000 per person, an Accelerated Free Fall course costs Pta210,000 for eight jumps from 13,500 feet and a Free

Fall Progressive Course costs Pta60,000 for three jumps from 4,000 feet.

Accommodation: Not included, but the centre will help to arrange it locally.

Food: Available at centre.

Equipment supplied: All specialist skydive equipment is provided.

What to take: Suitable footwear.

When to go: Weekends only throughout the year, depending on weather.

Established: 1989

Safety: All the centre's skydiving instructors are AFF, CPCL or CACL qualified (via the Spanish Aeronautical Association, FAE). The centre is a member of FAE and the Real Aero Club de España).

Insurance: Insurance cover is included in each course price.

Methods of payment: Travellers' cheques and cash.

Booking information: Two weeks' advance booking is recommended. A fully refundable 25% deposit is required for each booking.

Nearest airport: Santander.

Nearest rail station: Santander RENFE station.

SWITZERLAND

ALPIN RAFT
Postfach 78, 3800 Matten
Phone: +41 33 823 4100
Fax: +41 33 823 4101
Email: mail@alpinraft.ch
Website: www.alpinraft.ch

Jump over the Eiger
Where better to parachute jump than over one of the most famous mountains in the world. The North Face – or *Nordwand* – of the Eiger is the backdrop to this unique experience, which involves a tandem parachute jump from a helicopter thousands of feet above the valley floor. No previous experience is required as all necessary training will be given.

Activity prices: SFr380 per person.

Accommodation: Backpacker accommodation available at the centre.

Food: None provided.

Equipment supplied: All specialist equipment is included.

What to take: Normal hiking clothes.

When to go: April to October.

Established: 1988

Safety: All instructors are fully qualified and extremely experienced.

Insurance: Clients must arrange their own insurance.

Methods of payment: All common methods of payment accepted.

Booking information: Book by phone or email. Full payment is charged for cancellation on the day of trip.

Nearest airport: Bern.

Nearest rail station: Interlaken.

UNITED KINGDOM

ACORN ACTIVITIES
PO Box 120, Hereford HR4 8YB
Phone: +44 (0)1432 830083
Fax: +44 (0)1432 830110
Email: sales@acornactivities.co.uk
Website: www.acornactivities.co.uk

Parachuting over Herefordshire

Acorn Activities offer a choice of jumps, depending on just how far you want to drop. For first timers who want to go solo, the best option is a static line jump using a fully steerable square canopy. The course lasts one or two days, depending on the weather and the time of year, with the first day used for training. In the summer you may be able to jump at the end of the first day if conditions are suitable. For those who want to go higher, a tandem skydive takes you to 12,000 feet with an instructor conveniently strapped to your back. But for the ultimate rush, the way down is to do it alone: accompanied by two instructors, you will plummet from 12,000 feet while they give you direct, practical assistance throughout your free fall. At a little over 5,000 feet, with canopy control instructions given by radio, you will pull the cord . . . and breathe for the first time in two minutes.

Activity prices: £205 for a one or two-day course, depending on conditions and available light.

Accommodation: Not included in the price, but can be arranged locally.

Food: Not included.

Equipment supplied: No specialist equipment is required.

What to take: Warm clothes and sturdy shoes or boots.

When to go: Year round, weather permitting.

Established: 1990

Safety: All instructors are BPA qualified.

Insurance: Insurance is required, although this can be arranged through Acorn Activities.

Methods of payment: VISA, Mastercard, cheque and cash.

Booking information: Late bookings are welcomed. A non-refundable deposit of £10 per day is required. Cancellation charges apply on a sliding scale from 80% for over 43 days before departure to 100% for up to 14 days.

Nearest airport: Depends on jump site.

Nearest rail station: Depends on the itinerary.

SKYDIVE UNLIMITED
Chatteris Airfield, Manea, March, Cambs PE 15 0EA
Phone: +44 (0)1354 741197
Fax: +44 (0)1354 741204
Email: jump@skydiveunlimited.co.uk
Website: www.skydiveunlimited.co.uk

Skydiving in the UK, Spain and Florida
Owner Andy Parkin offers tandem skydives and accelerated free fall courses in the UK, Spain and Florida year round, from one day to one week in length. Tandem skydiving can be done whenever there's a suitable window in the temperamental British weather, but the eight jumps of the accelerated free fall course are best completed abroad where conditions are more reliable. Completion of the AFF (accelerated free fall) course entitles you to skydive on your own from 12,000 feet anywhere in the world. By the time you're qualified, the cost plummets almost as fast as you, to as little as £30 a pop.

Activity prices: The tandem flight with an instructor costs £185. The full accelerated free fall course costs £1,350 in the UK, £1,750 in Spain and £1,950 in Florida.

Accommodation: Spain and Florida prices include flights and accommodation.

Food: Not included in the price.

Equipment supplied: All specialist equipment is supplied.

What to take: Personal clothes and a good pair of shoes or canvas boots.

When to go: Year round.

Established: 1997

Safety: All the instructors have BPA ratings and the centre is approved by the BPA which is governed by the CAA.

Insurance: Third party insurance is included. Clients should arrange their own accident cover.

Methods of payment: Cash, VISA, Mastercard, etc.

Booking information: Bookings can be taken at any time and deposits are required. Cancellation penalties only apply if the client fails to show on the day without prior arrangement.

Nearest airport: Depends on the location.

Nearest rail station: Depends on the location.

SNOWBOARDING

Like big-wall climbing and mountain biking, the sport of snowboarding began in California in the 1970s. It is now one of the fastest-growing recreational activities in the world. In fact, snowboarding has for many become the preferred method of playing on, and off, the pistes.

The secret of snowboarding's appeal undoubtedly lies in its simplicity. It can be divided into two distinct types: freestyle boards have soft boots and bindings for maximum flexibility and feel off-piste, while Alpine boards have more rigid boots and bindings that allow for greater speed and control on piste.

Unlike skiing, snowboarding has only one plank of wood for beginners to think about, and no poles to plant in the way of rogue edges. In fact, many snowboarding schools guarantee that you'll be making simple turns on gentle slopes within a morning's boarding. Once you can wend your way down the nursery slopes, it's simply a matter of practice makes perfect. If you're really dedicated, there's no reason why you can't work on your skills year-round: the glacier runs of Tignes and Mont Blanc provide just as much excitement in July as they do in January!

FRANCE

MOUNTAIN ACTIVITY EXPERIENCE
93 avenue Michel Croz, 74400 Chamonix
Phone: +33 4 50 55 80 80
Fax: +33 4 53 48 50
Email: M.A.X@wanadoo.fr
Website: montblanconeline.fr/max/max.htm

Snowboarding in the Chamonix Valley

Within the team of instructors at Mountain Activity Experience you will find some of the pioneers of mono-skiing and snowboarding. They first made mono-skis and snowboards out of wooden planks and spent months running up and down Les Grands Montets, steadily perfecting a technique that has evolved into snowboarding as we know it today. It's not necessary to be a skier before you try snowboarding – in fact, it helps to come to the sport with no preconceptions at all. It only takes half a day to master basic turning on an easy slope, and with half-day taster sessions available for only FFr200,,you might be running out of excuses . . .

Activity prices: From FFr200 per person for a half-day (minimum four people).

Accommodation: Not included in the price.

Food: Not included.

Equipment supplied: None provided.

What to take: Boards and boots are not included, but can be rented at the centre.

When to go: Winter only.

Established: 1997

Safety: All instructors are nationally qualified snowboard instructors.

Insurance: Clients must provide their own insurance.

Methods of payment: Cheques and cash.

Booking information: A deposit is required to secure a booking. Cancellation within a month of the course forfeits the deposit.

Nearest airport: Geneva.

Nearest rail station: Chamonix.

SWITZERLAND

ADVENTURE'S BEST

PO Box 9, Via Basilea 28, CH-6903 Lugano

Phone: +41 91 966 11 14

Fax: +41 91 966 12 13

Email: info@asbest.ch

Website: www.asbest.ch

Snowboarding in southern Switzerland

Established in 1994, Adventure's Best organises a variety of outdoor activities in the region of Ticino, Switzerland's most southerly state or *canton*. Ticino offers over 3,000 sq km of untouched mountain wilderness and in winter is ideally suited to snowboard touring. From the first snow of the season (usually December) until May, nationally qualified Alpine guides will lead you off the beaten piste to experience some of the most remote runs in the region. Accommodation is not included in the price, but can be arranged at the centre at a budget to suit, from shared dorms to single rooms.

Activity prices: Contact the centre for the latest prices.

Accommodation: Not included in the price, but is available at the centre. Shared dorms cost SFr20 per person, a double room SFr40 per person, a double room with en suite bath/shower SFr50 per person and a single room with en suite bath/shower SFr60 per person.

Food: Not included in the price, but is available at the centre. Buffet breakfast costs SFr15 per person.

Equipment supplied: All specialist equipment is provided.

What to take: Personal clothing.

When to go: December to May.

Established: 1994

Safety: All instructors hold recognised qualifications from the relevant national or international governing body.

Insurance: Clients are responsible for arranging their own insurance.

Methods of payment: VISA, Mastercard, Amex, travellers' cheques and cash.

Booking information: No deposit required.

Nearest airport: Lugano-Agno (5 km).

Nearest rail station: Lugano (200 metres).

SNOWSHOEING

If you remember old black-and-white film footage of polar explorers trudging across snowy wastes with tennis rackets strapped to their feet then you would be shocked at how technology has revolutionised this kind of travel to the point where people now go out and do it for fun. Snowshoes work on the simple principle of spreading the load, thus stopping you from sinking into the snow. If you doubt your snowshoes' effectiveness, then try removing them and see how far you get! Modern snowshoes are lightweight, energy efficient and anti-clogging so that you can just concentrate on walking through pristine snowscapes and getting to parts of the mountain that would otherwise be beyond all but the fittest mountaineers. A popular snowshoe type is the one where your heel lifts off the base, making for a much more natural walking action. This is a great family activity, too, with equipment available for children and the fun levels being much higher than a normal walk in the park. That fresh snow makes great snowballs . . .

FRANCE

MOUNTAIN ACTIVITY EXPERIENCE
93 avenue Michel Croz, 74400 Chamonix
Phone: +33 4 50 55 80 80
Fax: +33 4 53 48 50
Email: M.A.X@wanadoo.fr
Website: montblanconeline.fr/max/max.htm

Exploring the Chamonix Valley by snowshoe
Learning to snowshoe is within everyone's reach, and it can take you to places so far off the beaten track that you'll think you've stumbled

into the Stone Age. Half-day and full-day excursions are offered, with outings costing as little as FFr110 per person (minimum five people). Virgin snow, miles and miles of wilderness and the most relaxing way to travel awaits anyone who wants to try something new . . . without losing a limb! Snowshoes are not included in the price, but can be rented for a nominal fee.

Activity prices: From FFr110 per person for a half-day to FFr170 per person for a full day (minimum five people in both cases).

Accommodation: Not included in the price.

Food: Not included.

Equipment supplied: None provided.

What to take: Snowshoes are not included, but can be rented at the centre.

When to go: Winter only.

Established: 1997

Safety: All instructors are nationally qualified high mountain guides.

Insurance: Clients must provide their own insurance.

Methods of payment: Cheques and cash.

Booking information: A deposit is required to secure a booking. Cancellation within a month of the course forfeits the deposit.

Nearest airport: Geneva.

Nearest rail station: Chamonix.

ODYSSEE MONTAGNE

101 Les Marmottières
74310 Les Houches
France
Phone: +33 (0)4 50 54 36 01
Fax: +33 (0)4 50 54 35 74
Email: odyssee@odyssee-montagne.fr
Website: http://odyssee-monatgne.fr

Snowshoe walking in the Alps

Traditionally the haunt of skiers and climbers, the mountains and forests of the Chamonix Valley are also ideally suited to travelling by snowshoe.

Snowshoes have been rediscovered in recent years by those who want to explore the winter wonderland of the Alps without the hustle and bustle of downhill skiing and the added expense of cross-country skiing. Modern snowshoes are comfortable to wear and extremely versatile. Odyssée Montagne offers three and four-day packages that combine guided tours of the Chamonix Valley and the Bernese Oberland with accommodation in cosy mountain huts. No experience is necessary as full instruction will be given and all specialist equipment is provided.

Activity prices: From FFr1,980 for four days and three nights.

Accommodation: Mountain hut accommodation included.

Food: All food is included in the price.

Equipment supplied: Modern snowshoes are provided.

What to take: Personal clothing for winter walking.

When to go: December to May.

Established: 1993

Safety: All mountain guides are members of the Ecole National de Ski et d'Alpinisme.

Insurance: Comprehensive insurance can be provided at an additional 5% of the full price.

Methods of payment: Travellers' cheques, VISA, Mastercard, Swift bank transfer, etc.

Booking information: A deposit of 30% is required at the time of booking.

Bookings will be accepted no later than 15 days before departure.

Nearest airport: Geneva. Collection available on request.

Nearest rail station: Saint Gervais.

SPAIN

CASA DE LA MONTAÑA
33556 Asturias
Phone: +34 8 5844189
Fax: +34 8 5844189
Email: casamont@mundivia.es
Website: http://personales.mundivia.es/casamont

Snowshoeing in the Picos de Europa

In winter, there's no better way to explore this relatively remote and untouched mountain range than by snowshoe. La Casa de la Montaña runs three-day exploratory trips which include accommodation and breakfast before departure, two days plodding through the Picos with a mountain guide, and meals and accommodation back at La Casa in between. La Casa includes a TV and lecture room, a kitchen and restaurant, an information office for those who prefer to make their own plans, a games lawn and mountain bike rental. Treks are not particularly strenuous and no specialist equipment is required: just a waterproof and windproof jacket, mountain boots, gloves, a scarf, sunglasses and suncream. Energy drinks and a thermos of something hot are also ideal.

Activity prices: A one-week trip costs around Pta59,000 per person (minimum six people), including transport, guided hiking and full board accommodation. Single days start from Pta4,000 per person, weekends Pta8,500 and multi-day trips Pta18,500, not including accommodation.

When to go: February to April.

Equipment supplied: Snowshoes provided.

What to take: Personal hiking equipment including boots, rucksack, waterproofs, etc.

Accommodation: Full board mountain refuge and centre accommodation is included in the price.

Food: All meals are included in the price.

Established: 1987

Safety: Mountain Guide Fernando Ruiz is a Professional Mountain Leader of the AEGM.

Insurance: Multi-activity insurance is available on request at an additional cost.

Methods of payment: Cash, VISA.

Booking information: A 30% deposit is required to secure a booking.

Nearest airport: Asturias & Santander (124 km). Pick-up from Santander Airport can be arranged for small groups at minimal cost.

Nearest rail station: Arriondas (22 km). Transfers can be arranged to and from Arriondas Station.

ADVENTURE'S BEST
PO Box 9, Via Basilea 28, CH-6903 Lugano
Phone: +41 91 966 11 14
Fax: +41 91 966 12 13
Email: info@asbest.ch
Website: www.asbest.ch

Snowshoeing in southern Switzerland
Nestling discreetly in the southernmost corner of Switzerland, Ticino
is an oft-overlooked winter wonderland of Alpine lakes, crystal clear
mountain streams and towering 3,000 metre peaks. Snowshoe
touring is available from the first snow of the season (usually
December) until the end of May, and the options are almost limitless.
Accommodation is not included in the price, but the centre has
private and dormitory rooms available on request.

Activity prices: Contact the centre for the latest prices.
Accommodation: Not included in the price, but is available at the centre.
Shared dorms cost an additional SFr20 per person, a double room SFr40 per
person, a double room with en suite bath/shower SFr50 per person and a single
room with en suite bath/shower SFr60 per person.
Food: Not included in the price, but is available at the centre. Buffet breakfast
costs SFr15 per person.
Equipment supplied: All specialist equipment is provided.
What to take: Personal clothing.
When to go: December to May.
Established: 1994
Safety: All instructors hold recognised qualifications from the relevant
national or international governing body.
Insurance: Clients are responsible for arranging their own insurance.
Methods of payment: VISA, Mastercard, Amex, travellers' cheques and cash.
Booking information: No deposit required.
Nearest airport: Lugano-Agno (5 km).
Nearest rail station: Lugano (200 metres).

SURFING

A clean, glassy-smooth wave rears up behind you. Paddling franti-
cally, you try to match the speed of the wave. Just when you think it'll
never arrive you feel the back of the board rise as the wave lifts you
and launches you towards the beach. You grip the rail, snap to your
feet, and suddenly you're accelerating forward under nature's
awesome power . . . before falling face-first into the wave in a
confusing maelstrom of froth and fibreglass.

As any aspiring surfer will tell you, few things in life compare to
catching your first wave, but falling off comes with the territory. The
more you surf, the less you fall off. At its best, surfing is clean waves,
warm water and weekends at the beach; at its worst it's a mushy
mess, with near-freezing water and weather that would make a seal
think twice. But as with anything worthwhile, the rewards more than
make up for the trials.

A good way to get used to waves is to try a boogie board first. A
boogie board is basically a shortened surfboard with a flat front that
allows waves to be ridden without the added frustrations of standing
up. In fact, boogie boarding is a well-established sport in its own right,
with experts performing all sorts of tricks, loops and flat spins.

If you don't need any convincing, the best way to get started is to
take an introductory course. It is possible to hire a board and teach
yourself, but a course will save you hours of frustration with a few
basic pointers. You will also learn something about waves, weather
and currents – many breaks can be dangerous if you don't know what
to look for. Most people manage to stand up by the end of their first
day. After that, it's all practice, practice, practice.

ACORN ACTIVITIES
PO Box 120, Hereford HR4 8YB
Phone: +44 (0)1432 830083
Fax: +44 (0)1432 830110
Email: sales@acornactivities.co.uk
Website: www.acornactivities.co.uk

Surfing in Cornwall and Pembrokeshire
Open to the Gulf Stream and the full force of the Atlantic swell, the Cornish and Pembrokeshire coasts enjoy some of the most reliable surfing conditions in Europe. Two, three and five-day courses are available, all taught by BSA qualified instructors. Wetsuits and boards are provided, and accommodation and transport to and from the beaches are included in the price.

Activity prices: £135 for a two-day course, £200 for a three-day course and £385 for a five-day course.

Accommodation: B&B accommodation is included in the price.

Food: Dinner costs an additional £14 a night.

Equipment supplied: Wetsuits and surfboards are provided.

What to take: Warm change of clothes, towel, etc.

When to go: Year round.

Established: 1990

Safety: All instructors are BSA approved.

Insurance: Insurance is required, although this can be arranged through Acorn Activities.

Methods of payment: VISA, Mastercard, cheque and cash.

Booking information: Late bookings are welcomed. A non-refundable deposit of £10 per day is required. Cancellation charges apply on a sliding scale from 80% for over 43 days before departure to 100% for up to 14 days.

Nearest airport: Depends on surf location.

Nearest rail station: Depends on the itinerary.

ADVENTURE SPORTS

Carnkie Farmhouse, Carnkie, Redruth, Cornwall TR16 6RZ
Phone: +44 (0)1209 218 962
Fax: +44 (0)1209 314 118
Email: holidays@adventure-sports.co.uk
Website: www.adventure-sports.co.uk

Ride the Cornish waves

Cornwall is home to British surfing and the waves at Newquay have been used for the World Surfing Championship series. Adventure Sports offers a range of courses to suit beginners and improvers with guidance from well-qualified and experienced board riders. They will get you standing on the board and riding your first wave in a reasonably short time. The company does not used fixed locations for its activities as weather and surf conditions vary around the Cornish coast. By staying flexible they can get you to the place where the waves are best. They also offer many other activities so you can mix surfing with other sports.

Activity prices: A three-day camping stay with two days of activities costs from £76 (low season) to £100 (high season) and prices go up to £329 for a seven night/seven activity days course.

Accommodation: Included in price. You have a choice of camping, self-catering chalets or a converted self-catering farmhouse. There are many social options nearby or on the site.

Food: Not included.

Equipment supplied: All specialised equipment is provided.

What to take: Swimsuit.

When to go: Summer months only.

Established: 1982

Safety: All instructors are nationally qualified and very experienced.

Insurance: Insurance is required. Policies are offered by the centre.

Methods of payment: VISA, cheque and cash.

Booking information: Advance booking is required. A £50 deposit is payable.

Nearest airport: Newquay.

Nearest rail station: Redruth. Transfers can be arranged.

FREETIME HOLIDAYS

Runnelstone Cottages, St. Levan, Penzance, Cornwall TR19 6LU
United Kingdom
Phone: +44 (0)1736 871302
Fax: +44 (0)1736 871302
Email: freetime@dial.pipex.com
Website: http://ds.dial.pipex.com/freetime

Surfing in Cornwall
With its temperate climate and reliable swell, Cornwall has long been at
the centre of British surfing, and offers some of the best waves in
Europe. Freetime's owner Chris South has 25 years of experience in
surfing and activity holidays, and as well as introductory lessons, he
runs the BSA Fin Awards course, for which certificates are awarded.
Most of the surfing is done at Sennen's Cove, but depending on
conditions both north and south coast beaches are within driving
distance. Courses vary from half-day introductions to six-day extrava-
ganzas, and accommodation can be booked locally at a budget to suit.

Activity prices: From £20 per half-day, £35 per full day and £80 for three days.
Group discounts also available.
What to take: Personal clothing, swimsuit and towel.
Accommodation: Not included, but can be arranged to suit.
Food: Not included in the price.
Equipment supplied: All specialist equipment is supplied, including boards and
full steamer wetsuits.
When to go: Year round.
Established: 1989
Safety: All instructors are BSA qualified and are Royal Lifesaving Association
National Beach Lifeguards.
Insurance: Third party liability is recommended and can be arranged if required.
Methods of payment: Cheque, VISA and Mastercard are all accepted.
Booking information: Advanced booking is essential, and a deposit is required.
Nearest airport: Newquay.
Nearest rail station: Penzance. Pick-up from the train or bus station in
Penzance can be arranged in advance.

TWR-Y-FELIN NO LIMITS

The TYF Group, 1 High Street, St Davids, Pembrokeshire SA62 6QS
Phone: +44 (0)1437 721 611
Fax: +44 (0)1437 721 692
Email: info@tyf.com
Website: www.tyf.com

Surf the Pembrokeshire waves

Based in Britain's smallest city, the TYF No Limits centre has access to some of the best coastline in the country and the surf quality is surprisingly high all year round. Whether it's the gnarly barrels of Freshwater West or the gentler rides at Whitesands and Newgale, there is usually a surf up to suit your ability. Their Introduction to Surfing course covers beach safety, basic paddling techniques, catching waves, board trim and steering, standing up, wave selection and rights of way. The BSA qualified instructors will guide you the whole way. The Improver Surfing course will help you fine-tune your technique and develop a wider range of moves. You will also get to study more about waves and the history of surfing.

Activity prices: The Introduction to Surfing course costs £240 for three days with full board or £132 for camping. The Improvers' course follows the same pricing plan.

Accommodation: Included in price. You can either camp or have B&B, half board or full board accommodation in the Twr-y-Felin Hotel, a beautiful converted 18th-century windmill.

Food: Included in hotel-based course prices (see above).

Equipment supplied: All specialist equipment is provided.

What to take: Swimsuit.

When to go: Year round subject to waves.

Established: 1986

Safety: All the surfing instructors are BSA qualified. The centre is approved by the AALA and the BSA and is a member of the Welsh Tourist Board.

Insurance: The centre has liability insurance but recommends that clients take out independent insurance against curtailment and cancellation of their course (available from the centre) and a personal accident policy.

Methods of payment: VISA, Mastercard, cheques and cash.

Booking information: Advance booking is required.

Nearest airport: Cardiff.

Nearest rail station: Haverfordwest. Transfers may be arranged.

WINDSURFING

With the possible exception of southern Spain, you might be forgiven for thinking that Europe isn't best suited to a sport that seems to involve as much time in the water as out. However, with a full steamer wetsuit and neoprene booties, shivering in the shadows of the sail has become a thing of the past.

Dozens of sailing and windsurfing centres all over Europe offer everything from two-hour taster sessions to week-long courses that culminate in a nationally recognised qualification. To start with you won't even need to get wet, as the basic principles are usually presented and practised on dry-land boards. Once on the water you'll probably find initial progress a bit limited as you fall first one way, then the other, trying to balance the sail. Since you're as warm as toast, however (see above) you have nothing better to think about than . . . well, getting better. An hour or so of perseverance in a gentle wind, and most beginners will be up and gliding along the surface, the waves skittering beneath the board and the wind filling the sail . . . right up until the point where they look down and flop over the top of the sail into the water. Each time you get up you spend more time on the board, and after just a few days you'll be tacking and gybing like you never needed a wetsuit in the first place.

Some sailing experience might be useful in grasping the basic principles of wind and sail direction, but it doesn't take long to figure out what you should be doing, and only slightly longer actually to do it. You don't have to be super-fit or a great swimmer either, since most of the time you'll be standing on the board and taking things easy! All you really need is a swimsuit, a towel, and a healthy helping of perseverance.

CLUB MISTRAL

Krumpperstrasse 21, 82362 Weilheim, Germany
Phone: +49 881 41544
Fax: +49 881 8675
Email: company@club-mistral.com
Website: www.club-mistral.com

A Greek sailing break
The Greek island of Karpathos is well known for its consistent wind conditions; the wind called the Meltemi originates from the north and rushes down through the mountains to the coast, at times reaching force 8. The German-owned Club Mistral has two centres in the Speed Lagoon and Devil's Bay areas, both ideal for windsurfing, with the former especially good for teaching beginners. The centre's qualified instructors can take you from a taster course that lasts for six hours all the way up to advanced racing lessons. The centre has a good variety of boards and sails that are always rigged up so you can swap and change to your heart's content.

Activity prices: Board hire costs US$120 for three days and US$225 for seven days. Hourly rates are also available. Tuition prices, including board rental, are US$320 for one week and US$470 for two weeks. An introductory course with 10 hours of tuition costs US$230 and a taster course lasting six hours costs US$150.
Accommodation: The Club Mistral Karpathos is located near the Long Beach Hotel, a small family-run hotel that has great seaviews over the Bay of Afiartis, a small restaurant and pool. One week in a double room, including breakfast, costs from US$176 to US$193 depending on season.
Food: Full board, half-board and B&B packages are available.
Equipment supplied: All specialist windsurfing gear is available at centre.
What to take: Swimsuit, sunscreen, towel.
When to go: April to October only.
Established: 1982

Safety: All the windsurfing instructors have national qualifications and are very experienced.

Insurance: The centre has liability insurance. Clients should arrange their own travel insurance.

Methods of payment: VISA, Mastercard, Eurocard, bank transfers and travellers' cheques.

Booking information: Advance booking is recommended.

Nearest airport: Karpathos.

Nearest rail station: N/A.

SPAIN

CLUB MISTRAL
Krumpperstrasse 21, 82362 Weilheim, Germany
Phone: +49 881 41544
Fax: +49 881 8675
Email: company@club-mistral.com
Website: www.club-mistral.com

Sail Europe's top waves
Tarifa, on Spain's southern coast near Cadiz, is a mecca for windsurfing aficionados and the German-owned Club Mistral is ideally located to take advantage of the conditions. The average wind speed is in excess of force 4 and peaks as high as force 9! Everything the windsurfer could possibly want is there with a wide variety of boards, including ones from Naish, Flow and Malibu, a range of sails, hire by the hour, day or week, and tuition for beginners or advanced surfers. The centre has over 60 boards and 100 rigs so it is easy to change between them to sample how the board affects your surfing. Tuition is provided by qualified instructors with great enthusiasm for the sport. The centre offers a range of courses including introductory and taster sessions, and jumping and wave riding for more experienced sailors. There is also a Club Mistral centre on Gran Canaria in the Canary Islands.

Activity prices: Board hire costs US$120 for three days and US$225 for seven days. Hourly rates are also available. Tuition prices, including board rental, are US$320 for one week and US$470 for two weeks. An introductory course with 10 hours of tuition costs US$230 and a taster course lasting six hours costs US$150.

Accommodation: The Club Mistral is attached to the Hurricane Hotel, a small Moorish-style building set in subtropical gardens. One week in a double room with a sea view, including breakfast, costs from US$315 to US$415 depending on season. Rooms with a land view are US$75 to US$100 cheaper.

Food: Full board, half-board and B&B packages are available.

Equipment supplied: All specialist windsurfing gear is available at centre.

What to take: Swimsuit, sunscreen, towel.

When to go: Year round.

Established: 1982

Safety: All the windsurfing instructors have national qualifications and are very experienced.

Insurance: The centre has liability insurance. Clients should arrange their own travel insurance.

Methods of payment: VISA, Mastercard, Eurocard, bank transfers and travellers' cheques.

Booking information: Advance booking is recommended.

Nearest airport: Malaga, Gibraltar or Jerez de la Frontera.

Nearest rail station: Jerez.

UNITED KINGDOM

ACORN ACTIVITIES
PO Box 120, Hereford HR4 8YB
Phone: +44 (0)1432 830083
Fax: +44 (0)1432 830110
Email: sales@acornactivities.co.uk
Website: www.acornactivities.co.uk

Windsurfing throughout the UK
With a berth in every port, it seems that Acorn Activities can provide windsurfing courses almost anywhere in the country. Two, three and

five-day holidays are offered with B&B accommodation in quiet, family-run hotels included in the price. For those who would prefer to make their own way to the centres each day, two and five-day course-only options are also offered. Those on the shorter two and three-day courses will learn the basics of rigging and sailing a windsurfer, while five-day veterans will get as far as more advanced skills, such as tacking and turning on the move. Wetsuits are provided for all courses.

Activity prices: £165 for a two-day course, £250 for a three-day course and £440 for a five-day course.

Accommodation: Family-run hotel accommodation included in the price.

Food: Breakfast is included, but dinner costs an extra £14 per person per night.

Equipment supplied: All specialist equipment is provided, including wetsuits.

What to take: Warm clothes and shoes that can get wet.

When to go: April to October.

Established: 1990

Safety: All instructors are RYA qualified.

Insurance: Insurance is required, although this can be arranged through Acorn Activities.

Methods of payment: VISA, Mastercard, cheque and cash.

Booking information: Late bookings are welcomed. A non-refundable deposit of £10 per day is required. Cancellation charges apply on a sliding scale from 80% for over 43 days before departure to 100% for up to 14 days.

Nearest airport: Cardiff or Birmingham International.

Nearest rail station: Depends on the itinerary.

ADVENTURE SPORTS

Carnkie Farmhouse, Carnkie, Redruth, Cornwall TR16 6RZ
Phone: +44 (0)1209 218 962
Fax: +44 (0)1209 314 118
Email: holidays@adventure-sports.co.uk
Website: www.adventure-sports.co.uk

Skim the Cornish waves

Cornwall is one of the best places in the UK for windsurfing with its exposed westerly location and the fresh Atlantic breezes. To take advantage of the varying weather conditions around the region, Adventure Sports do not have a fixed location for windsurfing. The centre's instructors are all nationally qualified and will take you through the principle of boardsailing and the techniques needed to manoeuvre out on the water. They also offer many other activities so you can try other sports during your stay.

Activity prices: A three-day camping stay with two days of activities costs from £76 (low season) to £100 (high season) and prices go up to £329 for a seven night/seven activity days course.

Accommodation: Included in price. You have a choice of camping, self-catering chalets or a converted self-catering farmhouse. There are many social options nearby or on the site.

Food: Not included.

Equipment supplied: All specialised equipment is provided.

What to take: Swimsuit.

When to go: Summer months only.

Established: 1982

Safety: All instructors are nationally qualified and very experienced.

Insurance: Insurance is required. Policies are offered by the centre.

Methods of payment: VISA, cheque and cash.

Booking information: Advance booking is required. A £50 deposit is payable.

Nearest airport: Newquay.

Nearest rail station: Redruth. Transfers can be arranged.

CALSHOT ACTIVITIES CENTRE

Calshot Spit, Fawley, Southampton SO45 1BR
Phone: +44 (0)23 8089 2077
Fax: +44 (0)23 8089 1267
Email: acocal@hants.gov.uk
Website: www.hants.gov.uk/calshot

Learn where the instructors learn

Being based on the shore of the Solent makes the Calshot Activities Centre a great place to learn to windsurf. There is plenty of sheltered water for the beginner yet there is also open water for more the more skilled boardsailor. There are a wide variety of courses on offer for all levels of ability. There is also a good selection of boards, rigs and simulators and the instructors are all RYA qualified. The beginner courses are taught on Hi-Fly Revo boards that are stable and manoeuvrable, aiding fast progress.

Activity prices: There are so many course options and package prices that you should call the centre with your specific requirements.

Accommodation: Included in price. There is space for 150 people at the centre with various room options.

Food: Included. Three cooked meals per day plus drinks with residential courses. Meals on other courses can be booked to suit.

Equipment supplied: All equipment is provided.

What to take: Swimsuit, suitable footwear.

When to go: April to October.

Established: 1969

Safety: All the centre's windsurfing instructors are RYA qualified. The centre is licensed by the AALA and is a member of the RYA.

Insurance: Insurance is required. Policies are offered by the centre which cover you from the day of booking for cancellation through sickness or injury.

Methods of payment: VISA, Mastercard, cheque and cash.

Booking information: Advance booking is required. Full payment is needed on booking for all courses of up to four days' duration. A non-refundable £25 deposit is needed for longer courses with balance paid eight weeks before arrival.

Nearest airport: Southampton or Bournemouth.

Nearest rail station: Southampton Central or Beaulieu Road, Brockenhurst.

HOVE LAGOON WATERSPORTS

Hove Lagoon, Kingsway, Hove BN3 4LX
Phone: +44 (0)1273 424842
Fax: +44 (0)1273 421919

Email: windsurf@hovelagoon.co.uk
Website: www.hovelagoon.co.uk

Windsurfing England's south coast

Ideally situated in a sheltered cove a few miles west of Brighton, Hove Lagoon offers the perfect environment for basic training, while the challenges of the open sea are only a stone's throw away. The best way to learn to windsurf is to do the RYA Level 1 course, which includes setting up equipment, getting the sail out of the water, getting moving and turning, not to mention theory and safety. If that sounds like too much to take on board, a two-hour taster session might be enough. More experienced windsurfers or those who need a refresher course can progress through the RYA qualifications at their own pace, and private instruction is available – a one-hour lesson costs £35 and includes an hour's free practice time after the lesson.

Activity prices: From £20 for two hours to £120 for a full weekend, including all instruction and specialist equipment. Private tuition, nationally recognised certification and group discounts also available.

Accommodation: Local B&B and hotel accommodation from £15 per night can be arranged, but is not included in the price.

Food: Catering facilities and a licensed bar are available, but are not included in the price.

Equipment supplied: All specialist equipment is supplied.

What to take: Personal clothing, swimsuit, towel and a pair of shoes that can get wet.

When to go: March to November.

Established: 1994

Safety: All instructors have qualifications recognised by the national governing body for the appropriate activity (e.g. RYA, BCU, etc).

Insurance: The centre is insured for all licensed activities.

Methods of payment: All common methods of payment are accepted.

Booking information: Advanced booking required by phone, post or email. A 50% deposit is required to secure a booking.

Nearest airport: London Gatwick.

Nearest rail station: Hove. Pick-up can be arranged for groups.

PEAK ACTIVITIES

Rock Lea Activity Training Centre, Station Road, Hathersage,
Hope Valley, Derbyshire S32 1DD
Phone: +44 (0)1433 650 345
Fax: +44 (0)1433 650 342
Email: admin@iain.co.uk
Website: www.iain.co.uk

Wet and wise in Derbyshire

If you fancy getting soaked on a wobbly board that seems keen to
throw you off at any given moment then sign up for a windsurfing
course at Peak Activities' RYA-approved watersports centre. It is
located just 40 minutes' drive away from the Rock Lea centre and is an
ideal place to learn to windsurf. Before hitting the wet stuff, you will be
instructed on a land simulator. Courses can be arranged to suit you,
varying from as little as two hours to a whole weekend. The boards used
are suitable for beginners though more advanced boards are available
for people looking to hone their skills further. To keep you safe, a high-
powered safety boat is on the water the whole time you are there.

Activity prices: Prices vary depending on group size and the length of course.
They start from £20 per person for a two-hour session.
Accommodation: Not included in the course price. There is a large range of
options within easy reach of the centre, ranging from hostels and B&B's to
farmhouses and hotels.
Food: Not included in course price but there are plenty of local eateries to suit
all budgets.
Equipment supplied: All specialist equipment, including wetsuits.
What to take: Swimsuit and suitable footwear. Full list supplied on booking.
When to go: Year round, though winter windsurfing is only for the hardy.
Established: 1979
Safety: All the windsurfing instructors used by Peak Activities are RYA
Boardsailing Instructors and have first aid qualifications. Staff carry radios and
first aid kits. The company is licensed by the AALA and is a member of the
Heart of England Tourist Board. Supplied specialist equipment is of a high
standard and regularly maintained and replaced.

Insurance: All Peak Activity tours are fully insured for public and third party liability. Optional additional insurance can be taken out to guard against cancellation, illness, loss of property etc.

Methods of payment: VISA, Mastercard, Eurocard, personal cheques.

Booking information: A 50% deposit is requested with all bookings.

Nearest airport: Leeds (45 mins), Manchester (45 mins), Birmingham (90 mins) or Sheffield (12 mins). Transfers can be arranged.

Nearest rail station: Hathersage. Transfers can be arranged.

WINDSPORT INTERNATIONAL

Mylor Yacht Harbour, Falmouth, Cornwall TR11 5UF

Phone: +44 (0)1326 376 191/363

Fax: +44 (0)1326 376 192

Email: windsport.international@btinternet.com

Website: www.windsport-int.com

Windy ways in Cornwall

Windsport International offers windsurfing courses at both of its centres (the other is in Rutland). They offer a range of courses to suit all abilities, from novice to semi-advanced board lovers. They have long boards which make it easier when you are learning and shorter sport boards for the more advanced. Their instructors are all nationally qualified and will ensure that you leave each session as a better windsurfer. The waters around Cornwall are some of the best in the UK for windsurfing – so hang on to your sail and let the wind whisk you away.

Activity prices: Contact the centre for the latest prices.

Accommodation: Clients to arrange own. There are plenty of options in Falmouth.

Food: Clients to arrange own.

Equipment supplied: All safety equipment and clothing.

What to take: Suitable footwear.

When to go: Year round.

Established: 1985

Safety: All instructors are RYA qualified and the centre is licensed by the AALA and recognised by the RYA.

Insurance: Insurance is required and a scheme is offered by the centre

Methods of payment: VISA, Mastercard, Switch, Delta, cheque with bank card and bankers' drafts.

Booking information: Advance booking is preferred, though tuition and boat hire are available on the day. A 25% deposit is required and cancellation policy may be applied.

Nearest airport: Newquay. Connections to London airports.

Nearest rail station: Truro.

ACTIVITY PRICES

A CURRENCY CONVERTER

All the prices in this book are given in local currency or the currency that the operator quoted on their questionnaire. Taking into account fluctuations in exchange rates, the local currency price is probably the one that will change least. To give you an idea of how these local prices convert, we have included below a currency conversion chart showing the major European currencies against English sterling. The rates are all for £1 sterling and were correct at the time of writing. This will give you some guide to equivalent sterling prices; however, the rates will have changed – maybe a little, maybe a lot – by the time you read this, so check out the latest details at your local bank.

Austria	20.86 schillings (Sch)	Malta	0.64 lira (LM)
Belgium	61.32 francs (BFr)	Netherlands	3.34 guilders (Fl)
Cyprus	0.87 pounds (C£)	Norway	12.56 kroner (NKr)
Denmark	11.34 kroner (DKr)	Portugal	302.88 escudo (Esc)
Euro	1.56 euro (euro)	Spain	252.21 pesetas (Pta)
Finland	9.05 marks (FM)	Slovenia	2.98 Prices are all
France	9.96 francs (FFr)		in Marks (DM)
Germany	2.98 marks (DM)	Sweden	13.21 krona (SKr)
Greece	495.96 drachma (Dr)	Switzerland	2.44 francs (SFr)
Ireland	1.19 punts (I£)	Turkey	793650 lira (TL)
Italy	2,953 lira (L)	USA	1.58 dollars (US$)

COMPANY INDEX

COUNTRY INDEX